SPORT SOCIOLOGY

10 QUESTIONS

JOHN PAUL

Wichita State University

MARK VERMILLION

Wichita State University

Kendall Hunt

publishing company

Cover image ©Shutterstock, Inc.
T-shirt image throughout design Courtesy John Paul.

Kendall Hunt
publishing company

www.kendallhunt.com
Send all inquiries to:
4050 Westmark Drive
Dubuque, IA 52004-1840

Copyright © 2018 by Kendall Hunt Publishing Company

ISBN 978-1-5249-0310-7

Published in the United States of America

BRIEF CONTENTS

CONTENTS

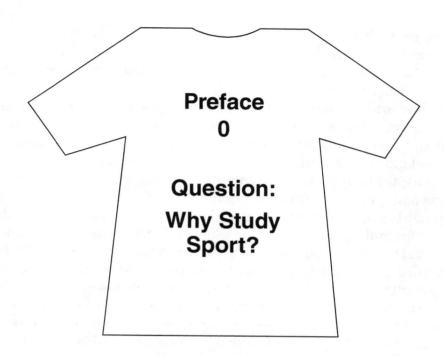

**Preface
0**

**Question:
Why Study
Sport?**

Through commonly asked questions such as "Does sport build community?," "Should college athletes be paid?," "What is the impact of women's sport on society?," and "Are sports mascots racist?," this book will explore the good, the bad, and the ugly about sport in society.

Specifically, *Ten Questions* provides empirical and uniquely sociological insights into the relationships between sports and the societal forces of gender, ethnicity, religion, the economy, and other institutions. While aspects of American sporting life are the core focus of this book, select international aspects of sport (e.g., the Olympics and other international sporting events) are also explored. Since the book is organized around various core and colloquial questions of sport, each chapter is designed to facilitate classroom discussion "right off the bat." Additionally, since the goal of each chapter is to ask a question and then answer it using sociological theories and concepts, students will gain an applicable skill in applying the sociological imagination to classic and contemporary events of sport.

WHY STUDY SPORT?

Sport is truly universal—There is no known human civilization that has not engaged in some sort of sporting activity. Indeed, participating in and being a spectator of various sports is an important aspect of most people's lives. In American society, nearly 40 million persons participate in organized sport activities each year and millions more participate by watching, either in person, on television, or via Internet streaming devices. Thus, it is fair to say that sport plays an important role in the lives of millions of Americans. Even if we do not play a sport, our lives are influenced by it, in part because we are inundated with the images and ideas about sport.

Indeed, sport is as much a part of American society as the institutions of the family, religion, education, economics, and systems of law and government. As Delaney and Madigan (2015:3) write, "To ignore sport is to overlook a phenomenon that extends into a multitude of social arenas, including the arts, mass media, the economy, the community, and international diplomacy." Further, sport reflects the norms and values of the culture that creates it.

So, what is our (sporting) culture? For some, it is identified in the notion of fair play, cooperation, team work, obedience to rules, hard work, and the notion of meritocracy—and these ideals help explain why so many people cherish sport. But, the culture of American society has also been identified by the slogan "winning is everything" and the "win at all costs" philosophy—and this then can lead to extreme competitiveness, the use and abuse of performance-enhancing drugs, exploitation of the athlete, an emphasis on rule bending ("it's only cheating if you get caught") as well as expressions of classism, sexism, racism, and nationalism. Thus, it is important to study sport from both of these perspectives and to recognize sport (and society) as having good, bad, beautiful, and ugly elements.

THE SOCIOLOGICAL PERSPECTIVE

Broadly stated, sociology is "the study of society" (a more detailed and workable definition is provided in Chapters 1 and 2). Sociology is a discipline that asks, "How is social life and society possible?," Why is our social world is the way it is?," and "Why do people think and act as they do?" In answering these questions, sociology requires us to examine various layers of our existence: specifically, we examine our individual lives, our communal lives, and the ways by which we interact to maintain or change our social world. Sociology assumes that we are, for the most part, products of our environment. To best understand this notion, we need to take a step back and try to imagine how our personal biographies and life histories are impacted by notions of our socialization, our geographic placement, our economic standing, our gendered and ethnic identities, and the values and expectations placed upon us by our community and nation. The ability to examine our own lives from these multiple viewpoints and social positions is known as the sociological perspective. However, this said, sociology also assumes that people have the ability to alter the social circumstances of their lives. We are, as Eitzen and Sage (1989:5) write, "both puppets of our society as well as its puppeteers." Stated differently, we are not simply robot-like creatures programmed by societal forces, but are individuals who, through collective action, have the ability to alter our own life courses and change the structure of society itself. Indeed, the sociologist gains insight into human behavior by utilizing the sociological perspective.

But again, what is the value of the sociological perspective in the study of sport? Mainly, in its ability to ask and frame questions such as: How does sport transmit culture and societal values—and what is the nature and impact of those values? How does sport organize us into groups and communities—and further, how does sport unite us and divide us? What is the impact and influence of sport on perceptions of race, gender and social class and how is sport experienced and used by persons in these differing social positions? How are sports used to alter the perceived destiny and life course of individuals? How has sport been used to challenge and/or change society?

Ultimately the sociological perspective gives us the ability to ask and answer these questions and more. The sociological study of sport is therefore of value, both for its own sake and for what it can tell us about individuals and societies in the broadest way.

UNIQUE FEATURES OF THE BOOK

Included in each chapter are cultural excursions that may take the form of: class activities, brief essays on popular sports movies, alternative sports, and interviews with athletes and scholars of sport, which link back to the principal themes expressed in the section under review.

Classroom activities: Ultimately this book is also designed to be both critical and fun. Within each chapter, students will find small experiential boxes that will ask them to reflect on the aforementioned themes and allow for a point of departure from traditional classroom lecture. Our hope is that these class discussions will facilitate debates (both serious and playful) about the obvious and not so obvious joys and challenges of sport.

Film and documentary recommendations: Since sport films and documentaries depict and reflect a myriad of sociocultural issues in society and serve as a purveyor of values, mores, and customs, movies become a useful way to illustrate sociological concepts and theories in an enjoyable and accessible way. Hopefully you can convince your course instructor to show a few of these in class ☺.

Sporting subcultures: By including a quirky collection of alternative and unusual sporting and recreational pursuits—from chess-boxing, to the sport of wife carrying, to prison rodeo, to competitive video gaming—this book seeks to challenge conventional notions of what sport is and what it is not within the sociological and societal context in which they are played.

Interviews with athletes and scholars: Interviews with select athletes and scholars of sports are included to give experiential and informative voice to individuals who have participated in various (and often mysterious) sporting worlds, thus educating us on the hidden realities of sporting life.

Extra-inning boxes: Finally, extra inning text boxes are sprinkled in here and there to: (1) recommend additional sources (and thought pieces) for students to discover and seek out other areas in the sociology of sport, and (2) highlight seminal figures (and key books) in the world of sport sociology.

Our hope is that this book will expose you to some of the core themes in the discipline and give you the critical and creative sociological thinking skills to encourage you to continue asking important questions once your class has ended.

ABOUT THE AUTHORS

John Paul received his PhD in sociology from Oklahoma State University. His teaching and research interests include the sociology of sport and the sociology of culture, as well as alternative sporting, religious, and artistic subcultures. In addition to his academic research, John engages in applied research, doing consulting work with various criminal justice agencies, using sport and art as modes of correctional reform.

Mark Vermillion received his PhD in sociology from Oklahoma State University. His teaching and research interests include the sociology and psychology of sport, sport management and ethics, and sport deviance and violence. In addition to his teaching and academic research, Mark engages in applied research, such as consulting with the NCAA and NJCAA affiliated athletic departments regarding survey methods or behavior development plans for student athletes. He has also worked with local sport organizations doing consulting and research services. Mark is currently chair of the department of sport management and executive director of the Partnership for the Advancement of Sport Management at Wichita State University.

REFERENCES

Delaney, Tim and Tim Madigan. 2015. *The Sociology of Sports: An Introduction.* 2nd ed. Jefferson, NC: McFarland and Company, Inc.

Eitzen, D. Stanley and George H. Sage. 1989. *Sociology of North American Sport.* 4th ed. Dubuque, IA: Wm. C. Brown.

**Chapter
1**

**Question:
What is Sport?**

Student Outcomes

After reading this chapter, you will be able to do the following:
- Understand the sociological definition and orientation of sport.
- Define and apply the terms "social construction" and "ethnocentrism."
- Describe the wedding of sociology and sport and the importance of the sociological perspective to sport.

What exactly is sport? The word derives from the 15th-century Anglo-French term *disports*, which means "pleasant pastime," or "activity that offers amusement or relaxation; entertainment, fun" (Brooke-Hitching 2015:2–3). For sociologists, however, sport is not just a game. It is a microcosm of the social world—which means that sport reflects our norms, values, and desires, has the ability to build and maintain social groups, and has the power to transform society itself. . . But more on this later. For now, we ask you, the reader, to consider the following question:

Class Activity

What is Sport?

©Eugene Onischenko/Shutterstock.com

(1) Please create two columns in your notes. In one of the columns, write out a list of "activities" that you do not consider to be sport. In the other column, make a list of activities that you do consider being a sport. Be prepared to defend your columns! Note that this exercise is not as clean cut as it may initially seem.

(2) Discuss your lists with the class and debate the categories and characteristics that define sport. Be nice to each other—these debates can get heated!

So, what do we have? Probably a long and impressive list of sports that may or may not have caused fair and foul word descriptions to be used among and at your classmates. In sociology too, there is often a lack of consensus on how to define sports—and simply being able to create a list of possible sports will not help us to fully understand sports from a sociological perspective. To better aid us in constructing a definition, let us begin with some common themes inherent in most sports. This will allow us to create a workable yet fluid definition that can be expanded throughout this course. First, we turn to Emma Witkowski, a researcher in game studies, who explored and compiled the various ways in which sports were defined in sociology, physical education, and kinesiology textbooks (See her text cloud on the next page to find the most common words associated with sport).

Following her compilation, we turn next to famed sport sociologist Stanley Eitzen, who writes, "sport is a rule bound activity organized and supervised by authorities and organizations to promote play" (2012:15). While we find this to be a good start toward our definition of sociology of sport, many of you probably noticed that the word physical (which is so prominent in the text cloud) is missing from

Figure 1 Cloud Description of Sport

Eitzen's definition. In fact, sport philosopher Steven Conner (2011:15) defines sport almost exclusively as games that involve bodily exertion and exhaustion. But is this always true? With these comparative and contrasting voices as a guide, let us now weigh in and suggest the following typology for a definition of sport:

Sports have rules.
Sports involve competition.
Sports identify winners and losers.
Sports involve strategy.
Sports are mental.
Sports are officially governed.
Sports are refereed.
Sports germinate excitement.
Sports involve training.
Sports express skill.
Sport expresses art and beauty.
Sport is drama/theater.
Sports require sacrifice.
Sports have fans.
Sports are playful (and playable).
Sports are physical.

Now return to your list and see if all of the listed activities meet these components. While we feel that all listed activities will meet (to varying degrees) these components, we imagine some of you are now saying something like, "But what about chess? It is not a sport because it is not 'physical!'" Let us explore this further.

Sport Case Study

Chess (and Its Varieties)

Sociologist Gary Allan Fine is most noted in the area of sport for his books: *With the Boys*, 1987 (a study of little league baseball) and *Players and Pawns*, 2015 (an examination about amateur and professional chess players). Speaking specifically to his book on chess, Fine reports:

> Chess can be a fight, an art, a sport, a life, or a war. . . . [like other] lifestyle sports, such as surfing, skateboarding and windsurfing, chess players display similar artistic expressions, stylistic nuance, and creative invention . . . Further, chess can be symbolically bloody, as pieces live and die and this reality thrills players, motivates improvement, and entertains the crowd. . . . Finally, for players in tournaments they must have sufficient stamina . . . research suggests that blood pressure and breathing rates rise during competition and players may lose as many as 10 to 12 pounds during a tournament . . . To be a champion chess player one's body as well as one's mind has to be in top condition – you can't separate mind from body (Fine 2015:6,10,14,35)

Based on the above description, chess appears to meet the all of the requirements that we laid out previously for sport. Thus, a lesson we wish to impart is this: sport is many things to many people, and from this, we learn that definitions of sport are, in large part, dependent upon the participants' ability to recognize and define it as such. In this way, sports are a social construction (which means, a created game that exists within the shared and agreed upon beliefs, values, and rules of behavior within a cultural group or society). Interestingly, this notion of sport as a social construction is more present than ever, as media and sports giant ESPN has started to broadcast (and therefore define) activities like spelling bees and video-game contests as sport.

Furthermore, this also forces us to recognize that different groups, cultures, and subcultures have different perspectives on what constitutes a sport, and perhaps we should be careful not to be **ethnocentric** when arguing what is and is not sport. In this case, **ethnocentrism** is the inability or unwillingness to see value and meaningfulness in the action/activities of another's culture. Since people are accustomed to the activities of their birth and socialized culture, it can be difficult for them to view the behaviors of people in differing cultures and social circles as being "worthy." So, next time you say, "That's not a sport!" we ask you to pause and apply these understandings to your thought processes.

For another example of sport as a social construction, check out the unique chess-hybrid below.

Case Study Continued: Chess-Boxing

Chess-boxing is as it sounds: a hybrid fighting sport that combines two traditional sports, chess and boxing. The competitors fight in alternating rounds of chess and

paul prescott/Shutterstock.com

boxing. The sport was created by Dutch performance artist, Iepe Rubingh, after reading *Froid Équateur* (French for "Cold Equator") by the French cartoonist Enki Bila who imagined the fictional sport in his graphic novel. According to Rubingh, the goal of the sport is to blend "brain and brawn" to create the ultimate intellectual and physical athlete. A match consists of eleven rounds. One round equals 4 minutes of speed chess (10 seconds max are allowed to make a chess move), followed by 3 minutes of boxing, for a total of six rounds of chess and five rounds of boxing. The match can be won with either a knockout, a technical knockout out, or a checkmate. In the event of a tie, a winner will be declared based on their results in boxing (punches landed, quality hits). The boxing fight wins the chess-boxing bout on boxing points. Interestingly, if the boxing fight also ends in a draw, the fighter playing the black chess pieces wins.

In order to ensure that the athletes are equal in competition, the regulatory body (the World Chess Boxing Organization, http://www.wcbo.org/chessboxing/) requires participants to be physically gifted, fit into a weight class, and be ranked as a "near expert" on the U.S. Chess Federation scale.

THE WEDDING OF SPORT AND SOCIOLOGY

In the wedding of sociology and sport, we must first acknowledge the sociological perspective, which includes: (1) the study of face-to-face interaction and communication (the ways by which we convey thoughts, feelings, and information to each other); (2) the study of groups and their unique cultures and worldviews; and (3) the study of larger scale social institutions (e.g., family, government, education, military, media, and sport) and how they organize and "hold" people and groups together into an immense unit we call society.

Indeed, sports are a pervasive reality in almost every society around the globe. If we look hard enough, we will find a reflection of sports in such universal features as: the dynamics of individual and collective play; a part of community life and development; a source of family unity and the creation of "tribal" affiliations; as a significant feature of radio and airplay devotion and the bulk of the mass media in general; a source of economic development; metaphors for military campaigns and symbolic (and real) acts of war; and as a feature of international diplomacy and world-building.

Further, as noted earlier, sports are a microcosm of society. This means again that we are able to find in sports the various reflections of ourselves and our society. Through the prism of sport, our norms and values and what we generally cherish (as well as what we despise) about our social interactions, our cultures, and our society get reflected. As sport sociologists, Delaney and Madigan (2015:3) note:

> Sport may reflect the notions of cooperation and teamwork, fair play, sportsmanship, hard-work, dedication, reaching to achieve personal excellence, obedience to rules, commitment and loyalty. . . . but sports may also reflect, particularly in American culture, the excellent exemplar of the cherished quote "win at all costs." Further this prevailing attitude often leads to elitism, sexism, racism, nationalism, extreme competitiveness, use of drugs (including performance enhancing drugs), gambling and a number of other deviant behaviors.

Class Activity

Take some time to give examples of what you have just read. How do sports reflect the aforementioned universal features of social life, as well as the good, the bad, and the ugly of sport?

Give historic and contemporary examples of the good, the bad, and the ugly in sport—how and why are these events socially important? Again, what do they tell us about society?

The fact that sport is good, bad, and ugly should not turn you away from the study of sports. We recognize that most of you use sports as a form of entertainment and an escape from the day-to-day realities, drudgery, and various hardships of life. Truly, in this way, sports can be a joy and a source of entertainment, artistic appreciation, and celebration of life. For example, in recent years, ESPN has been running commercials aimed at teaching the positive aspects of sports. In one such older commercial, a female jogger runs within an urban environment followed by numerous people who have significant demands on her time (her family, her boss, and symbolic representations of the pressures of being a woman in contemporary society). The commercial is accompanied by the catchphrase, "Without sports, how would we escape?" In a number of more recent commercials, ESPN humorously and playfully shows some of the "religious fervor" embedded in sports fandom, and suggests that sports are a quasi-religious experience that helps build community and offers a place to share, celebrate, and experience the pain of loss and defeat together. These commercials are accompanied by the slogan, "It's not Crazy—It's Sports."

Sport Case Study

Noodling (Hand Fishing)

©David Ryznar/Shutterstock.com

Because the first author grew up and studied in Oklahoma, he would be remiss if he did not introduce the sport of noodling and celebrate the"It's not Crazy—It's Sports" idea.

Noodling is the most common term applied to catching a live fish by hand—and it is also considered the "official" adventure sport of Oklahoma (the biggest hand fishing tournament in North American is held annually in Pauls Valley, Oklahoma, see http://okienoodling.com/). The origin of the term "noodling" is not actually known, but multiple theories exist regarding the contemporary etymology of the word. One idea holds that it derives from slang for jazz to *noodle* meaning make "improvised music." Thus, when one is without rod or reel, one improvises (using one's body as bait and spear). Another possible origin is from the Flemish *noedel* meaning "simpleton, stupid person"—as if you're a noodle (a fool) to submerge yourself underwater and insert your hand in an underwater hole to attempt to wrestle out a catfish (catfish occupy such holes at times year-round, but are most likely to hole up during spawning season when laying, guarding, and fanning their eggs). Other origins suggest that wrestling with a slippery, squirming fish is like trying to grasp a wet noodle. Finally, the way the fisherman wiggles his or her fingers to lure the catfish is like waving wet spaghetti.

Native American historian James Adair left a written record of the act of hand fishing when, in 1775, he described a "surprising method" of fishing under the edges of rocks among Southern Indians. He writes:

> They pull off their red breeches, or their long slip of Stroud cloth, and wrapping it around their arm, so as to reach the lower part of the palm of their right hand, they dive under the rock where the cat-fish lie to shelter themselves from the scorching beams of the sun, and to watch for prey: as soon as those fierce aquatic animals see that tempting bait, they immediately seize it with the greatest violence, in order to swallow it. Then is the time for the diver to improve the favorable opportunity: he accordingly opens his hand, seizes the voracious fish by his tender parts, hath a sharp struggle with it . . . and at last brings it safe ashore (p. 405).

In his account, hand fishing was both a means of survival and a test of masculinity and fortitude (my own extended family members introduced me in my youth to noodling as a masculine rite of passage). How did this become a sport? Scholar Todras-Whilehill (2006) notes that during the great depression many people turned to noodling to put food on the table. After that, it became family custom, a skill passed down through generations. To become a noodler, you must be brave enough (or foolish enough) to reach into an underwater hole and extract the occupant. At times, this is simple. The occupant becomes infuriated by your intrusion and chomps on your hand and you attempt to pull it to the surface. One hopes the creature is a catfish rather than a snapping turtle, a beaver, or a snake. For these reasons, as well as the high risk of drowning while wresting a catfish underwater (they can grow to more than 100 pounds), the sport has been banned in most states.

Crazy? Yes, to some. But for others this is a tradition and an act of pleasure. Please remember sociology argues that sport is culturally bound and has meanings beyond play. So, what does noodling tell us sociologically? For some it is a mode of hunting, for others it's a family tradition. Still others experience it as a rite of passage and a test of mettle—some see it as an adrenaline sport and a game to make and break records, as well as a way to find status and honor. Finally, after hand fishing tournaments, it becomes a "fish fry" and a celebration of community and nature's bounty.

In truth, regardless of how crazy they may seem to an outsider, sports can bring us together in a wide range of emotions (think of the famous quote by Jim McKay: " . . . the thrill of victory . . . and the agony of defeat . . .") and can form an identity that binds us together in ways that rival our connections to family. At the same time, sports also have the power to create division—note the soccer "hooligans" who engage in violence against fans of another team as a way of showing their ethnic, class, and national loyalties.

It is also important, from the sociological perspective, to question society and sport. We need to also challenge the rigidity of sporting traditions and ask if sport has outmoded concepts that should be changed. For example, when tennis player Billie Jean King battled Bobby Riggs in the nationally televised 1973 "Battle of the Sexes" she used that tennis match to challenge the sporting establishment, gendered stereotypes, and heterosexism (Shoup 2016). When LeBron James, Kobe Bryant, and other athletes in the NBA wore T-shirts protesting the extrajudicial killing of unarmed black men and women by police officers, they used sport to challenge the continued existence of racism, police militarization, and the social order (Greenberg 2015).

Finally when collegiate football players at Northwestern University attempted to unionize in 2014, they did so not to anger fans, nor to disrespect the game of football; they did so to highlight various inequalities that athletes in high-profile sports often face—namely, the stated inability to pick one's own major degree and course of study, the lack of extended healthcare (despite the fact that they were sacrificing

Tim Clayton/Contributor/Getty Images

their body and long-term health for the university), and the recognition that a "full scholarship" rarely covered the actual cost of attendance and cost of living expenses in contemporary society (Nocera and Strauss 2016).

As sociologists, we will examine all of these realities: the good, the bad, and the ugly. We will celebrate sport and show its positive features in building and maintaining individual relations, group existence, and positive societal presence. We will, however, also explore the bad and the ugly. Being critical will enable us to examine the negatives surrounding sport, for the goal is to seek positive and workable change to improve this "vital, interesting, and exciting aspect of social life" (Eitzen 2016:21).

To this end, please read the following interview with Dave Zirin, a noted journalist and critic of sport. The goal of Zirin's writings has a twofold purpose: (1) to encourage a recognition that sports can, and often do, create architectures of inequality, pain, and misery, and (2) that once people become aware of said injustices, we will act as agents of reform and change to make sport (and society) a better place.

An Interview with Dave Zirin, a Critical Sport Journalist

Dave Zirin is the sports editor for *The Nation*, as well as the author of numerous books on the politics of sports (including *People's History of Sports in the United States: 250 Years of Politics, Protest, People, and Play*, 2009, *Game Over: How Politics Has Turned the Sports World Upside Down*, 2013, and *Brazil's Dance with the Devil: The World Cup, The Olympics, and the Fight for Democracy*, 2014). He has been named one of UTNE Reader's "50 Visionaries Who Are Changing Our World," and is a frequent guest on ESPN and other media outlets.

How would you describe what you do?

DZ: I'm a sports writer by trade and I try to write in the language and style of sports writing, which has its own vernacular, to be sure. My beat is that messy, jagged place where sports and politics smash together . . . Politics are an enduring, constant, and historic presence in sports. [My] goal is to try and get the mainstream sports media, athletes, and fans, to acknowledge this, and—if they happen to be unhappy with the politics of sports—challenge it to change.

So much of sport journalism is apolitical and non-critical; what drives you to examine sport and politics?

DZ: For far too many people, politics is what the people with the bad haircuts do on CSPAN. But politics are of course the food we eat, the air we breathe, and yes, the sports we watch and play. People aren't alienated from sports the way they are from formal politics. Therefore, we often get a more honest discussion about issues like labor rights, racism, sexism, and homophobia, through the prism of sports . . . That's what I find just endlessly fascinating.

You've devoted much energy to defending, celebrating, and encouraging political athletes. What makes an athlete a political athlete and why do you think it so important to focus on them?

DZ: [Athletes are often told to] "Know your role and shut your mouth." Stay in your box . . . Athletes that are political defy the box. Many of them, in my experience, would say more if they felt that there was a media that would take them seriously. We need more writers and academics that do. . . . I'm fascinated by the way we have strong associations of Jackie Robinson with the Civil Rights Movement, Muhammad Ali with the anti-war and black power struggle, and Billie Jean King with the women's rights movement.

Even though sports are supposed to be "bread and circuses," they can acquire the power of the transformational. Politically committed athletes face a couple very tough obstacles. There is a history of punishing athletes who speak out . . . [and] many political athletes don't speak out because of fear [they] will either be slammed by the press or—perhaps worse—ignored.

What can scholars who study sport do to reach a broader public and make a difference in sport and society?

DZ: I find so much of sports sociology remarkable in its breadth and power [to] "debunk" accepted truths . . . [I think] every sports sociologists' department should also . . . have a sports and society column in their college paper. Every sports and sociology student should try to intern in their athletic departments. Let's get [sociological] ideas out there in the oxygen . . . Further, if we wish to reclaim sports, we must look at history, learn the role sports play in our world, and listen to the athletic rebels of today.

Excerpted from: "Toward a Radical Sport Journalism—An Interview with Dave Zirin," by Richard King, *Journal of Sport and Social Issues*, 32(4), November 1, 2008, pp. 333–344. Copyright © 2008 by SAGE Publications. Reprinted by permission of SAGE Publications, Inc.

CHAPTER SUMMARY

The goals of this chapter have been several. Our first goal was the introduction of the unique and alternative perspectives employed by sociology in the definition and study of sport. Ultimately, we want students to understand that all sports are social constructions—that is "made up" games created by different groups, cultures, and subcultures for various particular purposes. All individuals and groups have different perspectives on what constitutes a sport. We have urged mindful, thoughtful, and intellectual awareness when arguing what is and is not sport—and we have provided several subcultural examples to challenge your notions of sport.

Our second goal was the awareness of sport as a microcosm of the social world. This means that the world of sport is "society in miniature"—all that may be found in society will also be found in sport. In this way sport is always more than mere play, it will reflect our norms, values, and desires; it will reflect the good, bad, and ugly of society; and it will hold the ability to build and maintain social groups as well as the power to transform society itself. To restate Zirin, "sports are the food we eat, the air we breathe . . . and the way through which we actually talk about politics and issues like economics, racism, sexism and homophobia. . . . That's what I find just endlessly fascinating"(King 2008:335). We agree, sport and sociology is endlessly fascinating.

Discussion Questions

*Given what you read in this chapter, has your view of what is and is not sport changed? Why or why not?

*Based on the definition of sport used in this chapter, most everyone watches and/or participates in something that could be considered a sport. What role does sport play in your life and how does it connect you to the larger society based on what we learned in this chapter?

*How may the terms "social construction" and "ethnocentrism" be used in sport?

*Dave Zirin purposefully addresses the political components of sport in his writing. There have been arguments that athletes in particular should stay away from politics and controversial issues and do what they are paid for—which is to play their sport and nothing more. While we will explore this in greater depth in a future chapter, what is your opinion about the role athletes should (or should not) play in addressing the issues facing society?

Extra-Inning: The Professional Football Player and the Professional Sociologist

Herbert George Blumer (1900 to 1987) was a prominent American sociologist whose main scholarly interests were symbolic interactionism (the systematic study of forms and impacts of socialization and human social interaction—more on this in Chapter 2) and qualitative (focusing on lived, experiential rather than survey) methods of social research.

He was a beloved professor at the University of Chicago who eventually left to found the Sociology Department at the University of California, Berkeley. In 1952, he became the president of the American Sociological Association.

Bettmann/Contributor/Getty Images

But he was also a professional football player. During much of the period that Blumer was at the University of Chicago, from 1924 through 1933, he played football professionally for the Chicago Cardinals (now the Arizona Cardinals). In 1925, Blumer won a league championship and was selected to the All-Pro Team in 1929. Sociologists Manning and Smith (2010:37) state that he "literally rubbed shoulders with the football greats of his era: Red Grange, Bronko Nagurski and Jim Thorpe." His students (several of whom became professional sociologists) would tell stories of him coming into class on Monday morning covered with bandages from the Sunday game.

The ideas and work of Herbert Blumer still very much influence the teaching and practice of sociology today. In the photograph above is Red Grange of the Chicago Bears (at the far left) trying to get through the Chicago Cardinals line. This was Grange's first professional game as a member of the Bears (Blumer is out there somewhere beyond the frame ☺).

Reference

Manning, Phillip and Greg Smith. 2010. "Symbolic Interaction." Pp. 37–55. *The Routledge Companion to Social Theory*, edited by Anthony Elliot. New York, NY: Routledge.

CHAPTER REFERENCES

Adair, James. 1775. *History of the Indians*. London: Edward & Charles Dilly.

Brooke-Hitching, Edward. 2015. *Fox Tossing: And Other Forgotten and Dangerous Sports, Pastimes, and Games*. New York, NY: Touchstone.

Conner, Steven. 2011. *A Philosophy of Sport*. London: Reaktion Books.

Delaney, Tim and Tim Madigan. 2015. *The Sociology of Sports: An Introduction*. Jefferson, NC: McFarland Press.

Eitzen, D. Stanley. 2012. *Fair and Foul: Beyond the Myths and Paradoxes of Sport*, 5th ed. Boulder, CO: Rowman & Littlefield Publishers.

Fine, Gary Allan. 2015. *Players and Pawns: How Chess Builds Community and Culture*. Chicago, IL: University of Chicago Press.

Greenberg, Chris. 2015. "8 Athletes Explain Why Their Protest Matters." *HuffPost*, January 16. Retrieved November 4, 2017 (http://www.huffingtonpost.com/2015/01/16/athlete-protests-ferguson-garner_n_6367292.html).

King, C. Richard. 2008. "toward a radical sport journalism: An interview with Dave Zirin." *Journal of Sport & Social Issues* 32(4): 333–344.

Nocera, Joe. 2016. *Indentured: Inside the Story of the Rebellion Against the NCAA*. New York, NY: Penguin.

Shoup, Kate. 2016. *Billie Jean King: The Battle of the Sexes and Title IX*. New York, NY: Cavendish Square Publishing.

Todras-Whilehill, Ethan. 2006. "In the Jaws of a Catfish." *The New York Times*, April 21. Retrieved September 21, 2017 (http://www.nytimes.com/2006/04/21/travel/escapes/in-the-jaws-of-a-catfish.html).

Witkowski, Emma. 2012. "On the Digital Playing Field: How We "Do Sport" with Networked Computer Games." *Games and Culture* 7(5):349–374. doi: http://doi.org/10.1177/1555412012454222.

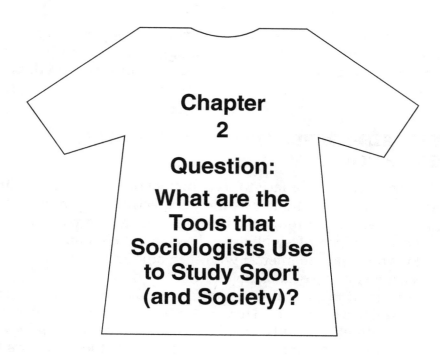

**Chapter
2**

Question:

**What are the
Tools that
Sociologists Use
to Study Sport
(and Society)?**

Student Outcomes

After reading this chapter, you will be able to do the following:
- Understand the meaning of theory.
- Learn the most common theoretical perspectives used in sport sociology.
- Use and apply theory to better understand and explain the role and place of in society.

Whenever we ask why our social world is the way it is (and by extension, why sport is the way it is) we are "theorizing" (hooks 1992). In simple terms, a **theory** is a set of assumptions based on observations that help us to make sense of our experiences and to issue predictions about our human behavior. They are distinct lenses that help us to look at and focus in on particular aspects of human social life. In Chapter 1, we defined sociology as: (1) the study of face-to-face interaction and communication (the ways by which we convey thoughts, feelings, and information to each other); (2) the study of groups and their unique cultures and worldviews; and (3) the study of larger scale social institutions (e.g., family, government, education, military, media, and sport) and how they organize and "hold" people and groups together into an immense unit we call society. In this chapter, we will take each of these layers and add a theoretical lens (and accompanying descriptive language) to show how they have practical and predictive applications in understanding and predicting human behavior.

THEORETICAL PERSPECTIVE (1): THE POWER OF SOCIALIZATION

We begin first with the idea of face-to-face interaction and communication. Sociologists term this first unit of analysis **the perspective of symbolic interaction**. This essentially means that through the learning of language, communication, and gesture (all various types of symbols and symbolic communication), humans acquire the skills necessary to interact with each other. As Vaughan (2001) argues, this is, in effect, a theory of socialization.

In terms of the importance of this to sport, one must keep in mind that athletes do not become athletes overnight. They go through a series of stages that socialize them into an athletic identity and into an appreciation of play and sport. These stages of interaction are termed *socialization*, or the processes by which persons, groups, and society present norms, values, knowledge, and desired ways of acting and feeling to the next generation. Socialization, in many ways, determines the method by which people construct their identities, worldviews, and modes of interaction in social relations. **Agents of socialization** are the individuals and groups that provide you with information in attempts to socialize you according to their own interests and beliefs. Agents of socialization include family members, peers and friends, teachers, coaches, members of community groups, and even media representations found in television programs, books, video games, etc.

Sport Case Study

Learning the Symbolic Interactions of the Sport of Rock, Paper, Scissors and its Variations

The familiar game of Rock, Paper, Scissors is played like this: You pound your closed fist into your other hand three times while chanting "rock-paper-scissors," then signal your choice by making a fist to represent "rock," pointing your index and middle fingers to represent "scissors," or opening your hand wide to represent "paper." The rule for winning is simple as well: A rock beats scissors, scissors beat paper by cutting it, and paper beats rock by covering it.

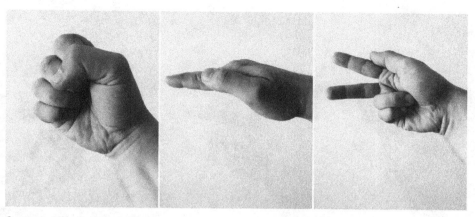

Courtesy John Paul.

If both players made the same choice of symbol, it is considered a tie and the game is played again until a winner emerges. In the past, various leagues have formed around this game. The most recent association, The United States of America Rock Paper Scissors League, was a national competition confederation which televised its national championship on ESPN—with the grand champion being awarded a $50,000 cash prize (Mayyasi 2014).

According to Belsky and Fine (2016: 122–123), the games origins date back at least to China's Han Dynasty, roughly 200BC to AD200." But though there were many different versions of this 'zero-sum game'—in which A is beaten by B, B is defeated by C, and C is toppled by A—the modern version Westerners know originated in Japan in the 19th century.

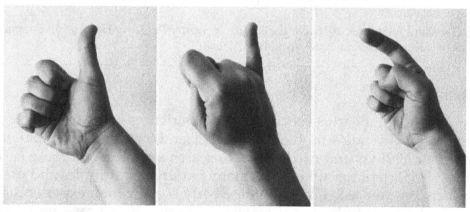

Courtesy John Paul.
frog (left), slug (middle), snake (right)

In the 19th-century Japanese game, frog is beaten by slug (originally a poisonous centipede), slug is killed by snake, and snake is defeated by frog.

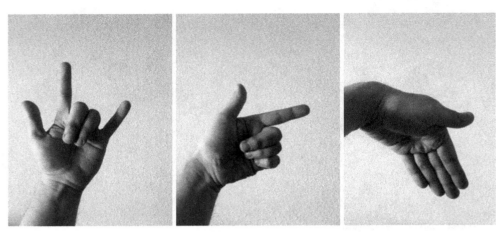

Courtesy John Paul.

fox (left), hunter (middle), elder (right)

In yet another version, trickster/supernatural Fox, is killed by a hunter with a gun, the hunter is halted by a village elder (essentially, with a hand gesture that reads, "stop"), and the elder is bitten by fox.

What other zero-sum variations can you think of or create (Rock-Paper-Scissor-Lizard-Spock, anyone?)

References

Mayyasi, Alex. 2014. "Inside the World of Professional Rock Paper Scissors." *Priceonomice*, September 5. Retrieved Oct 15, 2017 (http://priceonomics.com/the-world-of-competitive-rock-paper-scissors/).

Belsky, Gary and Neil Fine. 2016. *On the Origins of Sports: The Early History and Original Rules of Everybody's Favorite Games*. New York, NY: Artisan.

Early Socialization

For most people, their earliest socialization experiences come from their primary caregivers (typically one's mother and father and/or one's grandparents), and then later their siblings and early peers. Research suggests that these early years are the most important for influencing many of our later attitudes and predispositions. In sociology, we ask, how will these early socialization experiences craft or influence our basic attitudes towards the world—and in our case, toward sport?

Assignment: Agents of Socialization—Early Memory of Sport

In your notes, please describe the most powerful early memory of sport that you can remember. This memory can be positive or negative (good, bad, or ugly) and can involve any sport or sport-related activity. Further, it may be anything in which you were present as a participant or a spectator. It may involve you playing or watching (even via television of social media).

Detail this memory. Tell us if it is a good, bad, or ugly memory (and why), and what (if any) relationship it had on your early socialization into (or out of) sport.

We imagine your sports memories are widespread; some memories are probably about positive remembrances of family and peer bonding (e.g., watching the game with your dad). Some are probably of achievement and are celebratory in nature (i.e., remembering the time you scored the winning goal or basket), while some are also of failure, pain, and humiliation (the time you were picked last or "cut" from a game).

Regarding this notion of sport as painful memory, a student once told us that she did not expose her children to sports because of the negative experiences she had as a child. Her father would watch sports on the television, and if "his team" was doing poorly, he would yell, curse, and be verbally and physically abusive to her, her siblings, and her mother. "I didn't want to take the chance that my kids would become that, so I ignored sport altogether," she said. Obviously, this is an extreme example, but it helps illustrate the fact that for most of us, sport is solidly entrenched in our emotional and sentimental lives, again be it good, bad, or ugly.

Family Socialization

Are parents and caregivers supportive of their children's sports involvement? What is the level and degree of parental expectations, encouragement, and time spent participating with their offspring in sport? These are some types of questions a sport sociologist will ask. Let us continue this line of questioning by focusing on the idea of parental expectation. Using the exercise above, and the assignment below, is parental involvement always a positive thing?

Assignment: Athlete Sperm and the Attempt to Create a Sport Superstar

Tom Farrey, an ESPN senior writer and reporter, produced an investigatory documentary titled "Sperm U"—a short video that chronicled adults who purchased (and who later conceived children from) the sperm of elite Division I athletes. Their hope?—to birth children with tremendous athletic abilities and craft future "superstar athletes."

Olga Bogatyrenko/Shutterstock.com

Farrey notes:

> I think they were trying to create a better life for their children. Parents know that this is a society that values athletic achievement. Athletes are well-liked, they are generally good-looking (a societal advantage), and with athletics, children have a possible pathway to go to college. Additionally, the rewards for athletic achievement have grown dramatically . . . . Pro salaries have skyrocketed. So, parents have more incentive to develop the child who has shown interest in sports into an elite athlete (Sports Nation 2013: paragraph 7).

In the video, some of the parents are heard saying things like, "I wasn't interested in sperm donors with high IQs, only athletic ability;" and "I (of a two-year old child) have a Tom Brady in the making?"

But what happens if the "athletic genes" of the donor father are passed on, but not activated? What if the child wants to be an artist rather than an athlete? Are parents crafting unrealistic expectations of their children? What happens if the child comes to believe that they were "created" specifically to be an athlete? What might be the psycho-sociological impact of this, and finally, what does this say about our society? **Please organize yourself into groups and discuss these questions**.

Documentary Recommendation: *The Marinovich Project* (2012) is an ESPN's 30 for 30 documentary that explores the powerful impact of socialization, sporting identify, and family bonds. It details the relationship between father Marv Marinovich and his son, Todd. Marv was a former University of Southern California Trojan and Oakland Raider, and the first strength and conditioning coach in NFL history. He was obsessed with training methods and would seek out alternative and revolutionary theories to improve athletic performance and craft athletic perfection. Marv would later test his theories on his newborn son, Todd.

Specifically, he wanted to see what would happen to a child if they were raised under rigid and intense training conditions. Could the perfect athlete be crafted though intense sport socialization? Todd would go on to be labeled an "athletic specimen" and Marv would become the poster-child for the dangers of being an overbearing parent.

In time, Todd would go on to star at USC and be drafted by the Raiders—but would later battle drug problems and he actively sought to ruin/end his professional career. He states in the documentary, "Just because I was 'bred' to be great at something, does that mean I was supposed to be that for the rest of my life?" "Did I have a choice?" "What was my identity away from sport?"

As these exercises show, it is important to study the process of socialization into sport. As children's first socializers, parents play a primary role in the creation of beliefs and values by giving their children the first messages about one's identity and by providing them with opportunities and experiences that support the development of certain skills and competencies. In this way, are we socializing others into sport as a means to express bodily movement and sporting creativity, to bond and learn to play well with others, and to develop an appreciation of physical competency and health? Or do we learn to craft rigid and limited "jock" identities, such that sport acts as an end all be all mode to experience life?

Consider the research of Krystal Beamon (2010). A former collegiate athlete, Beamon has studied former and current professional athletes, asking them specifically if they thought sport was overemphasized in their socialization. Interestingly, the majority of athletes she interviewed reported feeling that their socializing agents and environment overemphasized athletics above other roles and the development of other skills and talents. For example:

> My next-door neighbor was the first Black quarterback at [a major university], and [our parents and community members] said you were gonna play a sport, you were gonna go to college, and that's what you were gonna do, you were gonna go pro. . . . It was just always understood that we were gonna play sports (p. 292).

> I really, truly believe we [African Americans] do overemphasize sports . . . and every time I get a chance to talk to athletes I often tell them that sports is secondary or even third to a lot of things. . . . We should focus more on education and other areas that we need to develop in our life and, and make perfect in our lives other than sports. I really do think that we overemphasize sports (p. 294).

Peers and media also had an influence:

> It's one thing to see people on TV but like . . . ya don't see no doctors, no lawyers . . . just ballplayers (p. 292).
>
> That's all we see on TV is Black males being athletes or rappers or entertainers. So, I think as a result, we condition ourselves to just be that . . . But that's from television. When I grew up, the only successful Black people we saw on TV was the Cosbys, a doctor, and a lawyer. Everybody else, I saw rappers and singers . . . athletes (p. 293).

She further argues that this may be especially damaging to Black men, as studies indicate that in comparison to their White counterparts, African American males are socialized by family and the larger community into sports deliberately and intensively by limiting exposure to other hobbies and role models, and by pushing sports as a possible career path early in life. It is suggested that the push toward athletics as seen within African American families is hindering the social and cognitive growth of African American youth. Beamon continues, saying that sport is often propagandized as the only "way out" and that these beliefs are particularly prevalent in poor and working class black communities. She argues that the expectations for professional success exceed the opportunities available. "Statistically speaking," Beamon states, "An African-American male is more likely to be a neurosurgeon than an NBA star . . . ultimately sports should not be the initial aspirations for children, but "an end to a mean" (cited in Johnson 2011: paragraph 8).

The Positive and Negative Effects of Sport Socialization on Women

Sports may help boys and girls socialize in different ways, and this may be either positive or negative. As Anderson (2009, 2010) notes, sports participation generally socializes boys into traditional gender roles, while similar participation socializes girls into nontraditional gender roles. Research indicates that sports have an additional social benefit for females, as participation in sports to be a way to break gender stereotypes, enhancing their sense of possibility (More on this in Chapter 9).

Video Recommendation

The Keepers of the Game (2016) is another sports documentary that explores themes of socialization and female empowerment. It is a story of the Salmon River High School girls' lacrosse team during their 2015 season. The team, composed completely of Native Americans players from the Mohawk nation, is forced to raise funds to finish its season and face off against gender-traditionalists who believe they shouldn't be playing lacrosse in the first place.

As ESPNW reporter, Katie Barnes (2016), writes, most sports films are: "reserved for the trials . . . facing young men . . . Yet *Keepers of the Game* carves out a space for women and girls to have iconic stories of their own" (Paragraphs 2–3).

kstudija/Shutterstock.com

The film follows the team throughout the season, chronicling its successes and failures, and is interspersed with the following research findings: "Compared to non-athlete peers, female high school athletes have greater self-esteem, goal-setting, and leadership and are less likely to suffer from depression" (Women Sports Foundation 2016:1). Indeed, sport scholar Lone Friis Thing claimed that female athletes' participation in sport creates a feeling of empowerment that involves "both a sense of bodily power and liberation and a sense of release of everyday stresses" (2001:284). Finally, to borrow the words, of Merleau-Ponty (2003:159), the "play" of lacrosse (and sport in general), "fosters a bodily experience of 'I can' instead of 'I cannot.'"

Assignment: Name and discuss sports films that focus of the female athletic experience. Focus on themes of gender socialization and female empowerment.

Learning to be Good or Bad

Stressing again the importance of socialization, sociologists routinely ask to what types of teachings and moral influences are children exposed. We argue that persons' behaviors are, in part, the result of exposure to the patterned, recurring actions and influences of powerful significant others. To this end, the behavioral direction and sway of a coach is no different. Please consider the following examples.

In 2015, a YouTube video showing two Texas high school football players purposively slamming into the back of a referee was viewed more than nine million times online (https://www.youtube.com/watch?v=uKd_sxbNhCw). The two players, who made the hit on the official, said that their assistant coach had encouraged the attack, saying something like, "That guy needs to pay for cheating us" (Workman 2015: paragraph 9). According to a signed statement of resignation, the assistant coach admitted that he told his players to strike the referee. The two teens have since apologized to the official and stated that the hit was "one of my biggest regrets of our lives" and the assistant coach was ultimately sentenced to 18 months of probation, ordered to pay a $1,500 fine, complete 120 hours of community service, and pay restitution for medical bills to the referee. A spokesperson for the school later said, "It is not the good sportsmanlike behavior that we teach students. . . . will not tolerate this kind of behavior" (Chappell 2015: paragraph 16).

Now to something more positive: In her final appearance as a college pitcher, Chelsea Oglevie of Florida Southern College had a 2-1 lead with 2-outs in the 7th inning. She was one out away from sealing her career with a win against Eckerd College in the last game of the season, and for seniors on both teams, it was the last game of their careers. Playing for Eckerd, Kara Oberer was up to bat (She had severely injured her knee earlier in the game while diving for a ball). Amazingly, Oberer hit a walk-off 3-run homer over the fence for the win. The only issue was that Oberer could not make it around first base due to her injury. NCAA rules state that no one on her team, including umpires and athletic trainers may touch her (aid her for help) or she would be called out. Chelsea Oglevie and one of her teammates, in an act of good sportspersonship, carried the game-winning home run hitter around the bases to end their season and for Oglevie, her career. In the end, Eckerd won 4-2 and the home run was the final pitch she ever threw. Eckerd College softball assistant coach Pat Affrunti said "everybody was pretty much bawling" and the act has created a powerful moment to teach proper sports play (Knight 2014: paragraph 3).

What is the significance of this for us? Again, it is the recognition that sport can be a powerful agent of socialization and sporting behaviors are not only learned, but also exist as agents of teaching and learning that transmit a group's expectations, norms, and values.

THEORETICAL PERSPECTIVE (2): GROUPS, CULTURE, AND CONFLICT

We now transition into our second theoretical perspective: groups, culture, and conflict. The second level of sociology is the study of groups and that this unit of analysis corresponds with the perspective of **conflict**—or speaking colloquially this identifies who is "part of the club" and "who is excluded from it." As Girard (1996:9) writes, "conflict is the process when two or more individuals or groups try to prevent one another from appropriating the object they desire through physical or other means."

Sport Case Study

Three-Sided Soccer and Conflict as the Mode of Play

Three-sided soccer is played with three teams instead of the usual two. It was devised as a thought piece by the artist Asger Jorn (1914–1973) to "play around" with concepts of cohesion and conflict—will it be every team for itself, or will two teams unify to go against one team, and how and why do these cooperative unions change? Three-sided football is, ideally, an exercise in conflict and negotiated cooperative behavior, with one side persuading another to join in a campaign against the third—thus breaking down the very basis of fair play.

First played in 1993 by the Glasgow Anarchist Summer School (to mock the notion of equity and meritocracy that sport is said to promote), the game has since grown to become a popular league activity that is (mostly) free of political and social commentary.

Played on a hexagonal pitch, the winning team is decided by that which concedes the fewest goals. See http://triball.strikingly.com/#triball

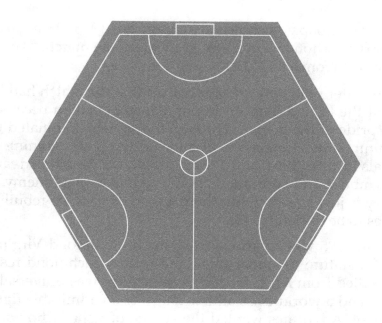

Indeed, the study of culture and conflict is often concerned with matters of belonging and difference, and the culture-conflict perspective essentially argues that society is made up of loosely integrated collections of people with contradictory interests. Hartigan, Jr (2010) writes:

> When we learn culture- we learn categories for making sense of the world around us. . . . and we learn categories of people too— 'nice' or 'bad'. . . and then 'friend' and 'stranger'(p. 11) . . . . We learn whether people belong with us or not. . . . We think culture is about determining the sameness; but in many ways it is about organizing and arranging degrees of difference within or across imagined cultural boundaries (p. 12).

A power example of conflict and belonging includes Bill Bullford (1991) study of football (soccer) hooligans. Bullford, found that football group affiliation was a powerful mode of identifying group belonging, as well as sources of conflict in society. Fans of various football clubs were organized primarily around themes of social economic class and religious ethnicity—and the violence and they expressed toward one another was "a rebellion of some kind—social rebellion, class rebellion, an outlet for feelings of illegitimacy and general frustrations without how society was organized" (p. 15).

Conversely, conflict can also promote group solidarity, and conflict can lead to a sense of peoplehood, social integration, and a sense of moral worth. Further, in this mode, as Ross Haenfler (2015:8) writes, "such cultural groups are known for rebelling in someway against society [generally] as a form of resisting the demands and pressures of their social, economic, and political systems." Several examples of this include:

(1) After soviet troops occupied Hungary in 1956, Hungarian nationals expressed their frustration in a hard-fought water polo match. "The pool was red with blood," writes Womack (2003:13). She continues:

> Hungarian water polo players later denied that the match had been that violent, but the legend lives on in popular imagination because it reinforces the pride of the people. Through the soviets dominated the Hungarian countryside, Hungarians dominated the pool, winning Olympic gold medals in 1956, 1964, and 1976 . . . there are decided advantages to fighting symbolic and sporting wars with against ones' enemy. The athletic victory is just as sweet, but there are no cities to be rebuilt or (usually) bodies to be buried (p. 13).

(2) The time in 1995 when various residents of Richmond Virginia fought the construction of a stature to tennis great, and former Richmond resident, Arthur Ashe. When he died from AIDS in 1993, Arthur Ashe was universally hailed as a man of wisdom and a world-class athlete and was an admirable figure worthy of with a monument. Advocates wanted the statute of Ashe (who was Black) to be

placed on Monument Avenue, the Boulevard whose only other statures included figures who had defended the confederacy during the Civil War. The Richmond city council held open podium public hearing on the issue on July 17, 1995, and though the debate was tense and full of racial rhetoric, the council voted to place the memorial to Ashe on Monument Avenue. On July 10, 1996, Richmond held an unveiling ceremony where a crowd of approximately 2,000 persons—more or less equally divided between black and white citizens—attended. However, not all in attendance were there to celebrate the occasion. A group of protesters waving Confederate flags and various posters and banners argued that the statute was a "hate crime" against the white Confederate men whose memories were being desecrated (Schultz 2012). The monument obviously became a focal point of racial tensions in the city and reminded audiences that racialized issues remained present in their community.

(3) Consider, finally, the protests at the University of Missouri in 2015. During that academic year, racial tensions at the University of Missouri arose when a Facebook post by Payton Head—then the president of the Missouri Students Association—reported that people riding in a pickup truck had shouted racial slurs at him as he walked near campus. Then, on October 5, members of the Legion of Black Collegians were verbally harassed during an on-campus rehearsal for homecoming festivities. A white male student, reportedly intoxicated, approached the students and referred them as "niggers." Three weeks later, on October 24, a swastika was drawn with human feces at a university residence hall.

On October 10, members of Concerned Student 1950 (a newly formed student group named for the year the first black graduate student was admitted to the university) blocked the President's vehicle as it moved through a homecoming parade. As reporters for *The Columbia Missourian* newspaper stated, "Wolfe did not respond to the group while he was in the car. His driver revved the convertible's engine, eventually (and perhaps unintentionally) hitting Jonathan Butler," a graduate student who is one of the group's members (Severn and Reese 2015: paragraph 7). The group demanded that he give a public statement about the racial incidents and the president responded with a rather poor response (captured on cell phone video footage) that seemed to dismiss the existence of racism on campus. The president met with members of the group a week later, and on November 6, he publicly apologized for the parade incident, saying, "Racism does exist at our university and it is unacceptable" (Koren 2015: paragraph 12). "Too little, too late," Butler then responded, as he began a hunger strike in protest of the school administration. Butler said he would refuse food "until either Tim Wolfe is removed from office or my internal organs fail and my life is lost," (Koren 2015: paragraph 6).

After this, 32 members of the Missouri Tigers football team also said that they would go on strike until the President of the University of Missouri resigned. The Mizzou players stated:

The athletes of color on the University of Missouri football team truly believe Injustice Anywhere is a threat to Justice Everywhere, We will no longer participate in any football related activities until President Tim Wolfe resigns or is removed due to his negligence toward marginalized students' experience. WE ARE UNITED!!!!! (cited in Thrasher 2015: paragraph 22).

Head football coach Gary Pinkel expressed solidarity on Twitter, posting a picture of the team and coaches locking arms. The tweet said: "The Mizzou Family stands as one. We are united. We are behind our players." The protesting players received the backing of their coaches and many of their white teammates said that they would stage a walkout, forfeiting the Saturday-scheduled game against BYU. The boycott would have could cost the university more than $1 million if the team had not played. Ultimately, the threat of a boycott by the Missouri football team forced Timothy M. Wolfe, the president, to resign. As Sports journalist Sean Gregory (2015: paragraph 5) writes, "Now, athletes realize they're not just the entertainment. They're not just a product of the world around them; they can shape it."

Michael B. Thomas/Stringer/Getty Images

Members of the University of Missouri Tigers Football Team return to practice at Memorial Stadium at Faurot Field on November 10, 2015 in Columbia, Missouri. The university looks to get things back to normal after the recent protests on campus that lead to the resignation of the school's President and Chancellor on November 9.

Finally, the group-culture-conflict perspective also suggests that groups are often in a continual struggle; they fight over resources (be them status and bragging rights, or economic or political power and access). Further, there is an assumption that such groups will often attempt to exploit those that are not in their group. For example, do college athletes have right to unionize if they feel like they have been economically—or, in terms of their health—exploited. Do they have a right to ask for monetary compensation regarding either of these concerns? Do owners of sports franchises and the right to ask the public to fund privately owned stadiums and teams? Can colleges and universities increase exorbitantly what they take from student fees in order to fund athletic departments? More on all of these questions later.

Using this mode of sociological thinking, we are able to ask these types of questions. In this context, sport sociologists ask, how does sporting culture and sporting groups operate in relation the larger social structures such as economics, race, religion, gender, nationality, etc.? Ultimately, we find that sport has an immense power to unite as well as to divide—and this is one of the main lessons we wish to impart: sport is more than sheer diversion, play, and escape. Sport can be a powerful force used to organize human beings into groups of productive or destructive forces.

Kneeling for the National Anthem: The Controversy of Colin Kaepernick

Colin Kaepernick (formerly #7 of the San Francisco 49ers) kneels on the sideline during the playing of the national anthem prior to the game against the Dallas Cowboys at Levi's Stadium on October 2, 2016. Before a preseason game in 2016, Kaepernick chose not to stand for the national anthem stating:

> I am not going to stand up to show pride in a flag for a country that oppresses black people and people of color. To me, this is bigger than football and it would be selfish on my part to look the other way. There are bodies in the street and people getting paid leave and getting away with murder (referencing a series of events that led to the Black Live Matter movement). I will continue to protest until I feel like [the American flag] represents what it's supposed to represent (Wagnoner 2016).

Kaepernick soon became highly polarizing as numerous people took public stances either supporting or maligning Kaepernick's actions. An NFL fan poll was taken during the beginning of the 2016 NFL season and Kaepernick was voted the "most disliked" player in the NFL (Rovell 2016). Yet, the sale of his jersey continued to be among the highest sought and sold (Andersen 2017).

Thearon W. Henderson/Stringer/Getty Images

Many NFL fans voiced displeasure (and threatened boycotts of the NFL) over his actions, arguing that his kneeling disrespected the flag—and by extension members of law enforcement and the US Military. However, a number of U.S. military veterans and law enforcement personnel have voiced support for Kaepernick's actions and mode of "protest" (Dator 2016, Wang 2017). This controversy (and the national conversation around issues of patriotism, inequality, and modes of protest) grew, when in September 2017, President Donald Trump sent out multiple tweets, advocating that NFL players should be either fired or suspended if they fail to stand up for the national anthem. In response, many NFL teams and players stood together to protest against Trump's opinion. The players knelt, locked arms, or even remained in the locker room during the playing of the anthem (Hoffman, Mather, and Fortin 2017).

Questions to Discuss

*When athletes speak out on social issues, they are often told to, "Shut up and Play!" What does this mean and why can't athletes (as citizens) have the power of political speech?

*Do you agree with Kaepernick and his form of protest? Why/why not?

*Do you believe his actions hurt his job prospects in the NFL? Why/why not?

*Do you think this outrage would exist is a white player kneeled to protest (or bring attention) to issues of social concern (such as the nation's opioid crisis, or veteran suicide rates?)

References

Anderson, Leigh C. 2017. "Colin Kaepernick's Jersey is Still a Top Seller." Salon, September 9, 2017. Retrieved November 4, 2017 (https://www.salon.com/2017/09/22/colin-kaepernicks-jersey-is-still-a-top-seller-benefitting-a-league-that-wont-sign-him/).

Dator, James. 2017. "US Military Members Are Showing Support for Colin Kaepernick with #VeteransForKaepernick." *SBNation*, August 31. Retrieved August 31 2017 (https://www.sbnation.com/2016/8/31/12726622/veterans-for-kaepernick-hashtag-protest-military-sit-during-anthem).

Hoffman, Benjamin, Victor Mather, and Jacey Fortin. 2017. "After Trump Blasts NFL, Players Kneel and Lock Arms in Solidarity." *The New York Times*, September 24, 2017. Retrieved September 24, 2017 (https://www.nytimes.com/2017/09/24/sports/nfl-trump-anthem-protests.html?mcubz53).

Rovell, Daren. 2016. "Poll: Kaepernick Most Disliked Player in League." *ESPN*, September 22, 2016. Retrieved July 4, 2017 (http://www.espn.com/nfl/story/_/id/17604958/san-francisco-49ers-qb-colin-kaepernick-most-disliked-player-nfl-according-poll-e-poll-marketing-research)

Wagnoner, Nick. 2016. "Transcript of Colin Kaepernick's Comments About Sitting During National Anthem." *ESPN*, August 28. Retrieved July 4 2017 (http://www.espn.com/blog/san-francisco-49ers/post/_/id/18957/transcript-of-colin-kaepernicks-comments-about-%20sitting-during-national-anthem).

Wang, Vivian. 2017. "New York Police Officers Rally in Support of Colin Kaepernick." *The New York Times*, August 19. Retrieved August 20 2017 (https://www.nytimes.com/2017/08/19/sports/football/colin-kaepernick-nypd-rally.html).

For a fuller discussion of Kaepernick's decision to kneel, please read Wagnoner (2016).

THEORETICAL PERSPECTIVE (3) SPORT AS A SOCIAL INSTITUTION

When sociologists explore social institutions (like the institution of sport), they study the ways in which that part of society contributes to society's overall operation. For example: On the morning of September 11, 2001, four commercial planes were taken over by hijackers who piloted the planes in coordinated terrorist attacks across America. Two of the planes flew into the World Trade Center buildings in NYC, while another targeted and hit the Pentagon. The fourth plane crash in Pennsylvania (presumably because of the passengers attempted to take over the plane from the hijackers). Approximately, 3,000 people were killed in these attacks. In the days to come, the nation coped by rallying around sports; fans, players, owners, and politicians used these athletic contests to build patriotic unity. As Eitzen (2012: 19–20) writes:

> from high school games to professional games, each was preceded by a variety of unifying symbolic acts—moments of silence, patriotic songs, the presentation of the flags (some as huge as a football field), military flyovers, And patriotic chants. . . . The message was the nexus of politics and sports, and nationhood

An analysis based on this perspective is termed **functionalism** and its lens focuses on the ways that the institution of sport helps the larger social system operate/function efficiently. In the preceding example, sport helped to promote harmony, collective healing, and domestic unity. Through a functionalist filter, we also explore how else sports connects to and impacts other institutions, such as the economy (as sport stimulates the economy as Americans spend more than $25 billion a year on athletics, Reilly 2012). Sport tends to dominate the social institution of media (with the largest portions of newspaper space being devoted to sport and sport typically brings in the largest TV audiences (Wood 2011). Sport also intersects with, and may become, quasi-religious, since sports can serve the functional equivalent of a religious ceremony that brings community together under a system of rituals and belief systems.

Sport can also be an arm and extension of government. Sport has been often used to open international diplomatic doors. Consider that, in the 1970s, when Communist China and the United States did not have diplomatic relations, the leadership of the two nations agreed that their athletes to compete in each country. After this exchange of athletic diplomacy, the two countries eventually established normal relations and a form of cultural, economic, and political diplomacy (Murry and Pigman 2013). In 2013, former NBA superstar Dennis Rodman and members of the Harlem Globetrotters visited the Democratic People's Republic of Korea (North Korea) as the guest of Kim Jong-un (then, the newly installed totalitarian dictator). At the time, several politicians and reporters joked that he, as a former sports star, was the only U.S. diplomat to North Korea in the contemporary era.

Unfortunately, the former basketball players' visit did not result in an established diplomatic relationship between the two countries but, as former White House press secretary Jay Carney said, "Sports exchanges can be valuable. Sports diplomacy can be valuable. And it's something that we pursue in many places around the world" (Harper 2014: paragraph 3).

As a final illustrative example of the functionality of sport, let us examine the use of sport in the nation of South Africa. Historically, a nation deeply divided, sport has helped to break down this division. First, when the whites in South Africa voted to dismantle apartheid (the system of institutionalized racial segregation and discrimination in South Africa between 1948 and 1991), one reason was the warning that the failure to do so would return the country to isolation in business and sport. Of the later, South Africa was barred from taking part in the 18th Olympic Games in Tokyo over its refusal to condemn apartheid. The ban was only lifted prior to the 1992 Olympic Games in Barcelona, when the international community became convinced that South Africa was irreversibly on the road to political transformation and the dismantling of the apartheid system.

When the World Cup in rugby was held in South Africa in 1995, President Mandela used the Rugby World Cup as an opportunity to bring various ethnic groups together within his country. The national rugby team, the Springboks, historically symbolized White South Africa, but Mandela encouraged Black Africans to think of this team as their team.

Movie Recommendation

Invictus (2009) is sports drama film about the events in South Africa before and during the 1995 Rugby World Cup following the dismantling of apartheid. Specifically, Nelson Mandela, in his first term as the South African President enlists the national rugby team in an attempt to unite the apartheid-torn Nation. When the Springboks went on to win the World Cup, for the first time in South Africa's history, Whites and Blacks found themselves unified by sport:

> Our Kind. Not black. Not White. South African. The rugby team became a symbol for the country as a whole. . . . Given the right time and place, sport is capable of starting such a process in a society. It is only a start, of course. The hard work lies ahead, after the crowds have dispersed and the headlines have ceased. South Africa is racial and economic woes are not behind it. Far from it. But thanks to the common grounds supplied by a rugby pitch, those problems appear less imposing than they [once] did (Swift 1995: paragraphs 8–10).

In sum, functionalism views society as a system of various interconnected parts (institutions) that help fuse society together, and sports are a necessary component of that "glue" that makes society possible.

Sport Case Study

Shrovetide Football

Every year, on Shrove Tuesday and Ash Wednesday, the town of Ashbourne in Derbyshire (England) welcomes thousands of people to brawl in the streets, turning the historic market town into something akin to a giant rugby scrum. Ashbourne is home to one of Britain's oldest and bloodiest sporting traditions: The Royal Shrovetide Football Match. The game, also known as "hug ball," has been played in the Derbyshire town since around 1667, though its origins are thought to date back to the 12th century.

The two teams that play the game are known as the Up'Ards and the Down'Ards—local slang for those that live north or south of the community river that runs through the town. During play, each team attempts to carry a ball back (thrown into the crowd from the town center) to their own goal rather than the more traditional method of scoring at the opponent's goal. The town goals are three miles apart and community members struggle to get the ball to their "home" goal. Players are allowed to hug and run with the ball (hence its alternative name), kick it, carry it, or throw it to get it back to their home goal. There are few rules, with the exception of acts to maim, murder, and attempts to hide the ball.

Roland Harrison/Contributor/Getty Images

When the ball is finally scored, the individual who made the winning goal (by knocking it three times against their millstone) is lifted on the shoulders of their colleagues and taken into the courtyard of The Green Man Royal Hotel (near the center of town). There, the player's name is immortalized in the community's recorded history.

How is this sport reflective of symbolic interaction, conflict, and functionalism?

The sporting event holds powerful **symbolic meaning** as it is played on Shrovetide Tuesday (a day of feasting and merry-making) and Ash Wednesday (traditionally a day to make confession and do penance for one's wrongdoings). Several symbolic and folkloric interpretations of the event suggest that the game is a community ritual celebration that reflects and strengthens the groups traditional Christian heritage. Cathcart (2016) argues that the game is similar to other ancient community sporting rituals (see, e.g., the game of Georgian of Lelo) that forces community members to experience and reflect upon the meanings of death, Easter, and resurrection. Symbolically, according to these folklorists, the community is participating in a sporting drama that invokes the Passion of Christ through physical suffering and a trial/test of one's worthiness. At the end of the sporting event, the community is also symbolically resurrected and has a strengthened sense of community identity by acting together in a physical ritualistic way.

Further, we may also argue that the game **functions** (i.e., allows) participants to release any tensions and stress that is built up over the year in a socially acceptable way—as one is expected to forgive any "transgressions" committed against them. (The idea is to gorge on violence one day, and repent for it on the next.)

Finally, other theorists suggest the game is nothing more than an expression of **conflict**: a rite of aggression built upon economic and social frustrations, with the uptowners and downtowners battling over access to wealth, jobs, and community pride (Williams 2015).

CHAPTER SUMMARY

The sociologist C. Wright Mills (1959) argued that sociology was valuable because it encouraged an imaginative and multi-leveled theoretical approach to knowledge about why people think and act as they do. Sociology, he argued, invited one to look for connections between the personal, cultural, and structural levels of our society and allowed us to see how the beliefs, decisions, and actions of individuals are shaped by our social world (shaped by socialization, group membership-including group unity and conflict, and our access to various social institutions). In turn, he also noted how our beliefs and our group actions might also change society.

This chapter provided you with a basic understanding of theory and identified the most common approaches sociologists use to study sport and society. But which approach is best when studying sport? The goal behind introducing the theoretical orientations in this chapter was to make us aware of the types of questions we ask and the types of issues we find important in the study of sport. In sociological research, we often employ all theoretical frameworks—symbolic interaction, conflict, and functionalist theories—to enable a holistic exploration and understanding of sport and society. Hopefully, you now find it impossible to ignore the central link between sport and society and note its impact in socialization, culture, and its power to tear or hold society together.

Discussion Questions

*When do you believe children learn the importance of competition—and do you believe our culture encourages "victory" to the negation of other values?

*How were you socialized into sport? Was this a positive or negative experience?

*Does sport unify more than it divides? Please provide examples using conflict and functionalist perspectives?

*Beyond the sport films/documentaries noted here, what other movies/biopics illustrate the themes of this chapter?

CHAPTER REFERENCES

Anderson, Eric. 2009. *Inclusive Masculinities: The Changing Nature of Masculinities.* London: Routledge.

Anderson, Eric. 2010. *Sport, Theory, and Social Problems: A Critical Introduction.* New York, NY: Routledge.

Barnes, Katie. 2016. "'Keepers of the Game' Breaks New Ground for Sports Storytelling Around Women." *ESPNW*, April 20. Retrieved October 21, 2017 (http://www.espn.com/espnw/culture/article/15273999/tribeca-espn-sports-film-festival-premieres-keepers-game).

Beamon, Krystal. 2010. "Are Sports Overemphasized in the Socialization Process of African American Males? A Qualitative Analysis of Former Collegiate Athletes' Perception of Sport Socialization." *Journal of Black Studies* 41 (2): 281–300.

Belsky, Gary and Neil Fine. 2016. *On the Origins of Sports: The Early History and Orginal Rules of Everybody's Favorite Games.* New York, NY: Artisan.

Buford, Bill. 1991. *Among the Thugs.* London: Vintage.

Cathcart, Will. 2016. "The Village Where People Celebrate Easter by Beating the Hell Out of Each Other." *Vice*, May 13. Retrieved November 4, 2017 (http://www.vice.com/en_us/article/kwka79/georgias-easter-bloodsport-lelo).

Chappell, Bill. 2015. "Police Look Into 2 High School Football Players' Hits On Texas Referee." *NPR*, September 8. Retrieved July 4, 2017 (http://www.npr.org/sections/thetwo-way/2015/09/08/438544495/police-look-into-two-football-players-hits-on-texas-referee).

Eitzen, D. Stanley. 2012. *Fair and Foul: Beyond the Myths and Paradoxes of Sport,* 5th ed. Boulder, CO: Rowman & Littlefield Publishers.

Girard, Rene. 1996. *The Girard Reader,* edited by James G. Williams. New York, NY: Crossroad.

Gregory, Sean. 2015. "Missouri President Toppled by the Power of the Student Athlete." *Time,* November 9. Retrieved July 4, 2017 (http://time.com/4104973/university-of-missouri-timothy-wolfe-athlete/).

Haenfler, Ross. 2015. Goths, Gamers, & Grrrls. New York, NY: Oxford University Press.

Harper, Jennifer. 2014. "Is Dennis Rodman a Diplomat or Just Spectacle?" *The Washington Times,* January 8. Retrieved October 1, 2017 (http://www.washingtontimes.com/blog/water-cooler/2014/jan/8/dennis-rodman-diplomat-or-just-spectacle/).

Hartigan, Jr., John. 2010. *Race in the 21st Century: Ethnography Approaches.* Oxford: Oxford University Press.

hooks, bell. 1992. *Black Looks: Race and Representation.* Boston, MA: South End Press.

Johnson, William. 2011. "Sociology Talks Life after sports for athletes." *The Short Horn,* Oct 19. Retrieved August 5, 2017 (http://www.theshorthorn.com/news/campus/sociology-assistant-professor-krystal-beamon-talks-life-after-sports-for/image_1c8d1b5e-55a8-59f8-b151-02377b500a2c.html).

Knight, Joey. 2014. "For Homerun Trot, Two Teams Become One." *Tampa Bay Times,* April 27. Retrieved July 4, 2017 (http://www.tampabay.com/sports/colleges/for-home-run-trot-two-teams-become-one/2177206).

Koren, Marina. 2015. "Mizzou's Football Team Tries to Sack the University's President." *The Atlantic,* November 8. Retrieved October 1, 2017 (https://www.theatlantic.com/national/archive/2015/11/missouri-football-racism/414819/).

Merleau-Ponty, Maurice. 2003. *Phenomenology of Perception.* Translated by Colin Smith. London: Routledge.

Mills, C. Wright. 1959. *The Sociological Imagination.* New York, NY: Oxford University Press.

Murry, Stuart and Geoffrey Allen Pigman. 2013. "Mapping the Relationship Between International Sport and Diplomacy." *Sport in Society.* 17 (9):1098–1118. doi: http://dx.doi.org/10.1080/17430437.2013.856616.

Reilly, Lucas. 2012. "By the Numbers: How Americans Spend Their Money." *Mental Floss,* July 17. Retrieved July 4, 2017 (http://mentalfloss.com/article/31222/numbers-how-americans-spend-their-money).

Schultz, Jamie. 2012. "Mapping America's Sporting Landscape: A Case Study of Three Statues." Pp. 166–172. *The Visual in Sport,* edited by Mike Huggins and Mike O'Mahony. New York, NY: Routledge.

Serven, Ruth and Ashley Reese. 2015. "In Homecoming Parade, Racial Justice Advocates Take Different Paths: One Group Chose to March in the Parade, Another Staged a Protest Along the Route." *Columbia Missourian,* October 10. Retrieved October 4, 2017 (http://www.columbiamissourian.com/news/in-homecoming-parade-racial-justice-advocates-take-different-paths/article_24c824da-6f77-11e5-958e-fb15c6375503.html).

Sports Nation. 2013. Chat With Tom Farrey. *SportsNation.* Retrieved October 4, 2017 (http://espn.go.com/sportsnation/chat/_/id/22115).

Swift, E.M. 1995. "Box to the Future with a United Nation Cheering: South Africa's Springboxs Won a Stirring World Cup Championship." *Sports Illustrated*, July 3. Retrieved July 4, 2017 (http://www.si.com/vault/1995/07/03/204437/bok-to-the-future-with-a-united-nation-cheering-south-africas-springboks-won-a-stirring-world-cup-championship).

Thing, Lone Friis. 2001. The Female Warrior: Meanings of Play-Aggressive Emotions in Sport. *International Review for the Sociology of Sport* 36 (3): 275–288.

Thrasher, Steven W. 2015. "Mizzou Revolt Strengthens as University President Concedes 'Change is Needed.'" *The Guardian*, September 9. Retrieved July 4, 2017 (http://www.theguardian.com/us-news/2015/nov/09/missouri-university-black-players-protest-support-grows).

Vaughan, Ed. 2001. *Sociology: The Study of Society*. Upper Saddle River, NJ: Prentice Hall.

Wagnoner, Nick. 2016. "Transcript of Colin Kaepernick's Comments About Sitting During National Anthem." *ESPN*, August 28. Retrieved July 4, 2017 (http://www.espn.com/blog/san-francisco-49ers/post/_/id/18957/transcript-of-colin-kaepernicks-comments-about-sitting-during-national-anthem).

Williams, Victoria. 2015. *Weird Sports and Wacky Games Around The World*. Denver, CO: Greenwood.

Womack, Mari. 2003. *Sport as Symbol: Images of the Athlete in Art, Literature and Song*. Jefferson, NC: McFarland & Company.

Women Sports Foundation. 2016. Benefits: Why Sports Participation for Girls and Women. Available: file:///Users/johnpaul/Downloads/benefits-why-sports-participation-for-girls-and-women-the-foundation-position.pdf

Wood, Ronald B. 2010. *Social Issues In Sport*. 2nd ed. Champlain, IL: Human Kinetics.

Workman, Karen. 2015. "High School Football Players Who 'Blindsided' Referee Say He Made Racist Remarks." *The New York Times*, September 9. Retrieved November 4, 2017 (http://www.nytimes.com/2015/09/10/sports/high-school-football-players-who-rammed-referee-say-he-made-racist-remarks.html?_r=0).

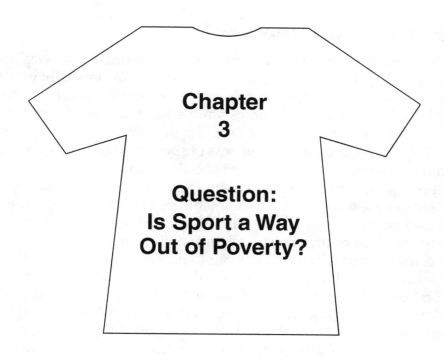

Chapter 3

Question: Is Sport a Way Out of Poverty?

Student Outcomes

After reading this chapter, you will be able to do the following:

- Understand the opportunity for social mobility through sport, including the access or barriers that social class places on sport.
- Recognize the impact that sport infrastructure has on lower, middle, and upper-class communities.
- Define and use the sociological concepts of "meritocracy," "stratification" and the notion of the "dirty trick" in sport.

Sport has long been emblematic of the American "rags to riches" success story and holds iconic status as embodying the American dream. Indeed, many believe that sports and sport participation are open to all people and that inequalities related to money, position, and influence have no effect on the games we watch and play. Yet, the truth is that watching, playing, and excelling in sport requires social and material resources. Thus, even in sport, social class differences exist and matter profoundly. In this chapter, we take a critical approach to the intersection of sport and social class and examine who benefits and who is disadvantaged by the ways sport (and society) is organized.

SPORT AND SOCIAL MOBILITY

Sport holds iconic status as embodying the American dream. As Washington and Karen (2010), note, sports achievement is believed to be the model of **meritocracy**—the harder one works, the more one achieves. They write "in sports, the competition is visible, public, and open to analysis and review . . . . And because it is public, we believe it to be on a 'level' playing field. Further, 'on any given day' the underdog can win" (p. xiv). Thus, the uniqueness of sport creates what appears to be the purest and most public model of upward social mobility.

Indeed, because sport heroes are among the best-paid and wealthiest icons of consumer society they serve as embodiments of the fantasy aspirations for the good life—and popular tales are replete with examples of how sports have provided persons with opportunities to enhance their economic positions and attain fame and fortune. And various sport's rag to riches stories abound. For example, American soccer star Clint Dempsey (who made $6.695 million in 2014—more than the total payrolls of 15 out of 19 Major League Soccer teams) grew up in a trailer park in Texas playing with migrant children from Mexico (Zaldivar 2014). LeBron James (considered the greatest active player in the NBA) grew up in the worst neighborhoods of Akron, Ohio with only his mother—who was 16 years of age when she had James (Helfland 2014). And Michael Oher, of The Blind Side fame, despite growing up in an environment of poverty and violence and with years of housing and family instability, still made it into the NFL and eventually became a Superbowl champion (Lewis 2007).

Video Recommendation

The Blind Side (2009)

The Blind Side is a movie based on the life of Michael Oher leading up to his college football and eventual NFL career. While Oher himself has publicly denounced how he was portrayed in the movie, it nonetheless provides a wealth of material for dissecting the intersection between poverty and sport.

In the movie, Oher was born to a mother with addiction issues and a father who spent more time in prison than with his son. As a result, he grew up in extreme poverty in a gang infested area of Memphis and went through bouts where he was homeless or placed in foster care. He is presented as someone with limited personal and academic potential whose only chance to succeed in life is through football because of his size. In fact, it is his perceived potential to excel on the gridiron that drives the movie's underlying theme that sport can lift people out of poverty. For example, he is provided with a tutor to help him get his grades up so that he can play football rather than because getting good grades can open doors to a college education and career options that could lift him out of poverty.

Another major piece of the film is the focus on the rich, white Tuohy family who take Oher in and "save" him from poverty. While the movie makes clear that the Tuohy family truly feels that Oher is a part of the family and love him as much as if he was their biological kin, there are nonetheless implications made in the movie that the family may have had ulterior motives related to his football potential in taking the actions that they did (i.e., as people with privilege, power and connections, they are instrumental in making sure that he is playing football in high school and gets recruited by top Division I programs including their own alma mater).

From a sociological perspective, The Blind Side brings up some interesting questions about social mobility. Current data show that it is not a common phenomenon for children from impoverished communities to get college scholarships for sports, let alone make it a professional career, so is this movie perpetuating a myth about common avenues out of poverty? Would Oher have had the same access to social mobility if he had not also had a rich, white family who supported him with their money, connections, and power? Does the movie perpetuate the stereotype that poor, black youth are only good at athletics and do not have the academic potential to succeed and gain social mobility in other ways?

Their rise from humble beginnings, along with similar tales of other athletes, create a widely-believed sports mythology, which suggests that if you have athletic ability, and ambition, you can come from anywhere and succeed. But this is not always the case.

STRATIFIED ACCESS TO SPORT

But while we love such stories of individuals overcoming adversity, it must be said that these scenarios of success by true grit alone are more myth than a steadfast reality. The truth is poverty and inequality keeps persons out of sport. This is because sport, like larger society, is highly **stratified**. Indeed, more than ever, it takes money to view sport and have the opportunity to play and develop sport skills. For example, in contemporary society, if one simply wishes to watch a sporting event in person, one finds that tickets can be quite expensive and limiting in opportunities for the direct experience. According to current statistics, the average cost for a family of four to attend an NFL game is just under $500 dollars (Greenberg 2014). Further, it's not cheap to go to a major-league sporting event either. Reports indicate that baseball tickets have increased "by as much as 344 percent since 1957, after adjusting for inflation" (Parker 2016: paragraph 1). Further, when one gains entry they find that spectators are often divided by social class. The wealthy and well connected sit in luxury suites and club seats, whereas fans who are less well-off sit in other sections with more distant and limited views, depending on their ability to pay for premium tickets or buy season tickets.

Additionally, it takes ever increasing levels of money to watch sports on television as cable and satellite connections come with ever-increasing monthly subscription fees and pay- per-view costs. Cable companies make deals to carry channels and channels make deals to carry sports. Big sports leagues, in an ever expanding media market, force channels to pay an exorbitant price for new contracts. For example, in September 2013, ESPN paid the NFL 70 percent more per game to carry Monday Night Football through 2021 (Thompson 2012: paragraph 9). Thus, whether you watch sports or not, you pay more for cable because cable providers pass the costs of these huge contracts onto viewers. In response, a growing number of consumers are ending their cable and satellite subscriptions and returning to antennas, broadcast TV, and the Internet for video programming. This means that money and economic power exert significant influence on who has exposure to sport, who becomes a fan, and who develops the knowledge necessary to understand and pursue sport.

Cycle Polo: The "Poor" Persons Version of Horse Polo

Horse Polo is not a cheap sport: It requires the purchase of an elite horse and requires maintenance, training and traveling costs. What separates polo is that it requires those who play it to own more than one horse (most polo players need about four horses in order to substitute tired horses. Horses must be exercised regularly and this usually requires two "grooms" (persons responsible for the care of the horses and the cleaning and management of the stables) at $2,500 a month. Tournaments can cost anywhere between $3,500 and $150,000. To be a patron and sponsor polo teams in tournaments can cost anywhere between $300,000 and $1,000,000.

Nikirov/Shutterstock.com

While horse polo is played on manicured grass fields with wooden mallets, cycle polo began in alleys and side streets on bicycles with mallets crafted from ski poles and PVC pipe. In fact, part of the fun of cycle polo is constructing and reconstructing your equipment. Cycle polo is a team sport with the game typically being played on a hardcourt. In this variation, teams composed of three players compete on tennis courts, outdoor basketball courts street hockey rinks, or whatever other surfaces are available. Commonly, a street hockey-ball is used and matches are played until one team scores 5 points or time (designated by the players) has expired.

There are three core rules of play: (1) In the case of a "foot down" or "dab" (touching the ground with one's foot) the player must "tap out" by riding to mid-court and hitting a designated area with their mallet. There is usually a tap-out located on either side of the court. (2) In order to score, the offensive player must hit the ball across the goal line using the narrow end of the mallet - this is called a "shot" or "hit"- hitting the ball across the goal line with the wide end of the mallet is called a "shuffle." (3) When your team scores a goal, you wait back in your end for the other team (player or ball, whichever comes first) to cross half before engaging in play again.

The exact origin of polo is unknown, but the first recorded match on horses was in 600 BCE in Persia. Since then the sport has been adapted to play on elephants (with an extremely long mallet), motorcycles, and even Segways. The modern bike polo version of the sport originated in Seattle, Washington in the early 2000s. The idea arose from bike messengers who spent their time in between deliveries playing early renditions of the game and was designed to be open to players of all ages, and economic incomes.

Class Participation and Sport Infrastructure

Even the play of sport requires facilities, equipment, and safe play spaces—all of which are more plentiful in upper and upper-middle income neighborhoods. Low income neighborhoods generally lack what is needed to initiate and sustain informal activities; families don't have large lawns at their homes, they don't live on safe cul-de-sacs without traffic, and well-maintained neighborhood parks are in short supply. The reality is that the higher the socioeconomic status of the individual, the more likely one will be able to actively pursue and play sport. There are several reasons for this reality. The most obvious is that many sporting activities are too expensive for the less well-to-do. The affluent also have access to private clubs and resorts where golf, tennis, and skiing and swimming are available.

Though the largest proportion of the tennis courts in are in now public parks, tennis clubs were once known for their exclusivity: At the higher end, membership in private clubs often require $100,000 or more in initiation fees and at least $10,000 in annual dues and monthly minimums for food and beverages. Beyond the excluding factor of money, clubs were also known for generally excluding women, and ethnic minorities. Indeed, women and ethnic minorities of the era who challenged these norms of exclusion were called "troublemakers" and were told that it's was a (white) man's sport and that's "that all there is to it" (Newton 1987: paragraph 3).

Documentary Recommendation

Althea (2015)

Althea Gibson, was the first African American to cross the color line playing and winning at Wimbledon in 1957 and 1958 and at the U.S. Nationals (precursor of the U.S. Open) in 1957 and 1958. "Althea" is a complex exploration of race, class and gender and traces Gibson's roots as a sharecropper's daughter to her emergence as a grand champion of the highly segregated tennis world. As the documentary's narrator states:

> Though a talented tennis player, Gibson was a street kid who lacked the genteel manner associated with the sport. It was under the tutelage of Dr. Hubert Eaton of Wilmington, NC and Dr. Robert W. Johnson of Lynchburg, VA, two African American physicians who loved tennis and helped young African Americans who wanted to play, that she flourished. She honed her skill, while receiving lessons in etiquette and the social graces, traveled and played in the segregated south, and even earned her high school degree. Her success in tennis earned her an athletic scholarship (basketball and tennis) to Florida A&M, where she received a BA in 1955 at the age of 27.

Bettmann/Contributor/Getty Images

And she was more than just a tennis "jock." Branching out to other areas, she recorded a jazz album, became an actor, and even took up golf, becoming the first African American woman to become a member of the LPGA (Ladies Professional Golf Association). Indeed, Althea's professional accomplishments put her in the forefront of the struggle to eliminate class, gender, and racial segregation in tennis (and beyond).

At first glance, the absence of a well-developed sports infrastructure open to the general public (i.e., more public golf, tennis courses) may not appear to represent social injustices. But we argue here that the absence of an infrastructure are social injustices suffered by individuals under the following societal conditions: (1) sports complexes have been found to be safe zones (particularly in high crime neighborhoods) for children to grow and thrive, (2) the majority of persons impoverished population lack access to safe fitness zones which may help to combat growing public health epidemics such as obesity and heart disease, (3) finally, limited public programs fail to counter the principle of social exclusivity that helps only to reproduce broader aspects of social inequality.

A more recent example of this is the construction of the new New York Yankees stadium (opened in 2009). As journalist Robert McClure (2012: paragraphs 1, 5, 8) writes:

> In the poorest Congressional district in the country, the nation's wealthiest baseball franchise took away kids' baseball fields in order to build the new stadium . . . The South Bronx baseball fields sat in Macombs Dam Park, across the street from the old Yankee Stadium . . . Kids too poor to attend a New York Yankees game at least could try to pitch a no-hitter in the shadow of the Bronx Bombers' aging palace. . . . During [the construction of the new stadium] crews also obliterated nearly 400 trees that helped clean the air in a neighborhood where hospitalization rates for asthma are five times what they are nationally.

New York State law requires that when parkland is taken away from the public's use, it must be replaced by new parkland nearby of equal or greater value. To meet the law, the Yankees (with tax dollars from New York residents) did rebuild park land. However, "instead of being set inside a large, green space surrounded by hundreds of mature trees, the fields were scattered on separate parcels, including the tops of parking garages" (Schwartz 2006: paragraph 3). Further, the taking of parkland for the stadium and parking garages also raised a number of public health concerns: the new recreational spaces would be closer to the highway and train tracks (thus producing an increased risk of noise and air pollution). Finally, concerning notions of racial and ethnic inequality, the taking of the park most profoundly affected Blacks and Hispanics who already had the lowest ratios of parkland space to residents (Matte et.al. 2007).

Documentary Recommendation

Battle for Brooklyn (2011) is a documentary that follows the stories of residents of a Brooklyn neighborhood as they fight to save their homes from being destroyed by an impending real estate project to build the Barclay Center, the new home of the Brooklyn Nets (formerly the New Jersey Nets). The film attempts to show the unjust outcomes that are possible when moneyed and powerful interests partner up with government entities to outweigh the rights of citizens.

In many ways, the documentary explores the use and abuse of Eminent Domain (the right of a government to take private property for public use) and the notion that sport stadiums do not bring significant economic growth (jobs or profit) to communities.

Regarding global society and sport infrastructure as social injustices, please consider the 2014 World Cup in Brazil. As the world enjoyed the televised games in Brazil, many within the country believed the global event was too much of a burden for the country's struggling economy. Activists across Brazil critiqued the government and football's governing body, FIFA (Fédération Internationale de Football Association), for exploiting Brazil and neglecting the needs of the poor (Zirin 2014). Specifically, activists critiqued the fact that 11 billion US dollars was spent to build stadiums and sports infrastructure—which could have instead been used to improve transportation, healthcare, and education.

Further, in preparation for the 2016 Olympics, it was reported that Brazil knocked down favelas (community dwellings most often defined in popular parlance as "slums") to build parking lots and removed people from homes to clear the areas, to present a sanitized (clean) image for a global audience. Romário, a Brazilian soccer star- turned-politician, called the entire project "absurd." He said, "There will be a couple games there, and then what? Who will go? It is an absolute waste of time and money . . . what will we do with the stadiums . . . one idea is to turn the entire stadium into a massive open-air prison. How ridiculous is that!" (Zirin 2014: paragraph 7).

The Eton Wall Game

Eaton College is an English independent boarding school for boys. It was founded in 1440 and is one of the oldest, most prestigious, and most expensive schools to attend. JK Rowling, the author of the Harry Potter series is rumored to have constructed her magical houses in part after the hierarchical dorms (and the status privileges they confer) that exist at Eton (Associated Press, 2015). In brief, the dorms are arraigned by those that receive a full scholarship versus those who receive partial or no financial support. Thus, this arraignment can create a class system when one is distinguished by wealth, a family name of power and status and a family name with no historical privilege or money.

In a playful yet critical review, the author Nick Fraser (2005) notes that Eton is a place that can breed class superiority:

Etonians can appear as . . . raving snobs . . . and 'exotic creatures' beyond the immediate comprehension of lesser mortals educated at state school. . . . Etonians tend to rub along with anyone they meet - because they can afford not to feel superior. . . . Eton flourished by establishing bed-and-breakfasts for the sons of the wealthy. Generations of aristocrats gave to Eton its distinctive, laidback culture of insouciance. Eton is a good school, coming near the top in the annual tables of exam results. . . . Attempts have been made to change the dress code, or introduce girls, but these have foundered. . . . The primary function of Eton over the centuries was to produce a more or less educated [male] ruling elite (paragraph 4, 8. 10).

And this battle of status exits too within Eaton as people often have to prove that they belong. Proving that one deserves to be at Eaton is often played out between the houses—and along "The Wall."

Leo Mason/Popperfoto/Contributor/Getty Images

View of various pupils of Eton College, watched by fellow pupils sitting on the wall, playing the Eton Wall game between house teams (Photo by Leo Mason/Popperfoto/Getty Images).

The main game consists of the two sets of players forming a rugby-style scrummage (called a bully) in which the teams attempt to advance a ball slowly along the Wall to the other side. Many players, particularly those whose position is actually against the Wall, lose the skin off their elbows, hips, and knees. Players within the Bully shove and push each other, mostly with their bodies but also by placing their fists against the faces of the opposition and attempting to lever them backwards and away from the Wall. Actual punching is not permitted, but players may soak their fists in the mud and grind the hardened soil again the faces of their opponents. If the ball falls out of bounds (which is anything beyond 5 meters away from the wall), play is restarted opposite where the ball stops after it had gone out, or was touched after it had gone out.

The game may last up to an hour, with two halves of 30 minutes each. Many games end 0-0. Since the ability to move the ball along the way is very difficult.

Question: With the game typically ending in a 0-0 tie, what is the purpose/function of the game? What is this about socially? Please use your sociological imaginations and debate this sporting and social spectacle.

**As a side: Debating at Eton has always been important and in some sense also considered sport? Do you consider debate (in terms of winning or losing an argument, a sport?).

The sport scholar Kendall Blanchard would. He studied "word dueling" among Inuit groups in the North American Artic. In actions, similar to that of a debate (or perhaps contemporarily, more similar to a "rap battle"), persons would meet in a head-to-head competition to settle an issue or grievance. He writes:

> The duel is a battle of words and wit. Combatants mimic, parody, and shout abusive, though often creative, insults at each other. Each puts on a show. . . . The object of the duel from the participants' standpoint is to gain sympathy and support from the audience. The one who is successful in working the audience so that it laughs with him and at his opponent is the winner of the competition (Blanchard 1995:28-29).

Question: Are there other examples of word games that our society considers sport? Remember, spelling bees are now shown on ESPN.

References

Associated Press. 2015. "JK Rowling talks 'Harry Potter' on Twitter." *The Boston Globe*, November 29. Retrieved October 5, 2017 (https://www.bostonglobe.com/lifestyle/names/2015/11/29/rowling-talks-potter-twitter/cn8FOD7XOwB2hjndRm5b0L/story.html).

Blanchard, Kendall. 1995. *The Anthropology of Sport*. Westport, CA: Bergin & Garvey.

Nick Fraser, Nick. 2005. "You can take the boy out of Eton . . ." *The Guardian*, November 22. Retrieved November 4, 2017 (http://www.theguardian.com/education/2005/nov/23/schools.uk).

SPORTS OF THE POOR: BOXING

Returning to a discussion of the U.S. sporting context, we now examine sports historically participated in by the poor. Of the sporting activities that persons with limited economic resources tend to participate in are those that are either publicly funded (such as community football and baseball) or those that require little equipment and limited space (such as boxing and basketball).

Consider for example the history and sociology of boxing: The first boxers in the United States were slaves and Southern plantation owners whom often amused themselves by putting together their "strongest chattel" and having them fight it out (Remnick 1998:221). Beyond this specter of forced fighting, the succession of persons who willingly pursued boxing were primarily the immigrant Irish in the 1800s and early 1900s. This athletic population transitioned to Jews in the 1920s, then to Italians and Blacks in the 1950s, and to Blacks and Latinos beginning in the 1980s. This pattern reflected the "acculturation strategies" of those ethnic groups located on the lowest rungs of the socioeconomic ladder. As each group moved up, it pulled its youth out of prizefighting and pushed them into more promising and meaningful pursuits (Wacquant 2006, Heiskanen 2014).

. . . and Basketball

Basketball prowess among the poor has been explained as of result of the game being accessible and inexpensive. As Pete Axthelm (2011:1–2) writes:

> Basketball demands no open spaces or lush backyards or elaborate equipment. It doesn't even require specified number of players . . . Basketball is the game for young athletes without cars or allowances . . . The game is simple, an act of one challenging themselves or another twisting, feinting, then . . . directing a ball toward a target, a metal hoop ten feet above the ground.

Indeed, basketball has been a sport at which urban and rural poor have historically excelled. But how true and realistic is this assertion, particularly for "average" (i.e., those who lack the talent and physical ability to play elite level basketball) players? Further, how realistic is this dream for those who do not have the right connections or proper exposure? Countless young persons from working-class family backgrounds view sport participation as perhaps their only hope and primary reason to achieve success.

The film *Hoop Dreams* (James, Marx and Marx 1994) and books such as Darcey Frey's *The Last Shot* (2004) and May's *Living Through the Hoop* (2009) document the emphasis that young men place on sports as a way out of poverty, crime and despair. But "the dream of financial success through a professional sports career is just that, a dream for all but an infinitesimal number" (Eitzen 2012:193).

Movie Recommendation

Hoop Dreams (1994) is a documentary that follows the story of two African American high-school students in Chicago and their dreams of becoming professional basketball players.

The documentary focuses on William Gates and Arthur Agee as they are recruited to a predominantly white high school with an outstanding basketball program. The teenagers are both poor kids from African American neighborhoods who have to travel approximately 90 minutes to and from their new school. As they endure long and difficult workouts and have to acclimate to a new cultural climate, the documentary records the struggles and successes of Gates and Agee.

djsknot/Shutterstock.com

Ultimately, the film raises a number of powerful issues concerning economic stratification, race and culture, and educational and aspirational values in America—especially in how sport is defined as the way out of poverty.

Consider the following data provided by the Nation Collegiate Athletic Association (NCAA), keeping in mind that being drafted by a professional is no guarantee that one will ever play at that level: 1.2 percent of male senior basketball players will be drafted by an NBA team (.03 of high-school seniors will be drafted by an NBA team—or 3 in 10,000) (NCAA 2013). Indeed, youth have a greater and more honest likelihood of upward mobility through focusing on science, math, and other academic pursuits. As Sociologist Jay Coakley writes:

> My best guess is that 6,000 African Americans, or about 1 in 6,600, are making a good living as professional athletes. Data from the US Department of Labor indicates that, in 2004, 18,640 African American men and women were classified as 'athletes, coaches, umpires, and related workers.' In that same year, 50,630 African Americans were physicians and surgeons, 44,840 were lawyers, and 69,388 were college and university teachers. Therefore, there were 36 times more African Americans working in these three prestigious professions than African American athletes in top level professional sports; and 9 times more African American doctors, lawyers, and college teachers than African Americans working in all sports. Furthermore, physicians, lawyers, and college teachers have greater lifetime earnings than most athletes whose playing careers, on average, last less than five years and whose salaries outside the top pro leagues rarely exceed 50,000 dollars (cited in Eitzen 2009:212).

Beyond this, basketball is quickly becoming a sport of the middle class. Scholars Joshua Kjerulf Dubrow and Jimi Adams (2012) studied the family dynamic and socio-economic backgrounds of NBA players from 1994 to 2004. They found that among African Americans, a child from a low-income family has 37 percent lower odds of making the NBA than a child from a middle- or upper-income family. Further, a black athlete from a family without two parents is 18 percent less likely to play in the NBA than a black athlete raised by two parents. As Dubrow and Adams put it, "The intersection of race, class and family structure background presents unequal pathways into the league" (p. 55).

Thus, contrary to popular perception, poverty and broken homes are underrepresented in the NBA, not overrepresented. For example, while 45 percent of black male children in the United States live in households earning no more than 150 percent of the poverty line ($22,050 for a family of four in 2010), just 34 percent of black athletes in the NBA grew up in that financial situation. As Keating (2011: paragraph 11) writes:

> The NBA of our imagination – a league that functions as a conveyor of inner-city hoop dreams – actually did exist at one point. In the 1960s and 70s, more than 90 percent of NBA players were from urban areas. But as the game grew more popular and attracted more corporate sponsors, pro teams and colleges expanded the search for talent, and suburban (and foreign) high schools began strengthening their programs.

The new reality is that it now takes more resources—a lot more—to compete at the highest level. "You need facilities, equipment and transportation, not to mention coaches and volunteers. . . . current research suggests that kids in cities are now much less likely to participate in sports than kids in suburbs" (Keating 2011, paragraph 11). Ultimately we convince ourselves the of transformative power of "hunger" and we believe that individual motivation is always greater than economic circumstance. But this is broadly a myth. With funding for school athletic programs decreasing across the country, it's important to understand one's family, community, and other support structures matter as much, if not more so, than talent.

Indeed, the popular image of the player rising from the "ghetto" to international fame and fortune misleads the public and the hopeful athlete alike. This false image is fueled, in part, by parents, community members, coaches and school supporters who push the young men to work harder on the court. The sociologist Reuben May (2009:151) has called all of this a **"dirty trick"**—or, institutionalized deceptions that perpetuate the fallacy of meritocracy through sport. He continues:

> Why would these young men believe in this hoop dream? First the media, and television programs . . . suggest to average players the viability of athletics as a means of mobility . . . these programs are highly suggestive, even inspirational, for young men. Second, the communities in which the young man have grown up support success through stereotypical means for black males. For those young men who seek mobility, the perceptions of opportunity are limited by the deleterious conditions of their communities. Third, the young men compete with other average players, providing them with an unrealistic measure of their skills [and] they can readily overestimate their abilities. The young men are blinded to the extensive pool of quality athletes who will be competing for the few opportunities for social mobility through basketball. . . . Finally, the coaches encourage basketball to the young men who pursue hoop dreams. The immediate benefit for coaches is that the players commit to developing their skills, working hard to develop what they believe is necessary for playing basketball at the next level (160-161).

Sport sociologist Krystal Beamon (2010), too argues that and sport is often propagandized as the only "way out" and that these beliefs are particularly prevalent in poor and working class black communities. She argues that the expectations for professional success exceed the opportunity available. "Statistically speaking," Beamon states, "An African American male is more likely to be a neurosurgeon than an NBA star . . . ultimately sports should not be the initial aspirations for children, but "an end to a mean" (Johnson 2011: paragraph 8).

Sports of the Poor Continued: Baseball and Soccer (Global Football)

Alan Whyte (2009: paragraph 1) writes:

> Originally developed in the United States in the 19th century, the game of baseball has become an increasingly global sport. And it is well known

that some of the best players in the world come from the Dominican Republic (DR), with multi-million dollar contracts in the US to prove it. In fact, some 15 percent of major league baseball players currently hail from the country.

For many young talented Dominican athletes, the game is far more than a means of recreation; it is "a vehicle by which to escape dire poverty" (Whyte 2009: paragraph 2). Indeed, Dominican players come to the United States hoping to earn a spot on a major-league team and dreaming of an economic windfall; the average salary of Major League baseball players in 2017 stands at $4.47 million (Statista 2017)—In the Dominican Republic, more than 40 percent of the people live below the national official poverty line and 30 percent of the population of 9.5 million are undernourished (Klein 2014).

But as journalist Ian Gordan (2013) points out, the nation is largely exploited by Major League Baseball as it tries to control access to the talent on the island. Further, the MBL often ignores most aspects of a player (even ignoring the vitally important need for teaching English and the integration into American culture) while simply focusing on baseball. In a rather damning appraisal of how Major League Baseball treats the Dominican Republic, he writes:

> It is a worst-case scenario in a recruiting system that treats young Dominicans as second-class prospects, paying them far less than young Americans and sometimes denying them benefits that are standard in the US minor leagues, such as health insurance and access to professionally trained medical staff. MLB regulations allow teams to troll for talent on the cheap in the Dominican Republic: Unlike American kids, who must have completed high school to sign, Dominicans can be signed as young as 16, when their bodies and their skills are far less developed (paragraph 9).

It is a reality that more than half of the Latin American players came from the Dominican Republic, the most from any country outside the United States. And yet, of the hundreds of Dominican prospects at the academies each year (along with Venezuelans and other Latin Americans also training there), less than half will ever leave the island to play even in the minor leagues, let alone in the majors, "where under 3 percent will eventually step up to the plate [and] more than three-quarters will drop out of baseball in four years" (Gordon 2013: paragraph 16).

It is true of course that US born players also face a long road to professional baseball. But nearly 70 percent of them will advance to the minor leagues at some point in their journeys and will have "more than four times the chance to crack a major-league roster" (Gordon 2013: paragraph 16). They are also far better paid at the outset: The average signing bonus for international players, is approximately half that of U.S. Americans (Klein 2014).

Global Football (Soccer)

Turning now the world's most popular sport (Kuper 2014), we explore too the powerful cliché and myth that is that it also is a way out of poverty. As Goldblatt writes, "Football is available to anyone who can make a rag ball and find another pair of feet to pass to" (2008: xiv).

Unfortunately, soccer is also a fairy-tale-like story that becomes a false hope to many young kids' futures of economic survival. As Chilean journalist, Juan Pablo Meneses, notes in his book *Niños Futbolistas* (2013), an extremely low percentage actually make it out of poverty and actually find stardom. Meneses investigates how young talented football players in South America are purchased and sold to various football clubs in Europe. He writes:

> I was watching the news and noticed that child footballers were being transferred at a very young age . . . Big teams like Barcelona and Real Madrid were assimilating very young children. To me, that sounded like child labor. . . . the rights to a boy under the age of twelve who plays for an amateur club in Latin America cost around two hundred dollars. If the boy is registered with a federated team the price varies between one thousand and six thousand dollars. Most of the boys are bought at around the age of ten. Thousands of agents are willing to sponsor them, with one main objective: to sell the boys with a big profit to clubs abroad. Once the transfer has been realized, their business is done. If (and more likely when) the child doesn't make it to the professional level, they just leave him behind regardless of his situation. . . . the children today consider football as a job instead of a game. Young and talented football players are trained only to play football. They 'forget' about their education. Their parents acquiesce in this, because they see it as their only option to escape poverty. . . . In most of the countries there is no other option. In the Dominican Republic there is baseball and in Mexico there is boxing, but in all other countries the only other option is to become a narco (cited in FIFPRO 2013).

Documentary Recommendation

Kicking It (2008) is a documentary that focuses on the experiences of homeless persons from Afghanistan; Kenya; Dublin, Ireland; Charlotte, North Carolina; Madrid, Spain and St. Petersburg, Russia as they train and compete in the Homeless World Cup.

The purpose of the homeless soccer organization is to use the play of soccer to challenge stereotypes of persons experiencing homelessness. Further, the organization uses soccer to facilitate change within the players (i.e., building self-esteem, getting them access to healthcare, group therapy) and in society (i.e., using the venue to encourage conversation on causes and consequences of homelessness and work toward its amelioration). In the documentary, viewers face the various causes of homelessness, including: homelessness due to drug addiction, family violence, extreme poverty, political disenfranchisement, migration and displacement due to war and economic collapse. In the end, this "sport documentary" helps raise consciousness and compassion on the issue of homelessness and encourages viewers to challenge their own conceptions about the issue.

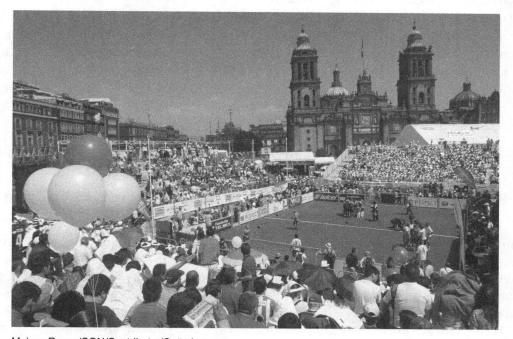

Moises Rosas/CON/Contributor/Getty Images

General view of the opening ceremony of the Homeless World Cup on October 06, 2012 at Zocalo Capitalino, Ciudad de Mexico, Mexico. (Fotopor Moises Rosas/Latin Content/Getty Images).

A "Slave-like" Class: Conditions in College Athletics

Other notions of class (and racial) inequities include scholarly works that call attention to the exploitation of the amateur athlete (Sperber 2001, May, Reuben 2009, Hawkins 2010). Indeed, many observers of college sports have an idealized version what it is like for young athletes to play football or basketball and a university with a big-time sports program. The belief is that these athletes accept an all-expenses paid college education for the joy and pleasure of playing in front of adoring fans—and that this all expenses paid opportunity will open the door for future career pathways. But participation in college athletics is never as it appears. There is an oft- overlooked dark side to big-time college sports. Eitzen (20012) writes:

> Let me use the metaphor of big-time college sports as a plantation system. I admit at the outset that this metaphor is overdrawn . . . Nevertheless there are significant parallels with slavery that highlight the serious problems plaguing college athletics . . . My argument is that athletes are persons exploited in a plantation system . . . and this involves several dimensions: (1) the athletes (slaves) are exploited economically, making millions for their masters provided only with a subsistence wage of room, bored, tuition and books; (2) they are controlled with restricted freedoms; (3) they are subject to physical and mental abuse by overseers; and (4) the master–slave relationship is accepted by the athletes as legitimate (p. 186).

How does the economic vitality of an area affect college football recruiting?

Paula Lavigne: Great recruits come from every part of the country . . . from every state. But in the past decade, more than 50 percent of the top high school recruits have come from one region—the South. . . . In the 1970s, top football recruits were more evenly distributed across the United States, with perhaps an emphasis coming out of the East and Midwest left over from the 1950s and 60s. Youngstown, Ohio, had great players, so did Pittsburgh. Philadelphia was very good, and New Jersey was always good and Chicago and Detroit. Flint, Michigan, had ball players back then. Now it's a ghost town.

Why?

Gary Laney: It's interesting to note that over time, as the nation's population center shifted steadily south and west, it seemed football started to be dominated more by teams from those regions . . . We've heard about the economic and population decline of the Midwest for years—the origin of the term "Rust Belt" is largely credited to presidential candidate Walter Mondale way back in 1984—and how, as factories closed in Detroit and Pittsburgh, workers migrated south for jobs, leading to future SEC athletes [But] to blame it solely on the Midwest's declining industrial base is an incomplete picture. There is also the decline of agricultural America, another staple of past Midwestern prosperity.

Will football dominance ever move back to the Heartland?

The Midwest will come back. Eventually, people will figure out that Detroit, Youngstown, Cleveland and cities like them are great sources of cheap real estate. That means companies will eventually locate there because, among other things, schools in the Big Ten will provide a highly educated work force.

Paula Levine is a staff writer for ESPN. Her words are excerpted from: Levine, Paula. 2012. "Top Football Talent Shifts South." *ESPN*. Retrieved July 5, 2017 (http://www.espn.com/espn/otl/story/_/id/7512012/top-college-football-talent-comes-south-shift-more-even-distribution-decades-ago).

George Laney is a sports writer that covers collegiate football. His words are excepted from: Laney, George. 2014. "Big Ten football a victim of shifting demographics, but can the conference rise again?" *Cleveland.com*. Retrieved July 7, 2017 (http://www.cleveland.com/osu/2014/09/as_demographics_shift_big_ten.html).

Ultimately athletes can make money for others but not for themselves. Amateur athletes are bound by rules that eliminate all economic benefits to the athletes: they may not they may receive only educational benefits (i.e., room for tuition fees and books); they cannot sign with an agent and retain their eligibility; they cannot do commercials; cannot receive meals, clothing, or transportation other than from family members. For example, shortly before University of Connecticut basketball player, Shabazz Napier lead his team to the 2014 Collegiate National Championship, told reporters he sometimes goes to bed "starving" because he can't afford food, despite that UConn's student-athlete guidelines include provisions for meal plans. He stated:

> We do have hungry nights that we don't have enough money to get food in. Sometimes money is needed. I don't think you should stretch it out to hundreds of thousands of dollars for playing, because a lot of times guys don't know how to handle themselves with money. I feel like a student athlete. Sometimes, there's hungry nights where I'm not able to eat, but I still gotta play up to my capabilities (Sherman 2014: paragraph 2).

The idea here is that big-time athletic programs are money making, commercial enterprises that generate revenue primarily though unpaid labor (thus making the athlete a wage-slave). To further this analogy, we also note that athletes are often forced to make public appearances for the schools and their photographs are used to publicize the athletic department and sell tickets but they cannot benefit. Schools sell memorabilia that incorporate the athletes' likenesses yet only the schools pocket the royalties. The athletes cannot receive gifts, yet their coaches and other receive the use of automobiles, country club memberships, housing subsidies and the like (Sperber 2001). Additionally, in order for schools to continue to profit financially from athletes, coaches and administrators often pressure athletes to enroll in so called "Mickey Mouse" courses (meaning, cartoonish and escapist; without rigor or relevance) in order to retain their athletic eligibility, thus hindering the actual attainment of a college degree (Gual 2015; Smith and Willingham 2015). As these scholars detail, coaches, athletic directors and even college presidents, are under such intense pressure to win, that they tend to diminish the student side of their athletes by pushing easy courses, encouraging them to enroll in less difficult majors, and cultivating relationships with "friendly" (easy) professors.

So why don't athletes fight to change the system? To be fair some have tried (and is a theme explored in Chapter 5). But broadly, athlete-students (a truer term than student-athlete) are resistant to challenging athletic authorities because they are preoccupied with making the team. Further the generalized submissiveness of athlete-students is that they are politically disenfranchised. Athletes who challenged the power structure often risk losing their scholarships. And athletes who have a grievance are "on their own; they have no union and no arbitration board" (Eitzen 2012:160). The coaches and athletic directors have the power over them as long as they are scholarship athletes. They're only option as several suggest (Hawkins 2010; Nocera and Strauss 2016) is to "leave the plantation" (Eitzen 2012: 186).

A Note on Terminology:
How did the term "Student-Athlete" come to be?

The following is excepted from a 2011 article written by Taylor Branch. Branch is the author of, numerous books on civil-rights movement. He has won the Pulitzer Prize and the National Book Critics Circle Award.

What is a Student-Athlete?

Taylor Branch: The term is meant to conjure the nobility of amateurism, and the precedence of scholarship over athletic endeavor. But the term "student-athlete" was written to help the NCAA in its fight against workmen's compensation insurance claims for injured football players.

Where did the term originate?

Taylor Branch: The term came into play in the 1950s, when the widow of Ray Dennison, who had died from a head injury received while playing football in Colorado for the Fort Lewis A&M Aggies, filed for workmen's-compensation death benefits. Did his football scholarship make the fatal collision a "work-related" accident? Was he a school employee, like his peers who worked part-time as teaching assistants and bookstore cashiers? Or was he a fluke victim of extracurricular pursuits? Given the hundreds of incapacitating injuries to college athletes each year, the answers to these questions had enormous consequences. The Colorado Supreme Court ultimately agreed with the school's contention that he was not eligible for benefits, since the college was "not in the football business."

How have schools used this this label?

Taylor Branch: Using the "student-athlete" defense, colleges have compiled a string of victories in liability cases. On the afternoon of October 26, 1974, the Texas Christian University Horned Frogs were playing the Alabama Crimson Tide in Birmingham, Alabama. Kent Waldrep, a TCU running back, carried the ball on a "Red Right 28" sweep toward the Crimson Tide's sideline, where he was met by a swarm of tacklers. When Waldrep regained consciousness. . . . He was paralyzed: he had lost all movement and feeling below his neck. After nine months of paying his medical bills, Texas Christian refused to pay any more. . . . His attorneys haggled with TCU and the state worker-compensation fund over what constituted employment. Clearly, TCU had provided football players with equipment for the job, as a typical employer would—but did the university pay wages, withhold income taxes on his financial aid, or control work conditions and performance? The appeals court finally rejected Waldrep's claim in June of 2000, ruling that he was not an employee because he had not paid taxes on financial aid that he could have kept even if he quit football. . . . The NCAA's "student-athlete" formulation is a legal shield.

Excerpted from: Branch, Taylor. 2011. "The Shame of College Sports." *The Atlantic*, October. Retrieved November 4, 2017 (http://www.theatlantic.com/magazine/archive/2011/10/the-shame-of-college-sports/308643/).

CHAPTER SUMMARY

Several main themes dominate this chapter. First, while sport has long been emblematic of the American "rags to riches" story, we find rather that this is more of a myth than a reality. In truth, very few people make it using sports as a medium of social mobility. Yet friends, family, coaches, colleges and universities, and the media propagandize sports as the way "out and up." The truth is, sports is often used and practiced as a form of exploitation—whether as an enculturated dreamscape or living spectacle that distracts us from the realities of social and class inequities.

Second, sport like society, is also largely stratified. Ultimately, socioeconomic status is related to the types of sports one watches and participates in, and we find that wealth, not hunger or drive for success, is a better achievement of sports achievement. Further, in the cultivation of sports franchises and venues, we often find that persons and place are regularly sacrificed to the institutions of sport (and economic and status capital). To this end, sport ultimately and unfortunately, does not benefit all—and we have tried to show this through a collection of scholarly and journalistic examples.

What Are Other Sports of the Poor? Prole Sports

The term "prole" is derived from Karl Marx's term for the working class—the proletariat (this term is also interchangeable with the common people, the lower classes, the masses). Indeed, adults with lower incomes are attracted to event like strong man competitions, arm-wresting contests, motor sports, mixed-martial arts, and World Wrestling Entertainment (WWE) (Sage and Eitzen 2016).

Why?

One core reason, especially in athletic forms such as wrestling and strength training, is that poorer persons (who typically lack access to specialized sporting equipment necessary for other activities) can turn inward and manipulate their own bodies, gaining strength and size (and thus status where may otherwise be denied in daily life). In terms of motor sports, an appeal may be due to persons' knowledge of the artifacts (tools, equipment) necessary to build and run vehicles (as the proletariat are more likely to labor in manufacturing and similar jobs that require knowledge of machinery to make things work). Another more symbolic explanation may be that automobiles and motorcycles are "symbols of liberation" (a form of speed/escape) for persons who otherwise feel trapped by her or her situation" (Sage and Eitzen: 119).

Regarding sporting events like WWE, viewers and fans are able to celebrate strength, fortitude, and rebellious acts in defeating larger and villainous actors (for many, a metaphor for life itself). Also, fans know that the "hero" will eventually prevail and the cosmic order of law and justice will be severed—a very heartening and symbolic necessity for "keeping on." Finally, spectators can identify with characters who are (or who play characters) like them: shared ethnicity, geographic background, cultural values, etc.

Reference

Sage, George H. and D. Stanley Eitzen. 2016. *Sociology of North American Sport*. New York, NY: Oxford University Press.

Discussion Questions

*We presented the notion that the economic vitality of an area affects college football recruiting. Do you agree?

*Have various class and ethnic groups used sport to become socially/economically mobile? Can you trace the mobility of various ethnic and class groups through sport?

*Is the promotion of sport as a way out of poverty a "dirty trick" in our society? Do families, media, and educational institutions (e.g., high-schools, colleges) over promote sport as a way out and up?

*How does social class affect one's choice of sport?

*What are additional "Prole Sports" not mentioned in this chapter?

*Amateur athletes are typically bound by rules that eliminate all economic benefits to the athletes. Do you agree with this? How might this economic arraignment be altered that benefits all parties? (more on this in the next chapter!).

Extra-Inning: The Sociologist Boxer

In the ring, his nickname was Busy Louie. In the classroom, Loïc Wacquant (pronounced Vah-KAAHN) is a professor of sociology. In his book *Body & Soul: Notebooks of an Apprentice Boxer* (2001), Wacquant details his time in Chicago as a graduate student who took up boxing at a predominantly Black gym to study the reality of poverty, the local job market, and how changes in the global economy effected the urban environment.

But he fell in love with boxing and almost gave up his study and academic career to become a pugilist—his trainer (boxing hall of famer, DeeDee Armour) convinced him otherwise. The book conveys the boxer's world by experiencing it firsthand (while also documenting the impact of sport and race and poverty on the local neighborhood). It is a powerful read on the now disappearing inner city gym and the place where self-discipline and the escape from the seductions of drugs, gangs and street crime can be found.

CHAPTER REFERENCES

Axthelm, Pete. 2011. *The City Game: Basketball from the Garden to the Playgrounds*. New York, NY: Open Road Media.

Beamon, Krystal. 2010. "Are Sports Overemphasized in the Socialization Process of African American Males? A Qualitative Analysis of Former Collegiate Athletes' Perception of Sport Socialization." *Journal of Black Studies* 41(2): 281–300.

Dubrow, Kjerulf and Jimi Adams. 2012. "Hoop inequalities: Race, class and family structure background and the odds of playing in the National Basketball Association." *International Review for the Sociology of Sports* 47(1):43–59.

Eitzen, Stanley D. 2012. *Fair and Foul: Beyond the Myths and Paradoxes of Sport.* Lanham, Maryland: Rowman & Littlefield Publishers.

FIFPRO. 2013. "For South American Kids, Football Means Business." *FIFPro: World Players' Union,* October 18. Retrieved July 4, 2017 (http://www.fifpro.org/en/news/for-south-american-kids-football-means-business).

Frey, Darcy. 2004. *The Last Shot: City Streets, Basketball Dreams.* Mariner Books.

Gaul, Gilbert M. 2015. *Billion Dollar Ball: A Journey Through the Big-Money Culture of College Football.* New York, NY: Viking Press.

Goldblatt, David. 2008. *The Ball is Round: A Global History of Soccer.* New York, NY: Riverhead Books.

Gordan, Ian. 2013. "Inside Major League Baseball's Dominican Sweatshop System." *MotherJones,* March/April. Retrieved November 4, 2017 (http://www.motherjones.com/politics/2013/03/baseball-dominican-system-yewri-guillen).

Greenberg, Jon (ed). 2014. *Team Marketing Report 2014.* Retrieved July 4, 2017 (http://www.team-marketing.com/public/uploadedPDFs/2014+NFL+FCI+Final+(2).pdf).

Hawkins, Billy. 2010. The New Plantation: Black Athletes, College Sports, and Predominately White NCAA Institutions. New York, NY: Palgrave.

Heiskanen, Benita. 2014. *The Urban Geography of Boxing: Race, Class, and Gender in the Ring.* New York, NY: Routledge.

Helfland, Zach. 2014. "LeBron James never forgot where he came from and they never forgot him." *Los Angeles Times,* Retrieved November 4, 2017 (http://www.latimes.com/sports/nba/la-sp-lebron-james-akron-20141028-story.html).

James, Steve (dir.) and James Marx, Frederick Marx (writers). 1994. *Hoop Dreams.* Kartemquin Films.

Johnson, William. 2011. "Sociology assistant professor Krystal Beamon talks life after sports for athletes." *TheShortHorn,* Oct 19. Retrieved July 4, 2017 (http://www.theshorthorn.com/news/campus/sociology-assistant-professor-krystal-beamon-talks-life-after-sports-for/article_6ec960a2-8ac9-5d34-b859-76ae732bd75b.html).

Keating, Peter. 2011. "The World of Sports runs on Merit, right?" *ESPN,* July 17. Retrieved July 4, 2017 (http://espn.go.com/espn/story/_/id/6777581/importance-athlete-background-making-nba).

Klein, Alan. 2014. *Dominican Baseball: New Pride, Old Prejudice.* Philadelphia, PA: Temple University Press.

Kuper, Simon. 2014. Soccernomics: *Why England Loses, Why Spain, Germany, and Brazil Win, and Why the U.S., Japan, Australia—and Even Iraq—Are Destined to Become the Kings of the World's Most Popular Sport.* New York, NY: Nation Books.

Lewis, Michael. 2007. *The Blind Side: Evolution of a Game.* New York, NY: W.W. Norton & Company.

Matte T, Ellis JA, Bedell J, Selenic D, Young C, and Deitcher D. 2007. *Obesity in the South Bronx: A look across generations.* New York, NY: New York City Department of Health and Mental Hygiene.

May, Reuben A. 2009. *Living through the Hoop: High School Basketball, Race, and the American Dream.* New York, NY: NYU Press.

McClure, Robert. 2012. "Public Parks for Sale: Kids Wait Six Years for Ball-fields Taken over by Yankee Stadium." *InvestigateWest*, Retrieved July 4, 2017 (http://invw.org/2012/06/11/explaining-yankee-stadium-1282/).

Meneses, Juan Pablo. 2013. *Niños Futbolistas.* Blackie Books.

NCAA. 2013. Estimated Probability of Competing in Athletics Beyond the High School Interscholastic Level. NCAA Research. Available: https://www.ncaa.org/sites/default/files/Probability-of-going-pro-methodology_Update2013.pdf.

Newton, James. 1987. "Bastion of Court Tennis Keeps Woman on Sideline." *New York Times*, March 28. Retrieved July 4, 2017 (http://www.nytimes.com/1987/03/28/nyregion/bastion-of-court-tennis-keeps-woman-on-sideline.html).

Nocera, Joe and Ben Strauss. 2016. *Indentured: The Inside Story of the Rebellion Against the NCAA.* New York, NY: Penguin.

Parker, Tim. 2016. "Why the Prices of Sports Tickets Vary so Much." *Investopedia*, Retrieved November 5, 2017 (http://www.investopedia.com/financial-edge/1012/why-the-prices-of-sports-tickets-vary-so-much-.aspx).

Remnick, David. 1998. *King of the World: Muhammad Ali and the Rise of an American Hero.* New York, NY: Vintage Books.

Schwartz, Anne. 2006. "Yankee Stadium Parkland Swap." *Gotham Gazette*, March 21. Retrieved November 5, 2017 (http://www.gothamgazette.com/environment/3192-yankee-stadium-parkland-swap).

Smith, Jay M. and Mary Willingham. 2015. *Cheated: The UNC Scandal, The Education of Athletes, and the Future of Big-Time College Sports.* Lincoln, NE: University of Nebraska Press.

Sperber, Murry. 2001. *Beer and Circus: How Big-Time College Sports Is Crippling Undergraduate Education.* New York, NY: Holt Publishers.

Statista. 2017. "Average player salary in Major League Baseball from 2003 to 2017 (in million U.S. dollars)" *The Statistical Portal*, No Date. Retrieved, November 5, 2017 (https://www.statista.com/statistics/236213/mean-salaray-of-players-in-majpr-league-baseball/).

Thompson, Derek. 2012. "If you don't watch sports, TV is a Huge Rip Off." *The Atlantic*, December 3. Retrieved July 4, 2017 (http://www.theatlantic.com/business/archive/2012/12/if-you-dont-watch-sports-tv-is-a-huge-rip-off-so-how-do-we-fix-it/265814/).

Veblen, Thorstein. 1889 [1994]. *Theory of the Leisure Class.* Mineola, NY: Dover Thrift Editions.

Wacquant, Loïc. 2006. *Body & Soul: Notebooks of an Apprentice Boxer.* Oxford University Press.

Washington, Robert E. and David Karen (Eds). 2010. *Sport, Power and Society: Institutions and Practices.* Boulder, CO: Westview Press.

Whyte, Alan. 2009. "Sugar: baseball and struggle." *World Socialist*, Retrieved July 4, 2017 (http://www.wsws.org/en/articles/2009/04/suga-a16.html).

Zaldivar, Gabe. 2014. "Clint Dempsey's $6.695 Million Salary Surpasses Entire Payroll of 15 MLS Teams." *The Bleacher Report,* Retrieved November 4, 2017). (http://bleacherreport.com/articles/2025066-clint-dempseys-6695-million-salary-surpasses-entire-payroll-of-15-mls-teams).

Zirin, David. 2014. "Brazil's World Cup will kick the Environment in the Teeth." *The Nation,* April 22. Retrieved November 4, 2017 (http://www.thenation.com/article/brazils-world-cup-will-kick-environment-teeth/).

Zirin, David. 2014. *Brazil's Dance with the Devil: The World Cup, The Olympics, and the Struggle for Democracy.* Chicago, IL: Haymarket Books.

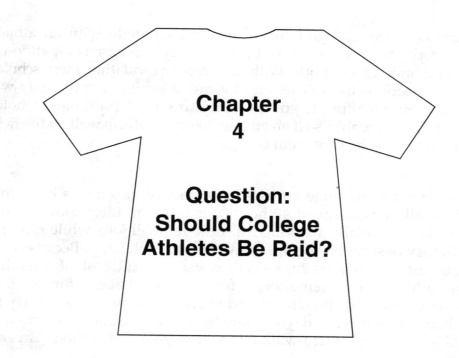

**Chapter
4**

**Question:
Should College
Athletes Be Paid?**

Student Outcomes

After reading this chapter, you will be able to do the following:

- Understand and describe the historical context surrounding the debate of whether to pay college athletes.
- Define and apply the concepts of power and authority to the debate of paying college athletes.
- Analyze and describe the historical development of amateurism.
- Explain the basics of Functionalism and how it can be applied to describe the current debate.
- Explain the basics of Conflict theory and how it can be applied to describe the current debate.
- Describe the "human costs" associated with intercollegiate athletics and organizational reforms.

In the September 16, 2013 edition of TIME magazine, Sean Gregory pens an article looking at the debate and issue of paying college athletes. The cover of this edition is of a college football player next to the bolded assertion: "It's time to pay college athletes." He writes:

In fairness, many college athletes are compensated—with an athletic scholarship. This attractive carrot drives today's intense competition in youth and high school sports. With tuition costs escalating, these scholarships are a serious meal ticket and for many families are the only way their children can afford to go to a four-year school. [But] most scholarships are also revocable, so if an athlete doesn't perform well on the field, he can, in a sense, be fired from college.

Further:

Academic work for some athletes is secondary: top men's basketball and football players spend 40 hours per week on their sports, easily. Players are essentially working full-time football jobs while going to school; they deserve to be paid more than a scholarship. Because even full-ride athletic scholarships don't cover the full cost of attending school, athletes are often short a few thousand bucks for ancillary expenses on top of tuition, room and board, books and fees: money for gas, shampoo and, yes, maybe a few beers. Some athletes are on only partial scholarship or are walk-ons still paying full tuition (Gregory 2013:36).

Within the remainder of the article, Gregory touches upon many topics salient to the debate of amateurism, paying student-athletes, market value of athletes' services, and the bifurcation between traditional revenue generating sports, such as football and men's basketball, and other less financially lucrative college sports. The article succinctly surveys the vast spectrum of topic-specific research and even attempts to develop rudimentary solutions.

Opening Conversation

Should Athletes Get Paid? Points to Ponder:

*Are there other forms of compensation besides money that should be offered for play?

*If this becomes reality, most schools would pay only football and men's basketball players, since those sports produce the bulk of the revenues. Is this fair?

*What are the risks and unintended consequences of paying athletes?

Let us carry this conversation throughout the chapter.

Read: Gregory, Sean. "It's Time to Pay College Athletes." *Time*, Retrieved August 1, 2017 (http://content.time.com/time/subscriber/article/0,33009,2151167-5,00.html).

One example to consider

Gregory Shamus/Staff/Getty Images

Jake Butt #88 of the Michigan Wolverines is tackled by Marshon Lattimore #2 of the Ohio State Buckeyes after catching a pass during the first half of their game at Ohio Stadium on November 26, 2016 in Columbus, Ohio. (Photo by Gregory Shamus/Getty Images)

When Jake Butt tore his right ACL after being injured in the Orange Bowl, his injury likely cost him a spot in the first round of the NFL draft. He sees his injury as a reason for college players to be compensated for what they do on the field. He states, "I should be the example of why college athletes should be getting paid in college or why I can't use my name to benefit off my likeness in college . . . Why can I see 'I Like Jake Butt and I Cannot Lie,' I see those shirts and I'm living paycheck-to-paycheck in college. Who knows? Heaven forbid something happens in the NFL, can I really benefit off of it when it was at the most? No, I can't." (Cited in Rothstein 2017).

Reference

Rothstein, Michael. 2017. "Heading to the NFL, Michigan's Jake Butt says college players should be paid." *ESPN*, March 24. Retrieved July 4, 2017 (http://www.espn.com/college-football/story/_/id/18995190/michigan-standout-jake-butt-says-college-football-players-paid).

In the TIME magazine article, Gregory (2013) notes that while the culture of remunerating college football players might be changing, NCAA rules are based on amateurism and deny athletes the opportunity to not only be paid for their services, but they also cannot benefit from licensing their image, including their signature on merchandise for financial gain. However, head football coaches' salaries for FBS (Football Bowl Subdivision) teams have seen staggering and sharp increases just in the last 10 years. Money and business-based relationships with college sport entities and athletic programs have been increasing steadily over the past few decades. Evidence for this can be seen in the lucrative broadcast rights agreements brokered between large conferences with broadcast groups such as ESPN. These numbers are in the billions! As Gregory (2013:38) states:

> The uncomfortable question has surfaced just as college sports are booming. Thanks to plush television-rights deals, like the 12-year, $3 billion contract the Pacific-12 conference signed with ESPN and FOX in 2011, vast revenues will keep rolling into university coffers. Coaches, admissions offices and university alumni operations profit from the stars. All kinds of people beyond campus are also making money from this lopsided system. Football-game days in particular drive college-town economies . . . But the players with the talent remain out of the money simply because a group of college presidents, athletic directors and conference commissioners set their wages at zero . . .

However, there is no consensus regarding the idea we should pay college athletes and the arguments against paying college athletes are numerous. John R. Thelin is a professor of education and policy that has written about many aspects of higher education and college athletics. Recently he wrote an article that was published on TIME.com about college athletes and the pitfalls—primarily financial—of paying them for their services. He noted the equity issues, tax implications, and the overestimation that coaches, sport journalists, athletes, and athletes' families make regarding an athlete's market value and worth (Thelin 2016).

There are many proponents and detractors when it comes to paying college athletes. As a result, contextualizing the debate with input from the social sciences assists those vetting all possible resolutions and solutions. The purpose of this chapter, then, is to outline some of the variables key to understanding the debate of whether college athletes should be paid. In order to do this, however, we will draw upon a vast array of sociological concepts, theories, and literatures to better inform our discussions. The chapter will not simply tell you "yes" or "no" regarding the question at hand; rather, it will provide specific viewpoints that you—as the reader and budding scholar—can fold into your worldview in order to make an informed opinion on whether college athletes should be paid.

Here's Why We Shouldn't Pay College Athletes
by John Thelin (2016)

*Salaries would replace scholarships (no in addition to). Given the requirement to pay tuition, room and board and healthcare would a salary give the student-athlete a better deal than a scholarship?

*In following all the "pay for play" contests, the skilled players would be pitting schools, accountants, and agents against each other for the best deal. Certain schools would be able to offer more, essentially killing competition and limiting the sport to a few schools.

What do you think about these arguments?

Reference

Thelin, John 2016. "Here's Why We Shouldn't Pay College Athletes." *Time*, March 1. Retrieved July 4, 2017 (http://time.com/money/4241077/why-we-shouldnt-pay-college-athletes/).

POWER, AUTHORITY, AND DEFINITIONS OF AMATEURISM

In the years following WWII college athletics was a "free for all" with boosters, community members, college athletic departments and college athletes taking full advantage of the unregulated environment. The NCAA, at the time, was a small and relatively powerless organization whose job was to simply promote college sports, especially men's college basketball (Thelin 2015). How did, then, such a small organization ascend to the pinnacle of power and authority within intercollegiate athletics here in the United States? To answer this question, however, requires someone delving into the political and socio-historical background of both the intercollegiate athletics landscape at the time and the regulatory dynamics at play within higher education. We will not be taking that road, but this does bring to light two very important ideas to understand when examining whether to pay college athletes or not: Power and authority.

Sociologist Max Weber (1922) provided important insight into understanding dynamics within social life that constrain individual actors, particularly that of the faceless bureaucracy. He discussed and wrote about many ideas, but his operationalization of power and authority serve as foundational elements for our needs. **Power** involves influencing or coercing other people to achieve your own goals, even if your goals contradict what others are trying to do. **Authority**, on the other hand, is a type of power associated with an institutionalized and respected position within an office, organization, or governance structure with clearly established guidelines, relationships, or expectations (Weber 1922). Using these definitions, we can see that the NCAA is a legitimate office and organization within the regulatory world of intercollegiate athletics.[1] Because their legitimacy (i.e., authority) is vested in them by the institutions of higher education they regulate, they are imbued with the ability to influence policy, regulation, timelines, and other basic rules and operations regulating (i.e., power) the colleges and universities within their designated system. The NCAA's power over athletes and athletic departments is a byproduct of their legitimate authority status as the premiere regulatory body in intercollegiate athletics. As a result, the NCAA has established what constitutes eligibility and amateurism appertaining to potential or current NCAA athletes.

Amateurism is an important topic for understanding the debate of whether to pay or not to pay college athletes. Each intercollegiate or amateur governance organization has their own criteria for determining participants' eligibility. Additionally, we are focusing our debate exclusively on intercollegiate athletic governance structures here in the United States avoiding the debate involving the International Olympic Committee (IOC) or other international federations' guidelines. For our purposes, we will use the NCAA as an example.

Class Activity

Break up into small groups. Next, locate the following intercollegiate athletic governance bodies' definitions of amateurism. How are they different? How are they similar?

NAIA (National Association of Intercollegiate Athletics)
NCCAA (National Christian College Athletic Association)
CCCAA (California Community College Athletic Association)
ACCA (Association of Christian College Athletics)
NJCAA (National Junior College Athletic Association)

Amateurism is crucial to the identified mission of the NCAA, since it helps to set the parameters for regulating competition, eligibility, and—ultimately—remuneration for services. According to the NCAA, amateurism involves a detailed eligibility certification process working with the athlete and their school (NCAA.org ND).

---

[1] We realize that the NCAA is not the ONLY intercollegiate regulatory body within intercollege athletics. For example, there is the NJCAA, the NAIA, and the NCCAA to name a few. We center our discussion primarily on NCAA athletics, but many of the processes and discussions contained within this chapter can be applied to other intercollegiate athletic governance structures.

According to the NCAA's amateurism guidelines (NCAA ND: paragraphs 3–4), an athlete must satisfy the following criteria to be eligible for competition within NCAA athletics:

> All student-athletes, including international students, are required to adhere to NCAA amateurism requirements to remain eligible for intercollegiate competition. In general, amateurism requirements do not allow:
>
> - Contracts with professional teams
> - Salary for participating in athletics
> - Prize money above actual and necessary expenses
> - Play with professionals
> - Tryouts, practice or competition with a professional team
> - Benefits from an agent or prospective agent
> - Agreement to be represented by an agent
> - Delayed initial full-time collegiate enrollment to participate in organized sports competition

While many may agree, or disagree, with the aforementioned definition of amateurism by the NCAA, nonetheless, it is the current definition in place. Certification of eligible amateur athletes began in 2007 (NCAA ND) with intercollegiate amateurism and corruption being concerns since the beginning of intercollegiate athletics here in the United States. For example, Nixon (2016: 200–201) provided some historical context on the issues of the beginning of intercollegiate sports regulation and amateurism by stating:

> In 1876, the popularity of football resulted in the formation of the Intercollegiate Football Association by Harvard, Yale, and Princeton. Despite regulatory efforts, a number of problems arose in college football concerning issues such as academic integrity, professionalism, institution control and injuries and even deaths of players.

Further:

> By 1905, concerns among faculty members, college administrators, and prominent officials had risen to a level where there were calls for abolishing the sport. The Intercollegiate Athletic Associate of the United States (IAAUS) was formed in 1905 to address these concerns and establish regulatory control that emphasized responsible and effective institution control, academic integrity, ethical behavior, and the welfare of student-athletes (Nixon 2016: 200–201)

Concerns from those outside of the realm of college sports reached an apex in 1929 when the Carnegie Foundation for the Advancement of Teaching produced a report on the "[s]tudy of the organization and control of college sports, which concluded that college and university presidents needed to provide the leadership to restore integrity to varsity sports programs that had become mired in professionalism and commercialism." (Thelin 2015: 4).

Indeed, Thelin (2015: 6) continued examining the Janus-faced nature of college sports when discussing the Ivy League in the 1950s:

> [T]he creation of the Ivy League in 1954 was a direct counter to the unprecedented excesses and abuses of college sports. . . . [Yet, these prestigious academic universities nonetheless] relied on an alumni slush fund[s], aggressive recruiting. . . . and the waiving of traditional admission requirements to field football squad[s]

Finally, Revisine (2014: 52), when discussing the issues of eligibility in college football observed:

> As the stakes involved in the games got larger, schools began to wrangle with the issue of who should actually be allowed to play on their teams. There had been some attempts at legislation in the early 1880s, with movements both to limit the number of years in which a player would participate and to ban professional athletes from intercollegiate contests. The enforcement was left to the individual schools, whose teams were essentially run by students and graduates. Not surprisingly, many of them chose simply to ignore the rules.

Lack of self-regulation and a failure of the "honor system" meant outside entities were needed for regulation. The regulation of intercollegiate athletic was borne out of a concern for the "fairness" of competition, which was aligned with the notion that amateurism highlighted the developmental aspects of college sports and competition. Additionally, members of the U.S. government and other social groups were concerned with issues of safety, purity, social and individual development, and regulating such a popular enterprise. The NCAA, as a result, became the entity charged with the task of doing such a thing. Indeed, Thelin (2015) noted while the U.S. government wanted regulation and change in intercollegiate competition, it did not feel it had the purview to enter into regulating mostly private institutions of higher education and their extracurricular activities, which is what college sports were designated as during the early days. As a result, terms like "student-athlete" were connoted to emphasize the educational association of sporting competitions and combat work-related liability, death and injury from participation in college sports (Branch 2014). Indeed, when quoting Walter Byers—the first director of the NCAA whom served from 1951–1988—Branch (2014: paragraph 1) noted:

> The term [student-athlete] came into play in the 1950s, when the widow of Ray Dennison, who had died from a head injury received while

playing football in Colorado for the Fort Lewis A&M Aggies, filed for workers'-compensation death benefits. Did his football scholarship make the fatal collision a 'work-related' accident? Was he a school employee?.... Given the hundreds of incapacitating injuries to college athletes each year, the answers to these questions had enormous consequences. . . . . Practical interest turned the NCAA vigorously against Dennison, and the Supreme Court of Colorado ultimately agreed with the school's contention that he was not eligible for benefits, since the college was 'not in the football business'.

Thus, the concept of amateurism is associated with a host of many socio-political factors contained within and associated with college athletics, as compared to being an issue of character as some critics say. What we can state unequivocally, though, is that amateurism and how the concept has been defined and applied over time within collegiate athletics is based on both power and authority. Additionally, amateurism and remuneration are two sides to the same coin regarding how to institutionalize or situate college athletes into a system based partly on education and partly on entertainment—both of which are rooted in a fiscal and political economic climate.

Sport Case Study

Amateur Sport: Collegiate Quidditch

What is Quidditch?

Quidditch was a fictional game created by author J.K. Rowling in her Harry Potter Series (published initially in 1996). The game, as depicted in the book series, involved two teams of magical wizards and witches, flying on broomsticks, playing against each other to throw balls through various hoops to score points. The fictional sport referenced real life elements of dodgeball, rugby, and flag football.

In 2005, taking inspiration form the Harry Potter novels, students at Middlebury College turned the fictional game into a real sport—and it has grown dramatically since. For example, in 2007, the first collegiate World Cup was held between Middlebury and Vassar (with Middlebury emerging victorious). In 2008, the second World Cup featured 12 teams, including the University of Washington, Louisiana State University, and the first international team, from McGill University. And in 2013 Quidditch was televised for the first time as a sporting event on the Buckeye Cable Sports Network, which aired matches between Bowling Green State University and the University of Toledo.

Sergei Bachlakov/Shutterstock.com

How is it Played?

Quidditch is a mixed gender contact sport, made up of two teams of seven athletes each (a team is limited to a maximum of four players who identify as the same gender) who play with brooms between their legs at all times (honoring the spirit of play in the fictional book series) as they try to advance a ball down the field through one of three standing hooped goals of various heights (typically made from PVC pipe). The game is won in the traditional way as whoever has the most points when the allotted time of play expires is the victor. The game is broken into three periods of 20 minutes each.

Specifically, three "chasers" (forwards) score goals worth 10 points each with a volley-ball called the quaffle. They advance the ball down the field by running with it, passing it to teammates, or kicking it. Each team has a keeper (goalie) who defends the goal hoops. Two beaters (defensive-like players) use dodgeballs called bludgers to disrupt the flow of the game by "knocking out" other players. Any player hit by a bludger is out of play until they touch their own goals. Each team also has a seeker (a free-ranging player) who tries to catch the "golden snitch." The snitch is yet another player who carries a small ball (typically a tennis ball in a sock) attached to and dangling from their waistband and uses any means to avoid capture. The capture of the snitch is worth 30 points (further, the capture of the snitch forces the end of the period). The snitch is released onto the field at the 17-minute mark of each period—and the seeker is released at the 18 minute mark (again his/her only goal at this point is to catch the snitch). Got it? Good! See https://www.usquidditch.org/about/rules/ for more information on rules.

During play, players are forbidden from taking certain actions, or fouls. Players who commit fouls face different consequences depending on the severity of the offense. A back to hoops foul indicates that a player must stop and return to their hoops, as though knocked out. A yellow card indicates that a player must spend one minute in the penalty box. A red card indicates that a player is barred from the rest of the game.

What Constitutes a Collegiate Quidditch Team?

According to the rules set by US Quidditch (the national governing body for the sport of quidditch), collegiate teams must be comprised solely of current students at one institution. Any currently enrolled student, including graduate students, may play for a collegiate team as long as they provide valid proof of enrollment. There is no minimum credit hour requirement for a player on a collegiate team. So, go get your friends together and start a team!

See https://www.usquidditch.org/about/mission/

In order to further examine the debate of paying college athletes, it behooves us to draw from some theoretical perspectives. We have seen there is a long history to understanding not only the NCAA but also the role college athletics play in both society and education. There is a lot of information in those views. But, we need a way of making sense of all of the facts, points of view, and history. Over the last 100 years, the debate of paying college athletes has been raging. Viewpoints, generally speaking, fall into two views: (1) (college) sports are developmental and as a result educational scholarships are fair remuneration for athletic services, or (2) athletes being given educational scholarships are being exploited for their athletic services and thus are not benefitting equally from the revenue and entertainment they provide or create. Drawing upon two structural sociological theories will help us to organize and understand the two viewpoints of paying college athletes so that you can not only form your own opinion, but also support whatever view you take or develop.

Should Athletes Be Allowed to Major in Sport?

In 1990, the economist William F. Shughart II asked an intriguing question in an op-ed essay in The Wall Street Journal: "Why should academic credit be given for practicing the violin, but not for practicing a three-point shot?"

Universities routinely give degrees in the performing arts, such as music, dance and theater—and public performances given to audiences paying for the privilege of seeing exceptional talent on display. Universities graduate art historians and cultural critics, so why not sport historians and critical sport commentators?

Beyond the general education requirements set by a college or university, an athletics degree could be a structured curriculum based on academic credit for both practice and play and for courses such as: sports history, sports law, sports finance, sports media, and of course, sport sociology.

What do you think? What are the pros and cons of this? Would this make the title "student athlete" more honest? Would this lessen the divide between athletics and academics, or expand it? How does this fit in to the argument over paying athletes?

AMATEUR ATHLETICS: FUNCTIONALISM'S TAKE

As noted in Chapter 2, functionalism is a large-scale theory examining major institutions and the functions that each institution (or organization) plays in society's composition. In terms of sport, Woods (2014:20) notes that functionalism ". . . looks at sport as a social institution that [can] positively benefit a community or nation [by giving them] something to strive towards and something to work on and play together." This means that—for example—participating in sports provides a host of individual and community-related benefits. Through our association with sports, people learn hard work, cooperation, how to deal with adversity, and how competition can be beneficial (Williams and Kolkka 1998).

A functionalist view of sport—on a social level—would see the "role" that sport plays in a specific society. Sage (1997) noted the close relationship between the growth of physical education, sport participation, and this functionalist view of sport that, beginning in the 1920s, focused on "social development." As a result, sport has a crucial function in society. Specifically, sport provides people the chance to learn important social values (e.g., integration and socialization functions) and how highlighting success leads to a meritocracy (e.g., instilling capitalist ideologies).

Robert K. Merton (1968) extended the functionalist perspective to note that all the actions and policies of all institutions produce **manifest functions** (intended consequences) and **latent functions** (unforeseen actions and unintended consequences). As identified by Merton and chronicled over the decades by many sociologists and other social scientists, manifest and latent functions are two useful concepts for examining amateur athletics here in the United States. Additionally, they serve as a nice starting place for contextualizing the chapter's question of paying college athletes. For example, if the original purpose of the scholarship was to incentivize and compensate student-athletes for their athletic services, the manifest function of this action was to reward student-athletes for their services, ensure a pool of labor to fulfill athletic obligations on university campuses (which became increasingly popular), and to provide high-quality competition (and entertainment) for spectators and potential students or donors.

The latent function, however, is that student-athletes' popularity and fame grew disproportional to the compensation of a full or partial educational scholarship. Now, you have billions and billions of dollars associated with intercollegiate sports, such as March basketball tournaments, bowl games, intercollegiate championships being broadcast on television, and the host of other business-related tie-ins (e.g., sponsorship and naming rights agreements and hundreds of millions of dollars from donors).

In the case of intercollegiate athletics and the paying of players, functionalism sees college athletes as contributing to the campus and university culture, the local community, the broader system of college athletics, and even to the United States as a whole (via national integration due to intercollegiate play). College sports is an environment where young men and women are not only integrated into society's values and normative processes, but also "developed" into strong members and leaders of society—similar to the "social development" argument Sage (1997) reviewed when discussing the similarities of organized sport and physical education practices here in 20th century America. Athletes are "paid" for their services with the social development inspired educationally based scholarship. Net worth and market value for hard services (e.g., playing in games on television or ticket sales) and soft services (e.g., image licensing to sell ancillary merchandise or further develop psychic income) however are developments that contradict the status quo and stability so valued by a functionalist view of sport. For example, Ed O'Bannon's class action lawsuit against the NCAA in 2015 or the Northwestern University's football players' attempt to unionize in 2014 show change and emphasize undercurrents of dissatisfaction with the current system of remunerating college athletes. In fact, a quick review of NCAA violations since the beginning of NCAA enforcement and infractions shows a large number of violations by schools or boosters for "impermissible benefits" to student-athletes as ways of recruiting the best athletes to their athletic programs (Vermillion and Messer 2011). This kind of behavior, systemic since the beginning of intercollegiate athletics, seems to belie the functionalist and utopian view of college athletics being an enterprise strictly for school pride and individual development with the athletic grants-in-aid fulfilling the necessary obligation of remuneration.

Interview with a Former Student-Athlete.
Experiences: Then and now.

Bio: Tyson Billings was a former collegiate distance runner who competed in nine NAIA National Championships and 11 Conference Championships. Billings enjoyed both team and individual success in Cross Country, Indoor and Outdoor Track. As a professional in the sports industry Billings has worked with Professional Football, Baseball, and Soccer as well as college athletics.

Billings currently works for the University of Nebraska in the Athletic Development and Ticketing Department where his duties include managing ticket operations for men's basketball, women's soccer, wrestling and baseball. This involves managing ticket sales at events, filling orders, renewal efforts, and customer service initiatives. Billings also assists with football and bowl game ticketing. Additionally, he is involved with analytical research and graphic design, while also developing ticket marketing strategies. The following is an interview of Billings, conducted by the second author:

Vermillion: As a former student-athlete, what were some of the pressures, burdens, or commitments you had to balance while competing at the highest level? About how much time did you spend in athletic-related activities per week?

Billings: As a student athlete, I felt significant pressure from many directions. Competing in a sport that can be directly compared to your counterparts leaves little room to hide poor performance. Especially from an individual perspective, I had to show consistent improvement on paper with times and places. In a sport like running you can compare results apples to apples which is very straight forward even with many factors contributing to your performance. With that being said, my performance was key in keeping my percentage of a scholarship which for everyone in my sport was far from a full ride. Since I competed in three sports my only off season was in the summer, which is when I was tasked with trying to earn money to offset the cost of college. You also spend a large amount of time physically taking care of your body. Injuries added a large amount of stress on me during my career as performance could be significantly hindered by injury. On an average school week I'd contribute 40–50 hours to athletic work between, practice, lifting, treatments as well as practice prep, event travel and competition. In the summer months, I had a job doing carpentry 40 hours a week and trained around 20–30 hours a week. For me it was essential to work in the summer to afford room, board, and tuition.

Vermillion: While competing as a student-athlete, how did you and your peers perceive the athletic scholarship?

Billings: To my teammates and I, we were thankful for the athletic scholarship we did receive as it directly offset our out of pocket cost to attend school. We paid for everything, (books, food, housing, clothes) so having a few, and I mean a few ($1,000–$5,000) per year definitely helped. We all knew we'd be in debt after our college careers with the feeling that athletic scholarships in our sports were capped no matter our performance. A few trips to National Championships may raise your scholarship $500–$1,000 over your career. Our team was very successful too as we would routinely compete with, and defeat Division I, professional, and international runners. We often would jokingly calculate how much scholarship we would earn per mile of training. The results of this measure were often very humbling. However, the academic and community sponsored scholarships were more important to seek out because those we felt actually had a significant difference in our out of pocket cost.

Not that the value was more on those, but the fact we were able to go out and seek additional funds made it worth the application effort.

Vermillion: What are some of the pressures, burdens, or commitments you see current FBS student-athletes dealing with on a weekly basis?

Billings: I think a big difference in what I experienced compared to the student athletes I am surrounded by is these athletes are dealing with media scrutiny and the millions of dollars invested with success. The media is on high alert, waiting for a slip up or a phrase out of tune from the generic "jock talk" response. Student athletes have unprecedented attention which can lead to pressure to do and say the right thing. They have to focus on not providing quotes that can be taken out of context or used for bulletin board material. The media wants to tell their own story regardless of what may be best for the student athletes. I am thankful I didn't have to answer why I didn't run my fastest time each week.

Secondly, the student athletes I have been around have expectations for success because of monetary value. You have individuals in the community literally investing large amounts of money in our athletes which is essential to run an athletic department in today's day but with those investments come the expectation of return on investment. It is hard to quantify what is a good return on a college athletics program because it's different for everyone. Despite what goals and values an athletic department may say is deemed as successful, your constituents often can have different opinions.

Vermillion: What is your view on the question of whether student-athletes should be paid?

Billings: In my opinion I don't believe student athletes should be paid with cash for their own personal financial gain. I understand that even at this point some universities stipend their athletes but I don't think that many athletes in college understand it's not just 4 years debt free when you have a college scholarship. A college degree is never free, it has a financial value. You are essentially getting a jumpstart on everyone who is in debt. I know I didn't realize how severe the burden of college debt plays on a young professional when I was in college. With the perspective that typical students are in debt for (fact check me) 10–20 years after their degree is in hand. It's a huge advantage to not be making loan payments 5–20 years after your playing days. I would have loved to earn money, but I think student athletes are receiving a huge value when their needs are taken care of in excessive quality by a university. For me as a former student athlete, if you have all your basic needs and then some (food, housing, books, academic resources, healthcare, travel) provided, you are already miles ahead of your traditional student. I enjoyed the gear we received and traveling the country but financial freedom immediately following graduation could impact decades of your life.

Class Exercise: Conduct an interview with a Student Athlete and ask their opinion/ experiences of this issue. What are their ideas/solutions to the notion of paying student athletes?

EXPLOITATION AND WORTH: CONFLICT THEORY WEIGHS IN

Conflict theory, in many ways, can be seen as the reaction to functionalism's focus on order, predictability, and stability. Delany and Madigan (2009: 26) note conflict theory is in stark contrast to functionalism and "examines the role of power and in the inequality found methodically throughout society." Additionally, Nixon (2016: 17) notes, in regards to conflict theorists: "[They] often . . . focus on broad patterns of inequality in society and how dominant groups or classes exploit or oppress less powerful and privileged people to benefit themselves and other people of high status." Finally, while Karl Marx (Carrington and McDonald 2009) did not develop conflict theory—because of its focus on economic dimensions of power and society—he is often associated with the theory.

A major contribution of conflict theory, generally speaking, is that conflict or discord is inherent in all social structures and life. That is, the social resources (wealth, power, and prestige) people strive for are not equally available to everyone at all times. As a result, conflict occurs between groups and influences social change in society. Conflict theory's examination of power, domination, economics, and class inequality can be easily applied to sport. Indeed, Delany and Madigan (2009: 28) note that conflict theory, when applied to sport, helps lead us to some of the following views:

1. Sport generates and intensifies alienation.
2. Sport is used by the state and the economically powerful as a tool for coercion and social control.
3. Sport promotes commercialism and materialism.
4. Sport encourages nationalism, militarism, and sexism.

Woods (2014: 20) continues the discussion of conflict theory in sport by adding that conflict theory "views sport as built on the foundations of economic power." It is easy, then, to see how some of conflict theory's key ideas (e.g., economics, power, authority, and unequal distribution of social resources) can be applied to sport. For example, the multibillion-dollar global sport industry concentrates a large part of power within most sports and sport organizations to a small, select group of people, such as wealthy team owners that are able to financially exploit the services of athletes. Ticket prices often increase after a team's winning season, and owners and corporations almost always make disproportionately more money than any athlete, coach, or front-office administrator.

Conflict theory's relationship to economic forces and how they impact societal relationships can be a useful way for examining the issue of whether or not college athletes should be paid. Understanding social relations from a political economy perspective illustrates how "[p]ower and wealth are inextricably intertwined and they dominate the rest of society. Social relations are the consequence of society's economic organization." (Eitzen 1988: 195). Within college athletics, it is easy to see how bureaucratically structured governance organizations benefit in innumerable ways from the labor of college athletes in order to increase profits, social status, and social power (Woods 2014). Sport grabs and focuses the attention of spectators and participants in such emotional ways that sport is said to be an "opiate" for the masses and desensitizing them to other societal and structural issues (Coakley 2014).

Class Activity

Exercise: Think of the amount of time you or people you know spend:

- participating in fantasy sports leagues
- watching college sports
- pre-game or postgame celebrations of college sports

Discussion Question: How does the assertion "Sport is an opiate for the masses of the general public" relate to your aforementioned exercise? What role do student-athletes play in your various forms of sport entertainment dealing with college sports?

College athletes participate on sports teams and in competitions generating billions of dollars annually for many organizations, such as the NCAA, television networks, and other business sponsors associated with specific intercollegiate athletic events or conferences. The commercialized entertainment of college athletes and sport has been rationalized by colleges and universities as attempts to recruit students, increase alumni donors, and raise or highlight the national and international prominence of the institution's brand (Nixon 2016). Indeed, Nixon (2016: 201–202) continues:

> The signature event in men's college basketball, so-called March Madness, reached a nineteen-year high in viewership in 2013, with the combination of CBS, TBS, TNT, and TruTV attracting an average of 10.7 million viewers per game. The championship game between winner Louisville and Michigan had an audience of 23.4 million. On the Alabama-Notre Dame BCS Championship game attracted more college sports viewers that year (26.4 million). The tournament also generated $1.15 billion in ad revenue.

Exploitation is a concept emanating from many social theorists' work, but most notably from Karl Marx's discussion on labor and economic relations. Specifically, he saw a two-class system composed of the bourgeoisie ("owners" with power and wealth) and the proletariat ("workers" and those with considerably less or no power and wealth). His view of exploitation involves the "means of production" and the roles and processes associated with both the proletariat—who produce most of the commodities sold for financial gain—and the bourgeoisie that own and control most processes and who benefit disproportionately from the products or services sold to the general public. For Marx, the workers' production exceeds their compensation. Marx's discussion of exploitation, then, highlights a useful concept for analyzing our topic. For our purposes (labor), exploitation has the following elements present:

- An actor or group using the work of others for their own gain.
- Gain could be explicitly financial or involving increased popularity and visibility (thus increasing financial gain)
- Power inequities with one person or group have a disproportionate amount of power as compared to other persons or groups.

Using the aforementioned working definition of exploitation, we can theoretically apply the concept to the example of intercollegiate athletics. For example, you have a large bureaucratically structured organization in the NCAA that benefits financially from the labor of student-athletes. While receiving some compensation for their efforts, e.g. athletic scholarship worth the varying prices of tuition, room and board, and other academic expenses, NCAA events such as bowl games or large basketball tournaments generate billions of dollars and have tens of millions of American viewers on television or through streaming broadcasts. From this line of thought, then, there could be a good argument that student-athletes, especially within the large, revenue-generating sports (e.g., football and basketball) are being exploited. This view, however, needs to be further examined with specific examples of exploitation and college athletes.

The discussion of whether to pay student-athletes often involves social critics, journalists, higher education administrators, and athletic directors. This dynamic is in keeping with conflict theory's view that powerful groups in society control not only how money is made or generated in society, but also which groups can weigh-in on the discussion. However, recently, student-athletes' views are increasingly being considered. Chavez (2014: paragraph 3), when discussing Northwestern University football players' right to unionize, noted the exploitation of college athletes, especially those in high-visibility sports:

> Sure, college players win full rides, with tuition and room and board. . . . But athletic programs are a huge source of funding for the schools. Northwestern raised an estimated $30 million for its football program—and the top earner, the Texas Longhorns, raised $139 million.

Coaches are frequently paid millions of dollars to coach amateur athletes that receive, in some cases, full athletic scholarships. Coaches are not the only ones benefitting, with many Athletic directors commanding large, six-figure salaries, as well (Chavez 2014). She goes on to say:

> All of this money is earned on the backs of the athletes, who risk life-altering injury every time they go on the field or court: concussion-related injuries, shattered bones, worn-out knees, hips and shoulders, torn muscles, ligaments and tendons. (Chavez 2014, paragraphs 6–9).

Chavez's (2014) view is similar, in part and process, to Gregory (2013) whom noted that—according to his calculations—during the 2012–2013 season each player for Texas A&M, regardless of position, could command about $225,000 based on an open market valuation. The $225,000 far exceeds the $40,000–60,000 in athletic scholarships many athletes receive calling into question the viewpoint an athletic scholarship is not exploitation.

When asking whether college athletes feel exploited, few have asked what student-athletes feel about the issue. To address this question, Van Rheenen (2012) examined student-athletes' perceptions of exploitation and the university's role in that process. He looked at differences and influences of race, sport played, gender, and whether the sport was considered a "revenue generating" sport (as compared to Olympic type sports or other non-revenue generating sports). Over 70 percent of revenue generating sport athletes and 25 percent of non-revenue generating sport athletes felt exploited by their university, with 35 percent of male and 24 percent of female student athletes feeling exploited. Over 60 percent of Black student-athletes, as compared to 26 percent of white student-athletes, felt exploited with there being very few differences between scholarship and non-scholarship athletes and their attitudes towards being exploited by their university. **For those college athletes reading this, what about you? Do you feel exploited by the system?**

Documentary Recommendation

Business of Amateurs (2016)

Written and directed by Bob DeMars, the *Business of Amateurs,* is a documentary focusing on student-athletes' rights and the forms of exploitation that occur within college athletics. The writer and director was a former football player at the University of Southern California (USC) and played for three coaches during his time there where he sustained injury, balanced educational demands, and balanced the increased demands of not only being a student-athlete, but also his coaches who were open about their view he was an athlete first, and secondly a student. According to the documentary's website:

> The NCAA is the face for college athletics, and it generates billions of dollars every year for the top universities in the United States. "The Business of Amateurs" is the first documentary that challenges the NCAA from the perspective of former student-athletes. (businessofamateurs.com ND).

It appears, then, there are a variety of factors playing in to an understanding or perception of exploitation. One's view on exploiting college athletes is probably associated with their view on whether college athletes should be paid. Regardless of exploitation and the conflict theory point of view, Thelin (2016) contends that paying players does not make good financial sense. Specifically, if their pay would be a salary as compared to a scholarship, then their salary would be subject to taxation. Students cannot deduct tuition or other college-related expenses because their salary, if they were paid at least $100,000, exceeds the deduction eligibility resulting in student-athletes earning little to no money for their services and no scholarship to pay for their education, too. According to conflict theory's views, once again powerful groups are able to control and constrain not only athletes' ability to be paid for their services, but also that the mechanisms already in place regarding salaries and taxation benefit other powerful groups leaving student-athletes powerless and with few, if any, ways to financially benefit from their athletic accomplishments.

Documentary Recommendation

Pony Express (2011)

Pony Excess is the title of an ESPN 30 for 30 documentary detailing the rise and fall of Southern Methodist University's (SMU) football program during the 1980s. The documentary illustrates how cheating, paying football players and even signing athletes, essentially, to professional contracts lead to the NCAA enforcing its repeat violators clause, known as the "death penalty" anecdotally. Eventually, SMU's football program was eliminated from the university for about two years before the long process of rebuilding could begin again. The cheating and corruption, though, was more than a few rogue athletes, coaches, and boosters over-emphasizing college football.
(Trailer: https://www.youtube.com/watch?v=IUFWMfMuLUw).

Indeed, Vermillion and Messer (2011) noted how concepts of **organizational deviance** helped to explain not only how we identify cheating and corruption in college athletics, but also how and why these types of problems have been consistently occurring for over 100 years. For example, Vaughan (1999) noted how bureaucratically structured organizations fall victim to inherent inefficiencies creating negative consequences for both organizations and individuals. She also noted that organizations (think of athletic departments, booster organizations, or governance structures) diffuse responsibility, while Erman and Lundman (1996) noted individuals are often blamed for systemic problems or failures, known as scapegoating. Finally, Vaughan (1996) identified that these organizations have "structural secrets," which inhibit communication and the flow of important information. The concepts of structural secrecy, scapegoating, and avoiding organizational responsibility are important ways for not only understanding some forms of cheating in college athletics, but are also on display in the Pony Excess documentary.

THE HUMAN COST OF PLAYING

Ronald Martinez/Staff/Getty Images

Shabazz Napier #13 of the Connecticut Huskies celebrates on the court after defeating the Kentucky Wildcats 60-54 in the NCAA Men's Final Four Championship at AT&T Stadium on April 7, 2014 in Arlington, Texas. (Photo by Ronald Martinez/Getty Images)

Shabazz led his team to victory in the NCAA championship game. But while he was at the University of Connecticut, Shabazz Napier told reporters he sometimes goes to bed "starving" because he can't afford food, despite that UConn's student-athlete guidelines include provisions for meal plans.

Hours before the 2014 NCAA Men's Basketball national championship game, the University of Connecticut guard, Shabaz Napier, opened up to reporters about NCAA high-profile athletes often going hungry adding fuel to the fire about the NCAA and how to compensate student-athletes. And when pressed further about these concerns, Napier also noted how he has a difficult time "playing to his best" because he doesn't have money for food, yet the university can be profiting off of his jersey sales. He noted how he doesn't feel players should be compensated in the "hundreds of thousands," but "when you see your jersey getting sold. . . . you feel like you want something in return" (Singer 2014, paragraphs 4–6)

Similarly, Fowler (2014) wrote about the University of Mississippi's quarterback whom whole heartedly agreed with Napier's sentiment. Bo Wallace, the Quarterback at the time, was speaking during the SEC media days when Fowler reported that a lot of guys did go to bed hungry. He further wondered how players with minimal resources pay for the suits and ties they must wear to media days. Schools can tap into a special assistance fund for help cover player expenses for special events. "If, I didn't have my parents [to help support me financially] I don't know what I would do" (2014, paragraphs 6–7)

These stories and quotes illustrate the human struggle behind much of the sports entertainment viewed by millions and millions of fans or consumers involving intercollegiate student-athletes. The NCAA addressed these news stories by instituting an unlimited meal plan, which was an immediate reaction to Napier's comments about student-athletes going hungry (Jessop 2014). Most recently, one major NCAA reform includes their new full "cost of attendance" scholarship. Specifically, the cost of attendance (COA) scholarship provides more financial support to student-athletes. According to Brutlag-Hosick (2015) of the NCAA, the COA includes tuition and related fees, books, room and board, academic-related supplies and expenses, transportation and other items normally associated with the cost of higher education. In her article Brutlag-Hosick (2015, paragraph 6) wrote and quoted several student-athletes with one in particular noting:

> 'On behalf of every athlete in this room, I want to thank you' said Oklahoma football player Ty Darlington . . . . 'I feel like the NCAA as a whole gets a bad rap like you're trying to exploit student-athletes. . . . Now I've seen that there really is a meaningful movement to help student-athletes.'

Each COA varies from state to state, city to city, and school to school with some areas being more expensive than others (e.g., public schools versus private schools). The COA discussion, predictably, has not ended the debate about whether this most effort satisfies the "paying college athletes" debate. Concerns have been raised as to whether the COA simply exacerbates the current arms race in intercollegiate athletics. Indeed, Katz (2015) surveyed over 130 NCAA Division I men's basketball coaches (about 1/3 of all Division I men's basketball program coaches) with many of them noting that the COA, which varies based upon institution, is becoming a recruiting tool for getting the best players. Many coaches and social critics now are left wondering if a recruit is looking for the highest paid scholarship offer as a way to compensate themselves for their potential and athletic exploits.

CHAPTER SUMMARY

The purpose of this chapter was to highlight tools useful for understanding the "paying college athletes" debate. Understanding how power and authority influence something as simple as the definition of "amateurism" or the invention of the term "student-athlete" help to contextualize and identify the dynamics at play within intercollegiate athletics. A brief historical overview of not only the NCAA but also intercollegiate athletics here in the United States has shown that issue of remunerating college athletes, cheating, exploitation, safety, amateurism, and corruption have been swirling around intercollegiate athletics since its inception. The entertainment quotient has always been leveraged as a rationale for not only extolling the virtues of competition, but also for recruiting donors and potential students for institutions of higher education.

In an attempt to better understand the debate and question of paying college athletes, we reviewed specific structural sociological theories and their related paradigmatic concepts. Functionalism, for example, speaks of manifest and latent functions and how those concepts impact our understanding of college athletics. Indeed, a functionalist orientation sees college sports—and the resulting athletes— as contributing to the over system of both education and sports-activities here in the U.S. Conflict theory is a different point of view highlighting how the political and economic environments influence definitions of success, exploitation, and how rewards are divided amongst those that develop the product or service, in this case, how athletes are rewarded for their athletic accomplishments serving as entertainment for millions.

In an effort to balance out the aforementioned structural theories, a discussion was entertained looking at the individualistic "cost" of participating in college athletics. The point of that section was to humanize the debate of financial remuneration, unionization, broadcast rights agreements, and the history of college athletic corruption with a few high-profile stories of the athletes themselves. Additionally, the NCAA attempted reform in the wake of these student-athlete reports giving us the current system of COA, which some see as not only recruiting incentives, but also the first step in officially paying student-athletes for their athletic services. However, as many scholars, critics, and sports entertainment personalities point out, there are many unanticipated consequences of dramatically overhauling the current scholarship-based system. Future scholars, administrators, and educators will need to weigh the benefits and costs as to whether college athletes should be paid.

Discussion Questions

*Think about the life—both on and off-campus—of student athletes. Would you say they have *power* and/or *authority*? Why or why not?

*Many of the discussions about whether to pay or not pay college athletes tend to focus on the revenue generating sports or football and men's basketball. Thinking about all student-athletes within all levels of intercollegiate athletics, are student-athletes being exploited? Using the concept from the chapter and recent examples, please defend your position.

*Currie (1998: 30) noted:

> Controversy about the role of student-athletes is nothing new . . . By 1890, many colleges were openly paying 'tramp'[or semiprofessional vagabond/traveling] players to join their teams. Some of these athletes even played for more than one school in a season. In 1902 the faculty at New York's Columbia University voted to make a football player ineligible due to poor grades. The athletic department did its best to overturn the decision, leading one college administrator to conclude that the football program was "incurable."

Who should be held accountable in situations such as the one described above? What role do faculty, college/university administrators, fans, and the general public play in how student-athletes are viewed on college campuses?

*Using the concept of *manifest* and *latent* functions, what would be some latent functions resulting from paying college athletes for their athletic services? Identify a list of 5–10 potential consequences.

*Using a conflict theory orientation, can be helpful—at times—for discussing the remuneration of student-athletes. We also know that most student-athletes do not have "full" scholarships to pay for their schooling. In order to address allegations of exploitation, what would be some ways of "paying" student-athletes in addition to their scholarships that would not involve a salary or hourly wage?

*Research the Ed O'Bannon class action lawsuit against the NCAA. How does this example illustrate the concepts of *power* and *authority*? Is the landscape regarding remunerating college athletes in the United States starting to shift?

Reference

Currie, Stephen. 1998. *Issues in Sports*. San Diego, CA: Lucent Books.

Extra-Inning: Sport Case Study—eSports: A New Generation of Student Athletes

"eSports aren't the future . . . They're the present. True skill at video gaming is just as impressive - and just as legitimate - as excellence in traditional sports."
~ Columbia College President Scott Dalrymple
(Schmidt 2015: paragraph 3)

"This is the new generation of student athletes. It's different because we haven't seen anything like this."
~ Maryville University Coordinator of Athletics and Recreation Jarrett Fleming
(Bauer-Wolf 2017: paragraph 17)

According to a 2017 article by Simon Hattenstone, the "world's fastest growing sport is live video gaming" (paragraph 1). eSports, as it is commonly called, generates revenues in excess of half-a-billion dollars a year and has a worldwide audience of over 350 million with North America making up the largest portion of the market (Newzoo 2017). In fact, eSports even has its own page on the ESPN website. With the growing popularity and potential revenue associated with it, it is likely not surprising to find that colleges are now fielding eSport varsity teams. In fact, it is projected that at least 50 colleges and universities will have official school sponsored varsity teams by the 2017–18 academic year (Smith 2017). One of the largest collegiate varsity programs in the United States is at Robert Morris University Illinois. With a team of 90 players (86 men and 4 women) and 16 paid coaches and staff members, the school boasts an $110,000 eSports arena (Parker 2017). It should be noted, however, that there are many more colleges and universities that compete in competitions through non-school supported club teams. For example, the University League of Legends (uLoL) boasts that over 300 college student run teams are registered members (uLoL n.d.).

As varsity eSports are not uniformly housed in college athletic departments (only about 40 percent are housed under athletics), the NCAA has not brought these teams under their governance even though these programs typically have full-time paid coaches, the players have stringent practice requirements that take a good share of their time, and the programs have an operating budget from the school including scholarships at a growing number of schools. This has opened the door for the creation of the National Association of Collegiate eSports (NACE) which represents approximately 95 percent of colleges with eSport varsity teams where, they report, player-athletes are currently averaging about $7,600 in scholarship money from their school (Bauer-Wolf 2017; Smith 2017).

While eSports varsity teams are typically dominated by male players, in April 2017, Stephens College became the "first women's college to sponsor a varsity eSports program" (Morrison 2017: paragraph 2). This has been hailed in the media as a barrier breaker for the sport of gaming, but what many do not realize is that women have:

. . . a long history of participation in collegiate esports. From the earliest days of collegiate esports, women have been actively involved in playing and helping organize the scene. The Collegiate Star League was, for example, founded by Princeton student and player Mona Zhang. Collegiate woman currently run a sizable portion of TeSPA clubs. (AnyKey 2016: p. 2)

In a sport which allows for an even physical playing field for men and women, it might be assumed that the ability to compete at the highest levels of the game would create a diverse player base, but this tends not to be the case. In response to this, a nonprofit organization called AnyKey (co-operated by Morgan Romine, the co-founder and captain of the Frag Dolls, a professional, all female gaming team) was established to "help create fair and inclusive spaces in esports for marginalized members of the gaming community . . . [and] build a gaming culture in which players are noted for their skills, not personal traits" (AnyKey 2016: paragraphs 1, 4).

Like more "traditional" sports, video gaming has the ability to consume the player and provide them with a sense of purpose and identity. In a 2017 Sports Illustrated article by Aaron Reiss about the Columbia College eSports program and its very first varsity eSports athlete, Connor Doyle, these themes become apparent. He originally attended an elite liberal arts college where he majored in math and economics. As a three-sport captain in high school, he also hoped to play Division III soccer, but failed to make the team. He reported that as a result of this, he lost his identity. He then tried to focus on academic goals, but when those too failed he turned to marijuana, Adderall and League of Legends which filled the "competitive void created by the loss of sports" (Reiss 2017: paragraph 4). Once he found his purpose, identity and passion again, he thrived and no longer needed the drugs. He currently "ranks among the top .07 percent of all League players" (Reiss 2017: paragraph 10) and hopes this will lead to a professional career.

Questions for consideration: Does the lack of physical activity or other aspects of the game, keep video gaming from being a "real" sport? If it is a "real" sport, should it then be housed under college and university athletic departments just like other sports? It has been argued that because of the lack of physicality, eSports are truly co-ed in that the gender make-up of the team does not (or should not) have an effect on the ability of the team to win . . . are there any other sports where this might be the case?

References

AnyKey. 2016. About. *AnyKey*. Retrieved July 4, 2017 (http://www.anykey.org/about/).

AnyKey. 2016. Diversity & Inclusion in College Esports Whitepaper. *AnyKey*, October. Retrieved July 4, 2017 (http://www.anykey.org/wp-content/uploads/Diversity-and-Inclusion-in-Collegiate-Esports.pdf).

Bauer-Wolf, Jeremy. 2017. "Video Games as a College Sport." *Inside Higher Ed*, June 9. Retrieved August 1, 2017 (http://www.insidehighered.com/news/2017/06/09/esports-quickly-expanding-colleges).

Hattenstone, Simon. 2017. "The Rise of eSports: Are Addiction and Corruption the Price of its Success?" *The Guardian*, June 16. Retrieved August 4, 2017 (http://www.theguardian.com/sport/2017/jun/16/top-addiction-young-people-gaming-esports).

Morrison, Sean. 2017. "Rising Stars: All-Women's Stephens College Breaks Ground with Varsity eSports Program." *ESPN*, April 20. Retrieved July 4, 2017 (http://www.espn.com/esports/story/_/id/19195390/all-women-school-stephens-college-adds-scholarship-esports-program).

Newzoo. 2017. Global eSports Market Report Light 2017 Highlights. *Newzoo*, Retrieved July 4, 2017 (http://newzoo.com/insights/trend-reports/global-esports-market-report-2017-light/).

Parker, Laura. 2017. "College eSports are Trying to Go Co-Ed, but Trolls Might Ruin Everything." *Vice News*, January 13. Retrieved *xxx* (http://news.vice.com/story/college-esports-are-trying-to-go-co-ed-but-trolls-might-ruin-everything).

Reiss, Aaron. 2017. "What it's Like to be a Varsity eSports Player." *Sports Illustrated*, January 4. Retrieved July 4, 2017 (http://www.si.com/tech-media/2017/01/04/varsity-esports-team-columbia-college-league-legends).

Schmidt, Rose. 2015. "Columbia College Unveils Competitive Video Game Program." *KOMU 8 News*, October 30. Retrieved July 4, 2017 (http://www.komu.com/news/columbia-college-unveils-competitive-video-game-program/).

Smith, Michael. 2017. "Colleges Flip the Switch on eSports." *Street & Smith's Sports Business Journal*, April 24. Retrieved July 4, 2017 (http://www.sportsbusinessdaily.com/Journal/Issues/2017/04/24/Colleges/esports.aspx).

uLoL. n.d. What is uLoL. uLoL. Online: https://ulol.na.leagueoflegends.com/what-is-ulol.

CHAPTER REFERENCES

Branch, Taylor. 2014 "How the Myth of the NCAA "Student- Athlete" Was Born." *Deadspin.com*, February 20. Retrieved June 5, 2017 (http://deadspin.com/how-the-myth-of-the-ncaa-student-athlete-was-born-1524282374).

Brutlag Hosick, Michelle. 2015. "Autonomy Schools Adopt Cost of Attendance Scholarships." *NCAA.org*, January 18. Retrieved June 5, 2017 (http://www.ncaa.org/about/resources/media-center/autonomy- schools-adopt-cost-attendance-scholarships).

Carrington, Ben and Ian McDonald (eds.). 2009. *Marxism, Cultural Studies and Sport*. New York, NY: Routledge.

Chavez, Linda. 2014. "How Colleges Exploit Athletes." *NYPost*, March 28. Retrieved July 4, 2017 (http://nypost.com/2014/03/28/how-colleges-exploit-athletes/).

Coakley, Jay. 2014. *Sports in Society: Issues and Controversies*, 11th ed. Boston, MA: McGaw.

Delaney, Tim and Tim Madigan. 2015. *The Sociology of Sports: An Introduction*, 2nd ed. Jefferson, NC: McFarland and Company, Inc.

Eitzen, D. Stanly. 1988. "Conflict Theory and Deviance in Sport." *International Review for the Sociology of Sport*. 23 (3):193–204.

Ermann, M. David and Richard J. Lundman. 1996. *Corporate and Governmental Deviance: Problems of Organizational Behavior in Contemporary Society*. NY: Oxford University Press.

Fowler, Jeremy. 2014 "Ole Miss' Bo Wallace: Shabazz Napier was Right, Players Go Hungry at Night" *CBSsports.com*, July 17. Retrieved July 4, 2017 (http://www.cbssports.com/collegefootball/news/ole-miss-bo-wallace-shabazz-napier-was-right-players-go-hungry-at-night/).

Gregory, Sean. 2013 "Should this Kid be Making $225,047 a Year for Playing College Football? That's What He's Worth, at Least. Athletes at Big-Time Football Schools are Cheap Labor Who Bring in Millions. It's Time They Got Paid for Their Work." *TIME*, September, 16. Pp. 36–42. *TIME*, Inc: New York, NY.

Jessop, Alicia. 2014. "The NCAA Approves Unlimited Meals For Division I Athletes After Shabazz Napier Complains Of Going Hungry: The Lesson For Other College Athletes." *Forbes.com*, April 15. Retrieved Novemeber 1, 2017 (http://www.forbes.com/sites/aliciajessop/2014/04/15/the-ncaa-approves-unlimited-meals-for-division-i-athletes-after-shabazz-napier-complains-of-going-hungry-the-lesson-for-other-college-athletes/#cc1cf7c15bd7).

Katz, Andy. 2015 "ESPN survey: Coaches Believe Differing COA Payments Will Impact Recruiting." *ESPN*, August 31. Retrieved July 4, 2017 (http://www.espn.com/menscollegebasketball/story/_/id/13549583/ncaa-coaches-believe-cost-attendance-allowance-recruiting-advantage).

Merton, Robert K. 1968. *Social Theory and Social Structure*. New York, NY: Free Press.

National Collegiate Athletic Association. ND. "Amateurism." *NCAA.org*. Retrieved November 4, 2017 (http://www.ncaa.org/amateurism).

Nixon, Howard L. II. 2016. *Sport in a Changing World*, 2nd ed. New York: Routledge.

Revsine, Dave. 2014. The Opening Kickoff: The Tumultuous Birth of a Football Nation. Guilford, CT: Lyons Press.

Sage, George H. 1997. "Physical Education, Sociology, and Sociology of Sport: Points of Intersection." *Sociology of Sport Journal*. 14:317–339.

Singer, Mike. 2014. "Connecticut's Shabazz Napier: 'We Do Have Hungry Nights'" *CBSsports.com*, April 7. Retrieved July 4, 2017 (http://www.cbssports.com/collegebasketball/news/connecticuts-shabazz-napier-we-do-have-hungry-nights/).

Thelin, John R. 2015. "From Sports Page to Front Page: Intercollegiate Athletics and American Higher Education." Pp. 3–13 in *Introduction to Intercollegiate Athletics*, edited by Eddie Comeaux. Baltimore, MD: Johns Hopkins University Press.

Thelin, John R. 2016. "Here's Why We Shouldn't Pay College Athletes" *Time*, March 1. Retrieved July 4, 2017 (http://time.com/money/4241077/why-we-shouldnt-pay-college-athletes/).

Van Rheenen, Derek. 2012. "Exploitation in the American Academy: College Athletes and Self-perceptions of Value." *International Journal for Sport and Society* 2(4):11–26.

Vaughan, Diane. 1996. *The Challenger Launch Decision: Risky Technology, Culture and Deviance at NASA*. Chicago, IL: University of Chicago Press.

Vaughan, Diane. 1999. The Dark Side of Organizations: Mistake, Misconduct, and Disaster. *Annual Review of Sociology*. 25:271–305.

Vermillion, Mark and Chris Messer. 2011. "The NCAA: An Enforcement Agency Involved in the Production of Organizational Deviance." *Journal of Contemporary Athletics* 5(1):1–21.

Weber, Max. 1922/2013. *Economy and Society*. Translated by. Guenther Roth and Claus Wittich. Berkeley, CA: UCPress.

Williams, Trevor and Tarja Kolkka. 1998. "Socialization into Wheelchair Basketball in the United Kingdome: A Structural Functionalist Perspective." *Adapted Physical Activity Quarterly*. 15:357–369.

Woods, Ronald B. 2014. *Social Issues in Sport*, 2nd ed. Champaign, IL: Human Kinetics.

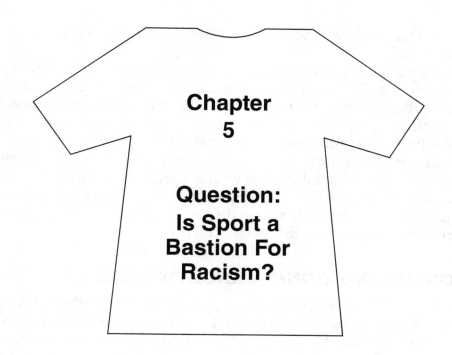

Chapter 5

Question: Is Sport a Bastion For Racism?

Student Outcomes

After reading this chapter, you will be able to do the following:

- Understand how sport is both a positive and negative force for promoting racial intolerance and racial justice in society.
- Speak with familiarity to the continued legacies of racial stereotypes and ideologies in sport.
- Identity racial controversies in sport mascot usage.
- Define and use the concepts of "racial and ethnic discrimination," and "stereotypes."

Contemporary sports are perceived by many to be a space where athletes of different races are freed from the constraints of racial conflict and division (Hoberman 1997)—in this way, sport is often thought to be an equal "playing field" free of racial conflict. This perception may be linked to the observation that athletes play on integrated, organized sports teams, and that an athlete's sporting identity often supersedes their racial identity. Indeed, racially and ethnically diverse athletic teams train, travel, compete, and win or lose together. Clearly, whites and their non-white teammates make friends across racial and ethnic lines through sport and majority and minority athletes are heroes cheered by their fans of all races. That is, fans tend to appreciate the athletes on their own teams, regardless of race.

Yet, despite this reality, sport continues to be an arena touched by race-related conflict and tension. In this chapter, we examine various sporting-related controversies to highlight the ways that sport and race continue to be inextricably linked with one another. Specifically, we document the prevalence and consequences of **racial and ethnic discrimination**, or unjust and prejudicial treatment. In terms of organization, we focus on the continued existence of institutional discrimination in contemporary sport. We follow this with a discussion of racial stereotypes and attempt to dispel some of the mythologies regarding the perceptions of race in sport. Finally, this chapter ends with a discussion of the lasting legacies of racial mascots and the controversies that exist in their use.

THE CONTINUING SIGNIFICANCE OF RACE

As an effort to highlight the continuing legacy of racial and ethnic discrimination that exists in the social worlds of sport and leisure, we offer the following historic incident: In 2009, despite having payed $1,900 for 1 day of swimming per week for the duration of their camp, a group of 56 campers (46 African Americans, and 10 Hispanics) were barred from the Valley Swim Club in Huntingdon, Pennsylvania. DeLuca (2013:340) writes, "following their first day at the club, the camp's money was refunded and they were asked not to return to the pool." The Valley Club claimed that the campers were banned because the facility "lacked the capacity or infrastructure to safely accommodate the group as originally anticipated" (Deluca 2013:340). However, during their time at the club, multiple campers explained to parents and camp staff that they heard pool members and staff making racist remarks while they were enjoying their time at the pool. Furthering the idea that campers were banned due to racist sentiments held by the mostly White club members, the club's president explained in a statement that "there was concern that a lot of kids would change the complexion . . . and the atmosphere of the club" (Arazia 2009: paragraph 8).

The incident at the Valley Club highlights a very real and significant racial disparity that exists within the sport and leisure activity of swimming in the United States. In addition to repercussions evident in racist attitudes, the consequences of access, or lack thereof, to swimming opportunities are manifest in other ways as well, one of which can be construed as a general public health concern. For example, the Center for Disease Control (2014) reports that Black children are more than three times as likely to drown as White children their age. Furthermore, economically underdeveloped neighborhoods experience more drowning fatalities, particularly among minority groups, and persons in these neighborhoods report a greater fear associated with swimming.

Ironically, the perception that Blacks and other ethnic minorities cannot swim is a longstanding **racial stereotype** (a widely held but fixed and oversimplified image or idea of a particular type of person or thing). In the past, it was believed that Blacks had inherent physical characteristics that hindered them from swimming. A 1969 study titled "The Negro and Learning to Swim," for example, concluded that Black men had low capacity for swimming because their bodies were "less buoyant than Caucasians" and their muscles functioned poorly in cold water (Allen and Nickel 1969). Contemporary scholars have mostly abandoned genetic and physical explanations for swimming disparities and pointed to social and cultural factors (Zinser 2006, Wade 2011).

Indeed, during much of the 20th century, non-whites faced widespread discrimination that severely limited their access to swimming pools. According to Wiltse (2014), the most consequential discrimination occurred at public swimming pools and took three basic forms:(1) Public officials and White swimmers denied non-Whites access to pools earmarked for Whites,(2) Cities provided relatively few pools for minority residents, and the pools they did provide were typically small and dilapidated. And, (3) cities closed many public pools in the wake of desegregation, just as they became accessible to non-whites.

In response to these closures, many (White) suburbanites turned to their backyards, building home-pools by the hundreds of thousands. As Wiltse (2014) continues:

> These residential pools . . . satisfied several desires that were common among the nation's burgeoning suburban middle class. They advertised financial success and upward mobility, enabled owners to control their social environment, and provided an ideal setting for family recreation and at-home entertaining. Backyard pools and swim clubs became so ubiquitous during this period that swimming and pool play became a common, almost every day, part of suburban life. This was a life, however, that few Black Americans could access (377).

Indeed few Black Americans lived in suburbs at the time, which meant that most were physically (and financially) cut off from backyard pools. As a result of limited access to swimming facilities and swim lessons, swimming did not become integral to the recreation and sports culture within minority communities. By contrast, swimming became broadly popular among Whites and developed "into a self-perpetuating recreational and sports culture precisely because they generally had convenient access to appealing swimming pools" (Wiltse 2014: 368).

Movie Recommendation

Pride (2007) is loosely based upon the true story of Philadelphia swim coach James "Jim" Ellis. Pride centers on the rehabilitation of a dilapidated city center swimming pool and the introduction of competitive swimming to the neighborhood youth.

One core effort in the attempt to save the swimming pool, is Jim's creation of the city's first all African American swim team, known as the P.D.R. team (Pride, Determination, Resilience). And true to the "inspirational sports movie" genre, the swim students stumble at first, but eventually overcome obstacles of overt racism, barriers of structural inequity, and smashes the stereotype that blacks cannot swim.

Of the film (and the social reality behind it), Jim Ellis states:

> [Society] had declared that black people lacked the buoyancy to swim . . . I would tell my athletes to face down stereotypes. . . . To those that did not want us swimming in 'their' White pools, I'd say, 'We are here. We're not going away. You can't close your eyes and we're going to be gone when you open your eyes. We're here, and we're going to stay here' (Greenleese 2007).

Reference

Greenleese, Nancy. 2007. "The Teacher Behind the Movie, 'Pride'" *NPR*, March 29. Retrieved Novemeber 4, 2017 (http://www.npr.org/templates/story/story.php?storyId=9209658).

CASUAL AND INSTITUTIONAL RACISM IN SPORT

On April 25, 2014, an audio recording of a conversation between N.B.A. Los Angles Clipper owner, Donald Sterling and his girlfriend was released to the public. In the recording, Sterling was heard making wide-ranging racist remarks. He was perturbed that his girlfriend had posted online pictures of herself with black men, including Magic Johnson, who played his Hall of Fame career with the Los Angeles Lakers. "It bothers me a lot that you want to broadcast that you're associating with black people," Mr. Sterling said. "You can sleep with [black people]. You can bring them in, you can do whatever you want but the little I ask you is . . . not to bring them to my games" (Prince 2014: paragraphs 8–9).

The N.B.A. had long been uncomfortable with Mr. Sterling. He was unsuccessfully sued by the team's former general manager, the N.B.A. great Elgin Baylor, for age and race discrimination in 2009. Mr. Baylor said in the suit that Mr. Sterling "had a pervasive and ongoing racist attitude" and ran the team with a "Southern plantation-type structure" (Branch 2014: paragraph 20) In the end, NBA Commissioner Adam Silver levied a lifetime ban against Donald Sterling, ultimately forcing him to sell the team.

Beyond Mr. Sterling's actions, scholars (Woods 2011, Dalaney and Madigan 2015, Eitzen 2016) argue that racism in sport is found far too causally among: (1) fans (via their sideline antics and often anonymous social media exclamations, (2) announcers (who express cultural xenophobia and spread longstanding racial myths), (3) owners (who express generational racism and treat players like property), and

(4) the professional sport leagues themselves (whose collective leadership often ignore diversity and limit professional leadership opportunities for minorities). To make this argument more concrete, please note the following examples:

- When Wayne Simmonds (a player for the Philadelphia Flyers and an African American) was dominating against the Rangers in the first round of the 2014 NHL playoffs, a significant number of racial tweets hit the web: "Porch monkey Simmonds is gonna learn" / "Go back to the jungle Simmonds you monkey" / "I hate Simmonds it was so great when a fan threw the banana at the ice when he was playing" (Bondy 2014: paragraph 3).

- Radio sportscaster Sid Rosenberg once remarked that the African American tennis superstars, Venus and Serena Williams were disgusting to watch. "I can't even watch them play anymore. I find it disgusting. I find both of those, what do you want to call them—they're just too muscular (Flay 2015: paragraph 5). Then, calling the women "animals," he then related a story when someone told him that the women would one day appear in Playboy magazine, to which he responded that they had "a better shot at National Geographic" (Kilgannon 2001: paragraph 2).

- Responding to the idea that NFL rosters are riddled with gang members, Radio host and former ESPN sport commentator, Rush Limbaugh said: "The NFL all too often looks like a game between the Bloods and Crips without any weapons" (Zirin 2013: paragraph 2).

- Former Cincinnati Reds owner Marge Shott used to refer to her black ball players as her "million dollar niggers" and once said that she said: "Hitler was good in the beginning, but he went too far" (Berkow 1992: paragraph 14, 20).

- In 2014 baseball star Carlos Beltran called out the MBL for their lack of Spanish interpreters, suggesting a degree of lack of cultural compassion and institutional neglect. Sportswriter Flip Bondy responded positively to Beltran's comments, writing: During the Yanks' glory years in the late 1990s, first base coach Jose Cardenal was forced to act as translator. Then when he left over a contract dispute before the 2000 season, an understandably resentful Jorge Posada was asked to translate for El Duque before and after games. Considering the resources available to professional teams, and that Hispanics now make up nearly 30 percent of major league rosters, it is ridiculous that Spanish-speaking players are getting very little help. If reporters aren't expected to speak Spanish, why are Latin players expected to speak English? (Castillo 2014: paragraph 21).

- In 2017, Baltimore Orioles center fielder Adam Jones said he was "called the N-word a handful of times" at Fenway Park. Many other black athletes were not surprised. NBA Hall of Famer Bill Russell, who won 11 championships as a player with the Boston Celtics, called the city "flea market of racism" (Wootson, Jr. 2017: Paragraph 5). Sportswriter Howard Bryant (2003) writes that many black ballplayers over the years, have all either expressed hesitancy about playing in Boston or inserted language into their contracts that expressly prevented them from ever being traded to the Red Sox. Why is this the case? Boston is more segregated than the average American city and this tends to create a symptom of intolerance.

- Also in 2017, Houston Texans owner Bob McNair made what many considered to be an inappropriate analogy about football players kneeling during the national anthem to protest racial inequalities. He said, "We can't have the inmates running the prison." With 70 percent of NFL players identifying as Black, many felt that the inmate comment perpetuated not only a stereotype of the violent Black male, but also suggested that they were persons without power. Some players suggested that the analogy made them the "property" of a white owner who saw himself as a prison warden. McNair later apologized once he was made aware that his comments could be interpreted as such (Belson 2017: paragraph 1).

Class Assignment

Please make a rejoinder to the above examples and create a list of positive racial stories in sport. Where has sport been "successful" in integrating disparate racial and ethnic groups and combating racial/ethnic prejudice?

CONTINUED LEGACIES: RACIAL STEREOTYPES, RACIAL IDEOLOGIES

Nearly two decades ago, former Dodgers general manager Al Campanis lost his job after stating on TV that blacks lacked the innate intelligence and intangables required of a general manager, because they were not "designed" with such leadership intelligence (Johnson 2007). Nine months after Campanis' faux pas, Jimmy "The Greek" Snyder was also fired from television after he argued that blacks' perceived athletic superiority was the result of "breeding experiments administered by slave owners" (Jones 2014: paragraph 14).

Again, though these statements were issued 20 years ago, the notion of genetic or natural differences in athletic ability between the so-called races is still present. There remain undercurrents of belief that blacks are physiologically different than whites, for example: the belief that blacks have a diminished ability to feel pain—thereby enabling them to engage in superhuman feats and endure physical pain (Gould 1981), or that they have extra muscles that allow them to jump higher, run faster, etc. (Hoberman 1997).

But what allows these myths to persist and why are so many people, apparently preoccupied with the question of whether there are racially linked genetic differences between black and white athletes? First, this is because people have learned to see race as a fact of life and use it to sort people into what they believe are biologically based categories. In truth, race is a biological myth based on socially created ideas about variations in human potential and abilities that are assumed to be biological. We know this because genetic research clearly shows that there is more biological diversity within any so-called racial population than there is between any two racial populations, no matter how different they may seem on the surface (Sussman 2014).

Indeed, famed sport sociologist Harry Edwards, when once asked whether black athletes were better than whites, he replied:

> How black does one have to be for this to make any sense? In other words, who does one put into categories of black and white? And even if we could totally eliminate social context from the consideration—an impossible task—how can we know which genes affect performance of a person who can trace her/his ancestors to Europe, Africa, and North America? (cited in Davis 1997:182).

Interview: Orlando Patterson on Jamaican Runners

Orlando Patterson is a professor of sociology at Harvard and the author of numerous academic papers and 6 major academic books including, *Slavery and Social Death* (1982); *Freedom in the Making of Western Culture* (1991); *The Ordeal of Integration* (1997); and *The Cultural Matrix: Understanding Black Youth* (2015).

Why does Jamaica dominate in producing so many world champion runners? It is race?

Orlando Patterson: It's not because of genetics, as some claim. A vast majority of Jamaicans' ancestors are from West Africa, which has relatively few outstanding sprinters. Nor can genetics explain why Jamaicans outperform other blacks in the Americas, especially in Brazil, which has 36 times as many of them.

If it's not race and genetics, what makes Jamaica so unique?

Orlando Patterson: First, it's because Jamaica is perhaps the only country in the world where a track and field meet is the premier sporting event . . . it is culturally ingrained into society. The British first introduced organized and informal athletics, and interscholastic competition, to Jamaica and other colonies in the late 19th century. . . . Jamaica quickly stood out from other Caribbean islands in extending these competitions from elite white schools to those of the non-white classes.

Second, Jamaica has an abundance of very healthy children and young people—the result not of Jamaica's mountainous terrain, as some have claimed, but of the extraordinary success of a public health campaign partly spearheaded in the 1920s by specialists from the Rockefeller Foundation. The program . . . emphasized hygiene, clean water and fecal and mosquito control. The old mantras "healthy bodies, healthy minds" and "cleanliness is next to godliness" took hold in the community and primary schools, whose teachers were recruited in the public health campaign. Running, as the cheapest sport, was the natural beneficiary of this movement. As a child, Usain Bolt received his initial training [in this health program]. . . . Ironically Jamaica is a poor country with the life expectancy of an advanced society.

The remarkable success of Jamaicans in building champion runners is due to the institutions of a globally dominant sports enterprise and a complementary system of public health . . . not race and genetics.

Excerpted from: Patterson, Orlando. 2016. "The Secret of Jamaica's Runners." *The New York Times*, August 13. Retrieved July 4, 2017 (http://www.nytimes.com/2016/08/14/opinion/sunday/the-secret-of-jamaicas-runners.html).

Second, instead of championing Black success in sport as a result of hard work, fortitude, and strategic preparation, such beliefs about genetic differences are issued as a way of dealing with a person's own threat of failure and lack of societal success. Several (Davis 1997; Markowitz 2004; Lavelle 2015) argue that this is typically a working class (and often White) cultural and social-psychological belief system—a mode of adaptation—for dealing with lack of social mobility in their own lives. As economic, educational, and social-political forces prevent, again, typically working class whites, from being socially mobile, racist attitudes are often employed for "answering" why some Blacks have become successful while they have not. Sport sociologist Coakley notes (2009:283), "When white athletes do extraordinary physical things, dominant racial ideology forces attention on social and cultural factors rather than biological and genetic factors."

Sport Case study

Soccer-Basketball (as an art project known as "The Rules of the Game II") is a hybrid sport/art project created by Gustavo Artigas, that combines basketball and soccer. The game is designed to combat ethnocentrism and the notion that different ethnic groups "can't get along."

Played on an indoor basketball court, the game had two soccer goals and two basketball nets and 4 teams. Initially "performed/played" in the year 2000 at the Tijuana/San Diego binational arts project, the hybrid sport involved two Tijuana high-school soccer teams and two San Diego basketball teams playing their respective sports simultaneously.

Given the ongoing concern of global immigration into the United States and the resulting cultural conflicts, Artigas wanted to create a game showing that (despite frustration, negotiation, and hard work) it is possible for two groups of people to occupy and figure out how to live together in the same space. See: http://gustavoartigas.com/ga/obras/las-reglas-del-juego-2/ for photographs of game play.

Documentary Recommendation

Race: The Power of an Illusion (2003)

While not a sport documentary, *Race: An illusion*, is highly recommended for tackling misconceptions about race and sport (i.e., the notion that race impacts sporting superiority).

Race, is a three-part series that examines contemporary science—including genetics—to challenges our common-sense assumptions that human beings can be organized into different groups according to their physical traits.

Further, it details the social roots of the concept of race and explores how persons have used the concept of race (despite the fact that it is not a biological fact) to rationalize, even justify, social inequalities. Ultimately, the series asks: If race is not biology, what is it? This series reveals that race resides not in nature but in politics, economics, and culture. It further reveals how our social institutions "make" race by disproportionately allocating resources of power, status, and wealth.

SYMBOLIC FORMS OF RACIAL IDEOLOGY IN SPORT: WHITE MASCOTS

This section begins by exploring the recent history and continued iconographic existence of Neo-confederate symbols (in particular, ethnocentrically designed White mascots) within sporting institutions. Indeed, at many educational institutions, sporting teams display symbol-systems that have historic links to political systems of racial oppression. Our argument is that these symbols remain as a historic celebration of white racialism and function to make "Whiteness" (and legacies of racial oppression) as the norm within sporting institutions. First some examples:

- At Nathan Bedford Forrest high school in Jacksonville Florida, athletes used to wear the Confederate Army's colors on their uniforms. They called themselves the rebels—and the school was originally named after the slave trade and Confederate general who became the original grand Wizard of the Ku Klux Klan. In 2014, the school changed in name to Westside and adopted the wolverine as its mascot. In the 21st century, the school was majority African-American, and many critics felt the name was a holdover of institutional racism. The local controversy drew national attention, and many city leaders felt it cast a poor light on the city of Jacksonville. In November 2006, the latest in a long line of petitions to change the name of the high school was submitted to the Duval County School Board. However, on November 3, 2008, the School Board voted 5-2 to retain the name. It was not until December 16, 2013, that the School Board voted unanimously to change the name, leaving the new name up to a student vote.

- In 2004, Nicholls State University retired their 42-year-old caricature of a white confederate soldier Col. Tillou (named for the university's founder, former Louisiana governor and Confederate officer Francis Redding Tillou Nicholls), after students raised concerns about its appropriateness as the "face" of the university. The original white-bearded, gray-uniformed mascot was retired after a student leader from the college's NAACP chapter raised concerns about its appropriateness. In particular, several students argued to change the logo, writing collectively: "As it is now, our mascot, the Colonel, is not something that we can identify with. It's a nineteenth-century war figure . . . that can in fact offend or bring back harmful memories to some people, and (for that reason) our mascot should be something people can identify with. I stand before you as a melting pot, and I can say that I personally cannot relate to the Colonel" (Percle 2004: paragraphs 1–16).
- In 2009 Ole Miss Chancellor Dan Jones issued a decision ordering the band to stop playing *From Dixie With Love* because some fans were chanting "The South will rise again" at the end of the song. The administrators at Ole Miss have struggled for decades to distance itself from Old South imagery, which they argue have hurt the school's academic and athletic recruiting (CNN 2011). Ole Miss teams are still called Rebels, but the university retired Colonel Reb in 2003 because critics said the goateed old "gentleman" looks too much like a plantation owner. In 2011, state lawmaker Mark DuVall crafted a bill requiring the Ole Miss band to play *Dixie* and a similar song, *From Dixie With Love*, during football and basketball games and to bring back Colonel Rebel as its mascot, in order to protect a unique part of southern culture (CNN 2011).

Indeed, a confederate celebratory culture continues to exist in much of the south (as well as in sporting symbols), and as much as defenders say these symbols are about protecting and promoting heritage, Newman (2007) argues that this is really about protecting and ensuring the white power structure and status quo:

> Such neo-confederate symbolic systems enact an anti-humane polity and ideology that to this day maps privilege and works to oppress the marginalized peoples of the region . . . they reflect themes of subjugation, oppression, and privilege woven through the material histories of slavery, civil wars, eugenics movements, segregation, civil rights, and new forms of racism (p. 316)

Returning to the racialist symbols of Ole Miss for a more in depth case study, we note that the practice of displaying the rebel battle flag and the singing of Dixie at football games began as a protest against civil rights legislation and movements toward racial integration. In protest to these trends, the University of Mississippi adopted the rebel flag, designated Dixie the schools fight song, introduced a mascot named Uncle or Confederate Reb (a caricature of an old South plantation owner), and officially designated all sports teams as "the rebels" in 1936 (Eitzen 2016: 50).

Truly the rebel flag in the same Dixie were symbols of defiance to use my supporters of segregation and civil rights (Eitzen 2016: 50).

So, it wasn't just that Colonel Reb "merely looked" like a southern gentleman plantation owner, it was that he was intended to be—he was a symbolic protest against attacks on the "genealogy of White supremacy in 'Dixie'" (Newman 2007:319). Newman continues:

> While attending an Ole Miss sporting event, one is meant to be symbolically transported to an imagined community which adheres to a patriarchal, genteel Old South dress code as many Ole Miss men customarily wear collared shirts and ties and women spectators typically don formal dresses. These Ole Miss fans chant the fight song 'Hotty Toddy' in support of their Rebels—a resistance song that became popular on the campus during the resistance to James Meredith's integration of the school in 1962. During the opening processions of each game, the White spectating throng welcomes the footballing combatants, almost all of whom are Black, to the battle by singing the Confederate anthem "Dixie"—a slave song which was co-opted by White entrepreneurs and incorporated into the blackface minstrels of the late 19th century. . . . All of these signifying acts—each of which perpetuates the conspicuous effect of Dixie South hegemonic Whiteness—is lorded over by the transcendental embodiment of sporting Ole Miss: the wildly popular mascot Colonel Rebel. More commonly referred to as "Colonel Reb" or "Johnny Reb," the mascot features a cartoonish physique of a mustachioed "gentleman planter" slouched over a cane, as if leisurely overseeing his plantation . . . Over time, the Colonel came to be known by other names, including "Johnny Reb" and "General Nat"—with the latter a reference to General Nathaniel Bedford Forrest (Newman 2007:319).

> **Excerpted from:** "Army of Whiteness? Colonel Reb and the Sporting South's Cultural and Corporate Symbolic" by Joshua I. Newman, *Journal of Sport and Social Issues*, November 1, 2007. Copyright © SAGE Publications. Reprinted by permission of SAGE Publications, Inc.

Further, contrary to popular arguments about "tradition," these symbols of Ole Miss, are relatively recent 20th-century creations. The university's inaugural football squad, established in 1893 played under the colors and moniker, "red and blue." Then, in 1929, the university sponsored a contest to rename the football team. The winning entry was the "Mississippi Flood," adopted in remembrance of the great flood of the Mississippi River that devastated the Mississippi Delta in 1927. The team nickname, "Rebels," was officially adopted in 1936 following a second contest sponsored by the student newspaper, the Mississippian. Of the 500 entries in a contest to choose a nickname, "Rebels" was (narrowly) selected over "Ole Massas" (a term often used by slaves to address their White plantation masters and overseers).

As noted earlier, despite significant protest, the mascot was officially retired by school administrators in 2003. Since then, the mascot at ole miss has been a bear (named Rebel), and most recently, a Landshark (Harris 2017). In an act of comical inventiveness, the mascot almost became Admiral Ackbar, the squid-like leader of Rebel Alliance from Star Wars (Malinowski 2010).

Richard Ellis/Contributor/Getty Images

In addition to the removal of Colonel Reb as the mascot, the University's Athletic Department ruled that in 2016 the song "Dixie", which was the unofficial anthem of the Confederate States of America during the Civil War, would no longer be played at athletic events due to its racialist (and potentially racist) interpretations.

Sport Case Study

The Redneck Olympics

As this is a chapter on race, it becomes important to remember that sport can serve to create and celebrate ethnic and class boundaries. Such is the case here.

There are no world-class athletes, but cold beer, barbecue, and sporting venues such as muddy tug-of-war, pig's feet bobbing, greased watermelon hauling, toilet seat horseshoes, and beer trot (an obstacle course that participants traversed while carrying a beer in each hand with the goal of not spilling a drop) are present. This is the Redneck Olympics (though formally the events' sponsors have to officially call it the "Redneck _____" because the real Olympics threatened to sue for copyright infringement).

What are the Redneck Games and isn't this offensive?

Redneck Games organizer Harold Brooks says the word redneck does not mean a: "person who's dumb or lazy . . . They're a hard-working group of people who can let loose and have a good time" (AP 2016: paragraph 5).

Sociologists note this term has been used historically to identify the disaffected white underclass, and redneck seems to be the only epithet for an ethnic/class minority that's still permitted in polite company. Ultimately, when this term is used by so called "non-rednecks," it suggests that Americans don't find class prejudice quite as shameful as racism (Nunberg 2016: paragraph 4).

But all stereotypes are reversible, especially when the people they're aimed at reclaim, redefine, and throw them back at their original users. In this way, "redneck" is reworked to becomes a badge of "working-class patriotism and authenticity" (Nunberg 2016: paragraph 12) and this is lived out in the celebration of the Redneck games.

AMERICAN INDIAN MASCOTS

During the past several seasons, there has been an increasing wave of controversy regarding the names of professional sports teams like the Atlanta Braves, the Cleveland Indians, the Washington Redskins, and the Kansas City Chiefs. The issue also extends to names of college teams like Florida State University Seminoles, University of North Dakota Fighting Sioux, and continues right on down to high-school teams such as the Tecumseh (Oklahoma) savages.

A coalition of activists, led by a number of Native American groups and sports writers, have protested the use of native names images and symbols as sports teams' mascots (King 2016). Ultimately they argue (ourselves included) that this is a racist practice that creates inauthentic identities and colonizes and distorts Native American history and cultural practices. Specifically, the concern is that American Indian symbolism is typically selected by outsiders for generic purposes that falsify and distort Native identity. As Joanna Bedard writes:

> What happens to a culture whose symbols are chosen by outsiders, by those who do not understand its deepest beliefs, structures and ways of life? What kind of interpretation of a society can come from symbols designed not to elevate conscious understanding to the highest of that society's ideas but to reduce that understanding to categories that debase or ridicule? Such symbols are not representations but caricatures (Joanna Bedard 1992:5).

A number of scholars and artists have attempted to highlight this racist practice by "flipping the gaze." For example, Ward Churchhill (1994:67–69) suggests:

> As a counterpart to the Redskins, we need an NFL team called Negroes to honor Afro-America. . . . Or a baseball franchise called the Sambos. How about a Basketball team called the Spear-Chuckers? A hockey team called the Jungle Bunnies? Maybe the essence of these teams could be the picked up by images a tiny black faces adorned with huge pairs of lips . . . and why stop there? There are plenty of other groups to include. Hispanics? They can be represented by the Galveston Greasers and San Diego Spics at least until the Wisconsin Wetbacks and Baltimore Beaners get off the ground. . . . Religious groups left out? Maybe, teams like the Kansas City Kykes . . . Issues of gender and sexual preference can be addressed through creation teams like the St. Louis Sluts for the Boston Bimbos . . . How about the Gainesville Gimps and the Richmond Retards so the physically mentally impaired will be excluded from our fun and games?

Otto Greule Jr/Stringer/Getty Images

Fans stage mascot protest before Game One of the 1995 World Series between the Atlanta Braves and Cleveland Indians at Atlanta-Fulton County Stadium on October 21, 1995 in Atlanta, Georgia. (Photo by Otto Greule Jr/Getty Images)

Indeed, a core problem with using Native Americans as mascots has to do with power. Lowen (2013: paragraph 14) writes, "of course other groups serve as mascots too. Think of the Minnesota Vikings, the fighting Irish Notre Dame, and the Vancouver Canucks. The last is even an ethic slur. "He continues:

> Each of these names was chosen with major input from the group to which refers. Proportionately more Norwegian Americans live in Minnesota and Jason states than anywhere else in the US. Irish-Americans have always had a special affinity for Notre Dame and I'm often headed the school. The NHL was born in Montreal; French-Canadians have long been a large proportion of its gators. If not we can Americans, Irish-Americans, or French-Canadians wanted to change the names they would do so whenever they please. In the meantime they cannot do take ownership of them (2013: Paragraph 14).

But this is not so with Native Americans. Changing team logos is often beyond their immediate control and it takes protest and education to try to change the minds of those in power.

Documentary Recommendation

In Whose Honor (1997), traces the history of the use of the Chief Illiniwek mascot at the University of Illinois, and other popular depictions of Native Americans in school athletics and professional sports franchises across the country. The film follows Charlene Teters* (a Member of the Spokane Nation) as a graduate student at the university and her evolution into a leading national voice against the merchandising of Native American symbols. The documentary shows the lengths fans will go to preserve their mascots and draws connections to other historical examples of stereotyped imagery such as Little Black Sambo and Frito Bandito.

Of her protest against the use of Native imagery in sports, Teters states:

> I am not a mascot. . . . Often, people think about Native Americans as we were envisioned at the turn of the century. If we're not walking around in buckskin and fringe, mimicking the stereotype in dress and art form, we're not seen as real. Native Americans are here, and we are contemporary people, yet we are very much informed and connected to our history . . . stop depicting us as "false" beings.

*As of this writing, Charlene Teters is a professor at the Institute of American Indian Arts in Santa Fe, New Mexico.

Chicago Tribune/Contributor/Getty Images

Consider the example of The Fighting Whites (alternatively identified as Fightin' Whites, Fighting Whities, or Fightin' Whities). The Whites were an intramural basketball team formed at the University of Northern Colorado in 2002 and named in response to a regional Native American mascot controversy (Graham 2002). The intramural college team attracted national attention because of its satirical protest about stereotypes of American Indians being used as sports mascots, particularly the "Fightin' Reds" of Eaton High School in Eaton, Colorado, not far from the University of Northern Colorado. The Reds' mascot (still in use as of this writing) is a caricature of an angry, loincloth wearing Indian with a large hooked nose, and an eagle feather in his hair. The Eaton Indian became part of a larger trend of using symbolic and fake Indians as mascots in the 1950s and 1960s in part to mock or condemn Native American protest movements of the era (King 2016). Further, according to Chad Shaw (2006), prior to the creation of the "Red" Indian mascot, the school was represented by the single letter "E" for 65 years—longer than the school's use of the Indian mascot—thus, challenging arguments for the continued use of the Indian mascot on grounds of "tradition."

Glenn Asakawa/Contributor/Getty Images

The intramural team, which included players of Native American, White, and Latino ancestry, adopted the name "Fighting Whites," with an accompanying logo of a stereotypical "White man" in a suit, styled after advertising art of the 1950s, as their team mascot. At first, the team's T-shirts used "Fightin' Whites" as the name of the team, but various media reports referred to the team as the "Whities" instead of "Whites." The plan to insult whites in the same way the minority students perceived Native Americans being insulted backfired on the group when the team's popularity skyrocketed. In response to customer demand, the team eventually began selling shirts under both names. The team added the phrase "Fighting the use of Native American stereotypes" to its merchandise to discourage the shirts from being worn by white supremacists, and arranged for an outside distributing company to handle manufacturing and sales of the clothing (Graham 2002).

The team sold enough shirts that they were eventually able to endow a scholarship fund for Native American students at Northern Colorado. In 2003, the team donated $100,000 to the University of Northern Colorado's UNC Foundation, which included $79,000 designated for the "Fightin' Whites Minority Scholarship."

As one last example of the anti-Indian trickster mascot, consider the Wednesday April 6, 2016, appearance of Bomani Jones (an ESPN employee and sports commentator) on ESPN's Mike and Mike. During the broadcast, Bomani wore a "Caucasians" shirt (which depicted a white face with an extremely exaggerated smile and a dollar sign in his hair, made to look like a eagle feather). The shirt design was an obvious parody of the Cleveland Indians' Chief Wahoo logo. Jones actually dedicated airtime to the shirt, which was supposedly "dominating the social media conversation" as the show progressed (Kalaf 2016: paragraph 1). After saying that he chose to wear the shirt because "it was clean," Jones discussed the idea behind it: It would be weird to have the Caucasians as a sports mascot, so why is a baseball team still called the Indians? Ironically many people tweeted in that they were offered by the shirt and Bomani was asked by unidentified executives at ESPN to zip up his hoodie (Kalaf 2016).

In the end, the critical analysis of Native American sports imagery highlights several critical points. First, these images serve as a socio-cultural mirror reflecting the form by which Native Americans are generally seen and expected to behave in mainstream culture. Morgan (1986:62) notes:

> In our not-too-distant past, grotesque racial caricatures and stereotypes of blacks were accepted in America as an ordinary form of humor [that] served to reinforce white notions of racial superiority. Even the less grotesque representations of blacks as servants or cooks had the same effect, driving home the concept that blacks were suited to menial jobs. The most objectionable of these caricatures are now out of circulation.

Unfortunately, racial caricatures of Native Americans have not fallen out of circulation, nor have their subsumed cues of racial inferiority disappeared. Further, the majority of these images are not only stereotypical but also oppressive. In specific, Native American sports images are commonly tied to systems of power in which Non-Natives appropriate Native cultural symbols as their own. The problem with this is that the general imagery of the "Indian" is a Euro-American creation born of generalized stereotypes. In this light, these creations never allow us to see actual Indians. Stereotypes negate our awareness of Native history, worldviews, and structural conditions—and this alone may be considered statements of ignorance and oppression.

One More Mascot: The Coachella Valley High-School Arabs and an example of Change

In 2014, a California high school, The Coachella Valley High School, agreed to change its team name and mascot from the "Arabs" to the "Mighty Arabs." The school district's board of trustees (in collaboration with the American-Arab Anti-Discrimination Committee, a civil rights group based in Washington, D.C.) agreed to amend the school's team name and mascot. The old mascot (similar to the Eaton Indian described above) was a grimacing, hooked-nose headscarfed "Arab" with a long and unkempt beard. Further, the school's representations of Arab culture included the use of "harem girls" and a belly dancer during marching band season—all deemed classic examples of Orientalism—or Western imaginations and depictions of Middle Eastern, North African, and Asian societies as backward and inferior (Said 1976).

The school's new mascot, is described in a statement issued by American-Arab Anti-Discrimination Committee as "a stoic, strong- jawed man with a neatly trimmed beard and was chosen with input from members of the Arab-American community" (Victor 2014: paragraph 7) The image was designed by Jesus Olivares and Sergio Espinoza, alumni and owners of a Screen Printing and Embroidery business in nearby Indio, California. The artists as well as many Arab-American families and business owners saw it as a way to turn something into a positive (Victor 2014). To view the old and new logos, please see http://america.aljazeera.com/articles/2014/9/12/arab-mascot-coachella.html.

But why the Arabs? The Coachella Valley is located about 2 hours east of Los Angeles and produces 95 percent of dates grown in the United States. Government officials introduced the crop—originally sourced from the Middle East—to the region in the late 19th century to promote economic growth. Its cultivation has allowed the California desert community to flourish and has even provided it with an Arabesque look that residents have been proud to promote (Victor 2014).

CHAPTER SUMMARY

As noted, sport continues to be an arena touched by race-related conflict and tension. In this chapter, we examined various sporting-related controversies to highlight the ways that sport and race continue to be inextricably linked with one another. Specifically, we documented the prevalence and consequences of racial and ethnic discrimination in society and the reality of institutional and symbolic discrimination in contemporary sport. In this chapter, we also attempted to dispel some of the mythologies regarding the perceptions of race—and racial superiority—in sport. Finally, this chapter ended with a discussion of the lasting legacies of racial mascots and sporting memorials to racialize violence and achievement—and again, per the larger goal of this work, we illustrate this with the work of contemporary scholars whom offer unique and critical insights into worlds of sport, play, and leisure.

Discussion Questions

*What are some examples of sport perpetuating racial inequalities—what are some examples of sport being used to undo racial inequalities?

*Following the above question, how is this reflected in film/media? What additional movie/documentary recommendations do you have on this subject?

*This chapter implies that group dominance in sport is not based on genetics or race, but cultural and institutional factors. Do you agree? Why/why not?

*Many race-based images are disappearing in sport. In your opinion is this a positive or negative reality?

*If sport is a reflection of society, then how do we eliminate racism from society? Is this fully possible?

Extra Inning: Harry Edwards, the first prominent sociology of sport scholar

Professor Harry Edwards is a famed sociologist who specializes his research (and activism) in the areas of sport, race, and protest. He has also written several books, including *The Revolt of the Black Athlete* (1969) and *The Sociology of Sport* (1973).

Corbis/Contributor/Getty Images

He has served as a staff consultant to the San Francisco 49ers football team and to the Golden State Warriors basketball team. He has also been involved in recruiting black talent for front-office positions in major league baseball. Edwards was also the architect of the Olympic Project for Human Rights, which led to the Black Power Salute protest by two African-American athletes Tommie Smith and John Carlos at the 1968 Summer Olympics in Mexico City. As a college athlete, Edwards had been a discus thrower on the San Jose State track team.

Edwards was born in St. Louis in 1942 but soon thereafter moved to East St. Louis, where he grew up and would go on to become a star athlete at East St. Louis High. He graduated in 1960 and was awarded an athletic scholarship to San Jose State University.

There, he graduated with honors and was awarded a Woodrow Wilson Fellowship to Cornell University, where he completed an M.A. and a Ph.D. in sociology. From 1970 to 2001, he was a professor at the University of California Berkley and now has the role of professor emeritus.

Most recently, he was interviewed for the documentary, OJ: Made in America (2016).

Professor Edwards continues to be a leading voice in the study (and use) of sport to change society.

Extra-Inning: The Redskins—Controversy and a Proposal of Compromise

dean bertoncelj/Shutterstock.com

The "Redskins" began in 1932 as the Boston Braves, a team that played in Boston, Massachusetts. In 1933, George Preston Marshall purchased the team and changed their name to the Boston Redskins to eliminate confusion with the Boston's baseball team of the same name (Smith 1987) and apparently to "honor" the then head coach William Dietz who identified as a member of the Sioux Nation (Hylton 2010).

In 1937 the team was moved to Washington, D.C., and though the team is now in Maryland, it is still considered Washington's team. From the perspective of the various owners of the team, the symbolism of the name is intended to honor the achievements and virtues of American Indians. For example, former Redskins owner Jack Kent Cooke said, "I admire the Redskins name. I think it stands for bravery, courage, and a stalwart spirit . . ." (Braiker 2013). And current owner, Daniel Snyder states that the name was chosen in 1933 to honor Native Americans and that it will never be changed (Synder 2013).

While owners claim that the name pays tribute to American Indians and reflects bravery, courage, pride, and a fighting spirit—the name has nonetheless stirred considerable controversy. For several decades, various Native American groups have protested the name insisting that the term is racially insensitive. This issue once again came to national attention with several prominent sports journalists making a public commitment to not uttering the team's name on air nor writing the term redskin in press because they considered the name offensive. They asserted that the

Redskins trademark is particularly derogatory because, unlike some of the other names ostensibly based on Native American culture, it is actually a racial epithet.

But from where does the word "redskin" originate? Early historical records indicate that redskin was used as a self-identifier by Native Americans to differentiate between themselves and Europeans. Throughout the 1800s, the word was frequently used by Native Americans as they negotiated with the Europeans and later the Americans. The phrase was largely benign until the zeal for westward expansion created conflict with Native tribes. At that point, the word redskin began to take on a negative, increasingly violent connotation that viewed Natives as "primitive" and warlike "savages."

Around the same time, the word redskin was becoming imbued with negative connotations, other Native American words and images were becoming increasingly popular symbols for sports teams. Team owners frequently began using words with indigenous connections in the 1850s to instill a sense of team spirit, unity and an "us against the world" type mentality for the sense of social solidarity (Hylton 2010). Later, Indian symbology was adopted because of a growing association (and stereotypical imagining) in the public mind with Indianness and athletic prowess. As Hylton (2010:896) continues:

> Thanks to the accomplishments of individual athletes like Jim Thorpe, Chief Meyers, and Chief Bender and of teams like the Carlisle and Haskell Indian Schools, the independent Nebraska Indians baseball team, and the Oorang Indians of the NFL, a new association developed between Indians and athletic proficiency. With such a perception embraced, names referred to Native Americans' acquired skills in American team sports rather than supposedly savage qualities. However, in the 1930s, the meaning of Native American nicknames changed again. Reinforced by powerful images of exotic, warlike Plains Indians in Hollywood films and a new widely adopted practice of associating team names with the ferociousness or guile of the players, Native American team names and logos took on a new meaning and became a source of crowd-pleasing pageantry.

Many journalists note that the original ownership of the Redskins team had a legacy of promoting racist ideology and segregation—thus, they feel that even if the naming was done to honor Indians, the owner's biased racial beliefs negated any positive symbolism intended and instead turned Indian imagery into symbols of a "minstrel act." In this regard, owner George Preston Marshall ordered team members to smear themselves with face paint before going out onto the field and the coach was made to wear feathers on the sideline (Gandhi 2013). Additionally, Marshall also resisted racial integration and the Redskins were the last team in professional football to sign and play a black player. As (Smith 1987) writes:

> Washington Redskins owner George Preston Marshall once quipped, 'We'll start signing Negroes when the Harlem Globetrotters start signing whites.' In 1961 the Redskins were the only team in professional football without a black player. In fact, in the twenty-five year history of the franchise no black had ever

played for George Marshall . . . Their owner was the one operator in the whole structure of major league sports who has openly flouted his distaste for 'tan athletes' (p. 189) . . . For the Redskins' owner, NAACP stood for 'Never at Any-time Any Colored Players' (p. 194).

Rhoden (2013: paragraphs 2–3, 13) writes that these words suggest "intolerance and a rallying cry for those who opposed civil rights, equal rights and human rights [and] years later, Daniel Snyder, the owner of the N.F.L.'s Washington franchise, is . . . aligning himself philosophically with George Preston Marshall." He continues:

Snyder might object to being placed alongside . . . Marshall. By his insistence on using a term that offends even one person, however, he contributes to an atmosphere of intolerance and bigotry. Snyder has an opportunity to get on the right side of history; though I don't expect [him] to change his team's nickname voluntarily . . . Snyder's fight is an economic issue, revolving around licensing, marketing and branding. His stridency is based in money, not morality (paragraphs 19–23).

When Native American symbolism is chosen, and applied to sport, it is generally done because such images are seen to reflect courage, pride, and ferocity. However, of concern here is the notion that Indian symbolism is generally selected by outsiders (non-Natives) for generic purposes. Further, because outsiders often select images, such images are not generally authentic to the particular cultures from which they are acquired (Black 2002).

In this light then, the Redskin is a racial caricature that is not only stereotypical but also oppressive. In specific, Native American sport images are commonly tied to systems of power in which Non-natives appropriate Native cultural symbols as their own. The problem with this, in our view, is that the general notion of the Indian as a Euro-American creation born of generalized stereotypes. Thus, the existence of the Redskin mascot makes it difficult to "see" actual Indians. Stereotypes negate our awareness of Native history, worldviews, and structural conditions—and this alone may be considered an act of ignorance and oppression.

Ultimately we have no power to force the team to self-censor or abandon its logo and name. Though we do consider the name offensive and feel it acts as a perpetuator of stereotypes, many Native Americans have gone on record as saying they support the logo because it is one of the few national symbols that "gives our people recognition" (Stapleton 2001). Given that less than one percent of the U.S. population identifies as American Indian, the logo can act as a strange and contradictory cultural beacon letting people know that Indians still exist (even if stereotypically perceived)—and in many ways, the controversy surrounding it is one of the few national platforms that gives voice to Native activists and a "symbolic place" to highlight Native American issues and realities.

Thus, for these reasons, we feel that a "comprising middle path" may be the best solution. We would be able to support the ownership's continued use of the logo and associated symbolism if the team creates honest and meaningful programs of outreach wherein they work with Native peoples to educate all about the realities and authentic identities of American Indians—and if they contribute a significant portion of the monies generated from logo sales to programs such as the American Indian college fund (see http://www.collegefund.org/). A similar of model of exchange can be found in the relationship between the Seminole Nation of Florida and Florida State University (FSU). In 2005, the Seminole Nation granted FSU "lasting permission" to use Native-Seminole imagery in return for limited academic scholarships for select tribal members and the construction of a Seminole Heritage and Culture museum on campus (FSU 2005: paragraphs 13–14).

We recognize that such a compromise would continue the "sustainability of acceptable racist imagery that becomes a portal for . . . White power structures . . . to maintain or advance their own [financial] interests" (Staurowsky 2007:72). But, if nothing else, such a comprise would also force the Washington Redskin franchise to acknowledge voices of protest, compel monetary concession for the appropriation and construction of Native imagery, and urge broader public recognition of American Indians beyond that of mascot fetishes and cultural imaginations.

References

Black, Jason Edward. 2002. The "Mascotting" of Native America: Construction, Commodity, and Assimilation." The American Indian Quarterly. 26, 605–622.

Braiker, Brian. 2013. "The Media Takes a Tomahawk to the Redskins." *Digiday*, August 9. Retrieved November 4, 2017 (http://digiday.com/brands/redskins-media-boycott/.)

FSU News. 2005. "Florida State University thanks Seminoles for Historic Vote of Support." Retrieved November 4, 2017 (http://www.fsu.edu/news/2005/06/17/seminole.support/).

Gandhi, Lakshmi. 2013. "Are You Ready For Some Controversy? The History Of 'Redskin'" *Npr. org*, September 9. Retrieved November 4, 2017 (http://www.npr.org/blogs/codeswitch/2013/09/09/220654611/are-you-ready-for-some-controversy-the-history-of-redskin).

Hylton, J. Gordon. 2010. "Before the Redskins Were the Redskins: The use of Native American Team Names in The Formative Era of American Sports, 1857–1933" North Dakota Law Review 86:879–903.

Smith, Thomas G. 1987. "Civil Rights on the Gridiron: The Kennedy Administration and the Desegregation of the Washington Redskins" *Journal of Sport History* 14:189–208.

Stapleton, Bruce. 2001. Redskins: Racial Slur or Symbol of Success? Bloomington, Indiana: IUniverse.

Staurowsky, Ellen J. 2007. "You Know, We Are All Indian": Exploring White Power and Privilege in Reactions to the NCAA Native American Mascot Policy" Journal of Sport and Social Issues 31:61–67.

Synder, Daniel. 2013. "Letter from Washington Redskins owner Dan Snyder to fans." *The Washington Post*, October 9. Retrieved November 4, 2017 (http://articles.washingtonpost.com/2013-10-09/local/42848059_1_native-americans-redskins-name-football-team).

CHAPTER REFERENCES

Allen, R.L. and David L. Nickel. 1969. "The Negro and Learning to Swim; The Buoyancy Problem Related to Biological Differences," *Journal of Negro Education* 38: 404–411.

Arazia, Karen. 2009. Pool Boots Kids Who Might 'Change the Complexion' Campers sent packing after first visit to swim club." *NBCPhiladelphia.com*, July 17. Retrieved November 4, 2017 (http://www.nbclocalmedia.com/news/politics/Pool-Boots-Kids-Who-Might-Change-the-Complexion.html#ixzz46YrfKpgx).

Associated Press. 2016. "Rednecks Hold Their 'Blanking' Summer Games." *TMJ4.com*, July 30. Retrieved November 4, 2017 (http://www.tmj4.com/news/national/rednecks-hold-their-blanking-summer-games).

Bedard Joanna. 1992. In D. Doxtator's *Fluff and Feathers: An Exhibit on the symbols of Indianness.* Brantford. Ontario: Woodland Cultural Centre.

Belson, Ken. 2017. "Texans Owner Bob McNair Apologizes for 'Inmates' Remark." The *New York Times*, October 27. Retrieved November 5, 2017 (https://www.nytimes.com/2017/10/27/sports/football/bob-mcnair-texans.html?_r=0).

Berkow, Ira. 1992. "Baseball; Marge Schott: Baseball's Big Headache." *The New York Times*, November 29. Retrieved November 5, 2017 (http://www.nytimes.com/1992/11/29/sports/baseball-marge-schott-baseball-s-big-red-headache.html?pagewanted=all).

Bondy, Filip. 2014. "10 Places where racism is still a major issue in sports." *Daily News*, May 3. Retrieved November 5, 2017 (http://www.nydailynews.com/sports/bondy-10-places-racism-major-issue-sport-article-1.1778178).

Bonner, Robert. E. 2002. *Colors and blood: Flag passions of the Confederate South.* Princeton, NJ: Princeton University Press.

Branch, John. 2014. "N.B.A. Bars Clippers Owner Donald Sterling for Life." *New York Times*, April 29. Retrieved November 4, 2017 (http://www.nytimes.com/2014/04/30/sports/basketball/nba-donald-sterling-los-angeles-clippers.html).

Bryant, Howard. 2003. *Shut Out: A Story of Race and Baseball in Boston.* Boston, MA: Beacon Press.

Castillo, Jorge. 2014. "Carlos Beltran speaks out against lack of interpreters for Spanish-speaking major leaguers." *NJ.com*, April 25. Retrieved November 5, 2017 (http://www.nj.com/yankees/index.ssf/2014/04/carlos_beltran_speaks_out_against_lack_of_spanish_interpreters_for_players.html).

Center for Disease Control. 2014. Unintentional Drowning: Get the Facts. *CDC.* Retrieved November 4, 2017 (http://www.cdc.gov/HomeandRecreationalSafety/Water-Safety/waterinjuries-factsheet.html).

Churchill, Ward. 1994. *Indians Are Us? Culture and Genocide in Native North America.* Monroe, Maine: Common Courage Press.

CNN. 2011. "Legislator pushes bill to restore Colonel Reb as Ole Miss mascot." CNN, January 28. Retrieved November 5, 2017 (http://www.cnn.com/2011/US/01/28/mississippi.school.mascot/index.html).

Coakley, Jay. 2009. *Sports in Society: Issues and Controversies.* Dubuque, IA: McGraw Hill.

Davis, Laurel R. 1990. "The Articulation of Difference: White Preoccupation With the Question of Racially Linked Genetic Differences Among Athletes." *Sociology of Sport Journal* (7):179–187.

DeLuca, Jamie R. 2013. "Submersed in Social Segregation: The (Re) Production of Social Capital Through Swim Club Membership." *Journal of Sport and Social Issues* 37: 340–363.

Eitzen, D. Stanley. 2016. *Fair and Foul: Beyond the Myths and Paradoxes of Sport*, 6th ed. Boulder CO: Rowman & Littlefield.

Fay, Kayleigh. 2015. "Let's talk about Serena." *Odyssey*, July 22. Retrieved November 5, 2017 (https://www.theodysseyonline.com/quotes-serena).

Graham, Judith. 2002. "Student team has mascot, message: Exasperated by Indian nicknames, squad turns tables." *Chicago Tribune,* March 14. Retrieved November 4, 2017 (http:// articles. chicagotribune.com/2002-03-14/news/0203140271_1_mascot-eaton-high-school-fightin).

Gould, Stephen Jay. 1981. *The Mismeasure of Man*. New York, NY: W.W. Norton & Company.

Harris, Bracey. 2017. "Ole Miss taps Landshark as new mascot" *Clarion Ledger*, October 6. Retrieved November 5, 2017 (http://www.clarionledger.com/story/sports/2017/10/06/ole-miss-landshark-mascot/739910001/).

Hoberman, John M. 1997. *Darwin's Athletes: How Sport Has Damaged Black America and Preserved the Myth of Race.* NewYork, NY: Houghton-Mifflin.

Johnson, Eric. 2007. "'Nightline' Classic: Al Campanis." *ABC News*, April 12. Retrieved November 4, 2017 (http://abcnews.go.com/Nightline/ESPNSports/story?id=3034914).

Jones, Bomani. 2014. "Sterling's racism Should Be News." *ESPN: Page 2*. Retrieved November 4, 2017 (http:// espn.go.com/espn/page2/story?page=jones/060810).

Kalif, Samer. 2016. "Bomani Jones Wears Shirt." *Deadspin*, April 7. Retrieved November 4, 2017 (http:// deadspin.com/tag/bomani-jones).

King, C. Richard. 2016. *Redskins: Insult and Brand*. Lincoln, NE: University of Lincoln Press.

Lavelle, Kristen M. 2015. *Whitewashing the South: White Memories of Segregation and Civil Rights.* Boulder, CO: Rowman & Littlefield.

Lowen, James W. 2013. "New Opposition to Old Sports Mascots." *History News Network*, April 5. Retrieved November 4, 2017 (http://historynewsnetwork.org/blog/151462).

Malinowski, Erik. 2010. "Ole Miss' Admiral Ackbar Campaign Fizzles." *Wired*, September 8. Retrieved November 5, 2017 (https://www.wired.com/2010/09/ole-miss-admiral-ackbar/).

Morgan, Hall. 1986. Symbols of America. New York, NY: Viking Press. Newman, Joshua I. 2007. "Army of Whiteness? Colonel Reb and the Sporting South's Cultural and Corporate Symbolic." *Journal of Sport and Social Issues* 31(4) 315–339.

Nunberg, Geoff. 2016. "A Resurgence of 'Redneck' Pride." *NRP,* September 6. Retrieved November 4, 2017 (http://www.npr.org/2016/09/06/492183406/a-resurgence-of-redneck-pride-marked-by-race-class-and-trump).

Percle, Dustin. 2004. "Students debate mascot controversy at forum." The Nicholls Worth – The Website, February 18. Retrieved November 5, 2017 (https://thenichollsworth.com/100467/uncategorized/students-debate-mascot-controversy-at-forum-monday/).

Prince, Rosa. 2014. "Donald Sterling: President Obama joins criticism of 'racist' remarks: Basketball team owner attracts fury from black players and leaders over recording of alleged racist rant." *The Telegraph,* April 27. Retrieved x November 4, 2017 (http://www.telegraph.co.uk/news/worldnews/northamerica/usa/10791580/Donald-Sterling-President-Obama-joins-criticism-of-racist-remarks.html).

Said, Edward. 1976. *Orientalism.* New York, NY: Vintage Books.

Shaw, Chad. 2006. *Eaton's Indian: From Arbitrary Creation to Beloved Caricature, 1966–2006.* Unpublished Masters Thesis. Available: https://drive.google.com/file/d/0Bz5mfCeDgjtVeWR5NUIT dnUybE5BRWZtUE5FNHFac3JQcDhj/view

Sussman, Robert Wald. 2014. *The Myth of Race: The Troubling Persistence of an Unscientific Idea.* Cambridge, MA: Harvard University Press.

Victor, Philip J. 2014. "California high school drops controversial Arab mascot." *AlJazeera America,* September 12. Retrieved November 4, 2017 (http://america.aljazeera.com/articles/2014/9/12/ arab-mascot-coachella.html).

Wade, Lisa. 2011. "Tragedy at Red River: Race, Privilege & Learning to Swim." *Sociological Images,* August 3. Retrieved November 4, 2017 (https://thesocietypages.org/socimages/2011/08/03/ the-red-river-tragedy-race-privilege-and-learning-to-swim/).

Wiltse, Jeff. 2014. "The Black-White Swimming Disparity in America: A deadly Legacy of Swimming Pool Discrimination." *Journal of Sport and Social Issues* 38(4): 366–389.

Zinser, Lynn. 2006. "Everyone Into the Water." *New York Times,* June 19. Retrieved November 4, 2017 (http://www.nytimes.com/2006/06/19/health/healthspecial/19swim.html?pa gewanted=all).

Zirin, Dave. 2014. "Is the NFL Really Stupid Enough to Hire 'Gang Tattoo Experts' to Examine Players?" *The Nation,* July 25. Retrieved November 5, 2017 (https://www.thenation.com/ article/nfl-really-stupid-enough-hire-gang-tattoo-experts-examine-players/).

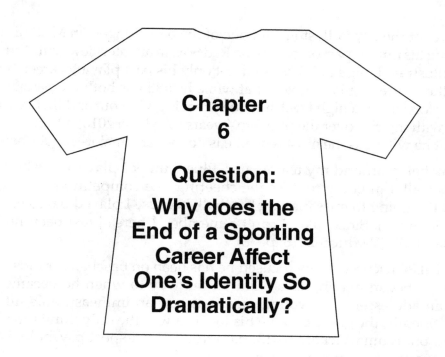

Chapter 6

Question:

Why does the End of a Sporting Career Affect One's Identity So Dramatically?

Student Outcomes

After reading this chapter, you will be able to do the following:

- Identify what is meant by the term "identity" and how sociological views of the "self" relate to athletes. How are these two concepts related, yet different?
- Explain and describe how socialization processes impact identity formation and maintenance.
- Describe how peer groups, status, and master status are associated with athletes and identity.
- Examine and describe the potential role and identity conflicts emerging from the label "student-athlete." That is, how is the "scholar baller" theory associated with student and/or athletic identities?
- Describe why "retirement" issues—from any level of sport—are difficult for many athletes.

INTRODUCTION

During the spring, summer, and fall of the 2016 MLB (Major League Baseball) season, David Ortiz chronicled his final year in the major leagues. David Ortiz, known affectionately as Big Papi, was a larger-than-life baseball player, representative and mouthpiece for the city of Boston, and one of the best sluggers in MLB history, especially during his time as part of the Boston Red Sox. In an interview with Tom Verducci of Sports Illustrated, Big Papi discussed not only his past playing career, but also his plans for the future. Big Papi noted that while he still has both the passion and acumen for performing at a high level, it is body that is giving out and that he fought and struggled with injuries over the past 3 to 4 years (Verducci 2016). Ortiz, when talking about what he will miss the most when he is no longer a major-leaguer noted:

> I think being around my teammates. Plus, I think I play for the best fans in baseball. I'm going to miss the cheering, the competition. But I don't think I'm going to miss playing baseball, because I played baseball for so long, so much. Since, like, I can't remember, [there's] just been nothing but baseball. (Verducci 2016, p. 36).

Big Papi also discussed how focused he has been on baseball for most of his life. The game he began playing as a child all the way to when he became a professional as an adolescent and young man, has had an immeasurable influence on him. Additionally, the game became his focus; it was the only thing for a long time he focused on. Emma Vickers (2013, paragraph 10), a sport psychologist, labeled this phenomenon as **tunnel vision** and asserted:

> A 'tunnel vision syndrome' affects many elite athletes to varying degrees at some stage of their careers. It is often the case that coaches, parents, professional sports agents and general managers are able to see it, however, athletes who are unaware that they suffer from tunnel vision spend far too much time thinking only of training, competition and results.

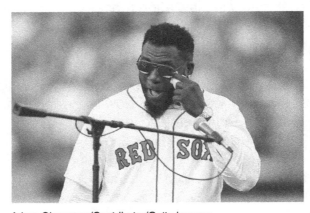

Adam Glanzman/Contributor/Getty Images

Former Boston Red Sox player David Ortiz #34 reacts during his jersey retirement ceremony before a game against the Los Angeles Angels of Anaheim at Fenway Park on June 23, 2017 in Boston, Massachusetts

As a result, athletes are left ill-prepared for the balanced perspective required of 'real world' career opportunities.

In his interview of David Ortiz, Verducci (2016) covers a wide range of topics spanning the career and list of accomplishments of Big Papi. Near the end of the interview, though, the topic of "what comes next" in the former major leaguer career comes up. It appears, however, that Big Papi has been preparing for this moment and noted the numerous activities that were going to keep him busy while enjoying his post-playing career. These activities include a production company, working as a commentator for baseball games on television, and spending more time with his family—all strategies conducive with positively transitioning from an athletic career into a life that is not necessarily 100 percent centered on sport participation (Vickers 2013).

Class Activity

High-profile retired athletes

With your classmates, please construct a list of retired high-profile athletes.

Take a look at the collective class list. What do you notice about this list and the athletes listed within it? What do they all have in common? Did the athletes retire on their own terms? Where they forced out, do to age, injury, salary cap? What are these athletes doing now?

Most of the athletes you listed were probably paid very well for their athletic services. Additionally, many of these well-known athletes retired from their sport on their own timelines. While injuries and physical health are always a concern, some of these athletes were able to "disengage" from their sporting careers on their own terms (see Kobe Bryant or Derek Jeter for example). Being able to retire of their own volition, however, is relatively unique as many athletes in power and performance sports have injuries or franchises that make the decision for them. For example, Chadiha (2012) wrote about the many **retirement and disengagement** issues for NFL players with some of them refusing to give up not only the dream of continuing to play, but also of waiting for a team call them and delay their post-retirement lives. It was, essentially, difficult to move on from the game they had played for so long. Many professional (and intercollegiate athletes) do not get the chance to decide when to officially retire. And, those that are privileged enough to make that decision often have difficulty knowing when and how to make it. Who can forget how Hall of Fame quarterback, Brett Favre, retired or contemplated (very publically) retirement from football, many times? Only to eventually play 20 years in the NFL.

Documentary Recommendation

Broke (2012), looks at the many ways athletes lose their money. The documentary begins with the following statistics (courtesy of Sports Illustrated):

> By the time they have been retired for two years, 78 percent of former NFL players have gone bankrupt or are under financial stress; within five years of retirement, an estimated 60 percent of former NBA players are broke.

How is this the case? Primarily, the athletes interviewed agree that because players most often turn pro by their very early twenties they generally have no business experience (and no skills training in investment and delayed gratification). Second, there is the "identify crafting" that comes with being a professional athlete. The culture of being a professional athlete is one that encourages excess spending as a way "telling" oneself and others that they "made it."

But beyond the bad investment decisions and extravagant purchases, the documentary also notes how family pressures (caring and supporting family members even after one's cash flow stops) and injury (exorbitant health care bills) can force one to go broke fairly quickly.

Finally, the average NFL career is less than 4 years and the average NBA career is less than 5—It doesn't take all that long to lose what one has earned in this limited career-span.

The purpose of this chapter is to examine the processes and dynamics associated with "retirement" from a sporting career. However, it should be noted that retirement (or disengagement) from sports is not a phenomenon associated exclusively with professional athletes. We will discuss the process of identity formation (both athletic and non-athletic identities) and maintenance of athletes from all levels. We will also employ a variety of theoretical tools and popular examples to better help not only understand how athletic identities impact individuals, but also build tools we as scholars, administrators, or practitioners can use to identify and support identity transition of athletes. In order to understand the retirement of athletes, then we need to understand their lives and how these identities are formed.

Activity

20-Statements Test

Who am I? It seems a relatively straightforward question. And, it is one that many philosophers, social scientists, and—increasingly—sport practitioners have to deal with, as sport becomes a larger and larger part of our society. The following test asks you one question, 20 times: "Who am I?"

Write out 20 answers to: "Who am I?" Do not write out your answers as you think others see you—write them out as you see yourself. Write out your answers as quickly as they occur to you.

Link: http://www.asanet.org/sites/default/files/savvy/introtosociology/ Documents/Twenty%20Statement%20Test.htm

Now that you have completed the Twenty Statements Test (TST), what do you notice about yourself? After others in class have shared, what are some commonalities? Over the years, many students and people tend to put down sociologically relevant ideas. For example, many people put down the "roles" they play in life, such as brother/sister, friend, sister, student, employee, etc. What does that tell you/us about how people view themselves? Was athlete part of this list? If so, how important is this identity to "making you who you are?"

WHAT IS AN IDENTITY AND HOW DOES IT FORM?

Any discussion on the topic of retirement, disengagement, or how athletes (and the general public) view themselves must begin with developing a vocabulary. It has become commonplace to speak of "taking a moment for myself" or hearing how "self-awareness" is a positive thing to have as a person, or how an athlete may "take time to work on themselves" after a high-profile gaff, incident, or mistake. Intuitively, these types of conversations begin with an understanding of what can be considered as the **self and identity**. Our focus, per this chapter's thesis, is to better understand not only the life, but also the retirement of athletes and how issues of identity are social issues. Additionally, once a focus and understanding is developed, then we can utilize social science to make a real and meaningful impact in the lives of not only athletes, but also those working within the institution of sport. Our first job, though, is to define the concepts important to this discussion and try to develop a basic understanding of identity formation processes. Finally, we highlight a brief discussion of theories useful for bringing all of these ideas together.

Sport Case Study

Bird-Watching as Endurance Sport

Jokes are often made that Bird watching is an activity for retirees, but the hobby or pursuit of watching birds has been turned into a competitive sport.

Welcome to the World Series of Birding (http://worldseriesofbirding.org/), a wild, 24-hour competition that is part scientific expedition and part grueling endurance event. The aim: to count as many species as one can in a 24-hour period.

And yes, there are birding superstars, birding groupies and a birding hall of fame.

About 85 million Americans enjoy observing, photographing or feeding wild birds. Birding ranks 15th on a list of the most popular outdoor activities, just below bicycling, according to a recent National Survey on Recreation and the Environment by the USDA's Forest Service (NSRE 2000–2002). About 18 million are serious enough to take trips exclusively to commune with other birders or count birds by sight or sound, according to the U.S. Fish and Wildlife Service's 2011 National Survey of Fishing, Hunting and Wildlife-Associated Recreation (US Department of the Interior, et al. 2011).

The first official World Series of Birding began at midnight on May 19, 1984, when 13 teams set out on a 24-hour treasure hunt. Their mission was to tally as many species of birds by sight or sound as possible. Their objective was to raise money for their favorite environmental cause, and to focus worldwide attention upon the habitat needs of migrating birds.

Why a World Series of Birding?

According to website of the World Series of Birding national organization, because: "it's a game, it's a marathon, it's a challenge, it's a heck of a lot of fun!" And because it: allows people to engage in such "citizen science" projects as sending bird counts to scientists and conservationists; draws attention to the habitat needs of migrating birds; gives birders a chance to put their birding skills to use for a good cause; brings together birders of all levels of experience, local conservation groups, schools and youth groups, and businesses that care about the environment, generates of lot of money for conservation causes, and focuses global media attention upon the challenge, adventure, and fun of birding.

Michael G. McKinne/Shutterstock.com

For more info please read:

https://www.usatoday.com/story/news/nation/2014/01/02/birding-sport-big-year-citizen-science/4261529/

And view: e-bird—A real-time, online checklist program where community members to report and accesses information about on bird abundance and distribution.

Reference

National Survey on Recreation and the Environment (NSRE): 2000–2002. The Interagency National Survey Consortium, Coordinated by the USDA Forest Service, Recreation, Wilderness, and Demographics Trends Research Group, Athens, GA and the Human Dimensions Research Laboratory, University of Tennessee, Knoxville, TN.

U.S. Department of the Interior, U.S. Fish and Wildlife Service, and U.S. Department of Commerce, U.S. Census Bureau. 2011 National Survey of Fishing, Hunting, and Wildlife-Associated Recreation.

Self and Identity

What is an identity? What is meant by the term self? Stryker (2002[1980]) discussed how questions of the self, identity, and how we—as people—situate ourselves into society's structural arrangement have been topics or questions for many, many years. For this chapter, we draw upon Gecas and Burke's (1995) definitions of these two foundational, social-psychological concepts. Regarding a definition of the self, Gecas and Burke (1995: 42) note:

> While the core of the self is the process of reflexivity, the concept of self is often used generically to encompass all the products or consequences of this reflexive activity. It would be more accurate to refer to the latter as the "self concept" or the phenomenal self. . . . The self-concept can be through of as the sum total of the individual's thoughts and feeling about him/herself as an object. . . . It involves a sense of spatial and temporal continuity of the person. . . . and a distinction of essential self from mere appearance and behavior. . . . It is composed of various identities, attitudes, beliefs, values, motives, and experiences, along with their evaluative and affective components (e.g. self-efficacy, self-esteem) in terms of which individuals define themselves.

For our purposes—and to keep all of the social scientific language as parsimonious as possible—this book will adopt the aforementioned definition of self-concept but use the word self to describe these attributes, activities, and resultant meanings. The self, as a result, is a view of how we as individuals see ourselves within society. This is an important idea, because the self, at its core, is individualistic, but also an arrangement within society and associated with social factors. Gecas and Burke

(1995: 42) continue to differentiate the self from what is meant by an identity: "Identity refers to who or what one is, to the various meanings attached to oneself and others." Identity, then, brings the concept of "self" further into the social word by illustrating how we define ourselves; how others define us; and how social factors can really impact how we see, feel about, or express ourselves as people. At this point, you can start to see how, for example, a professional athlete—whom has been seen and related to as a great athlete, as compared to as a student, a worker in a business, or a civic minded person in a community—might have some trouble adjusting to life in a post-sports (participation) career. What happens when how you define yourself for most of your life, e.g., as an athlete, ends suddenly? What do you do next? To further answer this, and many other questions, we need to have a basic understanding of how identities form.

Identity Formation: Theories and Processes

Symbolic interactionism (SI) is an important generalized theoretical framework for examining issues of not only the self and identity, but also how society's interaction with individuals (through the use of symbols, culture, norms/values, etc.) is a complex social process. Stryker (2002[1980]: 1) reviewed the history of symbolic interactionism asserting: "Symbolic interactionism has been regarded both as a general framework for the analysis of society, and as a relatively specialized social psychological theory addressed primarily to problems of socialization." Woods (2014), when reviewing SI, identified the usefulness of the theory for not only looking at micro-level social issues, but also how sport participation impacts people and their experiences. Relatedly, Cunningham (2007) noted the primary area of concern for SI was examining how people give meanings to their lives. One of the advantages of SI is that it can be summarized in three major points:

1. We interact with things in our (social) environment based upon the (shared or agreed upon) meanings we have of the people, expectations, and social dynamics present.
2. Meanings are not inherent and are based upon social interaction with others.
3. Meanings are always changing.

SI has become increasingly more important in not only understanding sport experiences, but also is being used more recently and applied within sport settings. It is an easy-to-use theory and becomes an important starting point for understanding athletes and how most people know them exclusively as athletes. For example, Vermillion (2010) examined how community college softball players' view of their dual roles (e.g., students and athletes) influenced their decisions to not only attend their community college to play softball, but also where they would transfer after their 2 years of competing and attending classes was done. The community college softball players were primarily known, especially on their community college campuses, as athletes. But, many of them noted that academics and student support resources were very important to them both in their decision to not only attend their current school, but also if/when they transferred to a 4-year institution. In this example, SI was a productive theoretical view for providing a basic explanation of how these softball players viewed themselves and additional societal expectations. SI is, as Stryker noted, a good starting point for examining the issues in this chapter because it is a general theory that can be combined or integrated well with other theories or concepts.

In keeping with our definitions of both the self and identity, Stryker (2002[1980]) reaffirmed how identities are embedded in the social fabric of our interactions and daily life. His view that identities ". . . are "parts" of self, internalized positional designations." (Stryker 2002[1980]: 60) illustrates how the previously mentioned socialization processes influence individuals by integrating them into their cultural and social surroundings. McCall and Simmons (1966) helped to blend the individualistic and psychologically specific aspects of who we are as people with their role-identity concept. Gecas and Burke (1995: 45) discussed McCall and Simmon's (1966) work noting a role-identity as the following:

> [T]he character and the role an individual devises as an occupant of a particular social position, thereby linking social structures to persons. In this way the multifaceted nature of the self (each facet being an identity) is tied to the multifaceted nature of society.

Essentially, the roles we play throughout the day are parts of who we are as people. This is important for understanding sports, in general, and athletes, coaches, or sport organizational personnel in particular. Extending McCall and Simmons (1966), Stryker (2002[1980]) built upon this line of thinking and developed identity theory, which illustrates how the person's self is simply a group of identities that are differentiated based upon both the salience (e.g., having an identity become dominant or activated in a social situation) and commitment (e.g., strength of interaction and relationships this identity has to other people in social situations). Essentially, Stryker is saying that the more committed a person is to an identity (such as being an athlete) then the more likely that identity becomes important to them over time.

Stryker (2002[1980]) also noted how each identity has a specific set of behavioral consequences associated with it. For example, Ericcson, Krampe, and Tesch-Römer (1993) stated that it takes about 10,000 hours of committed practice to a specific task to begin the process of mastering the task. If we apply that idea to sports, then we can see that athletes spend an inordinate amount of time on a particular activity. The activity, then, becomes a part of who they are and the more they practice this activity, then the more they display both commitment and saliency, as Stryker (2002[1980]) discussed. For example, Nagata (2014) examined how important and exclusive the athletic identity of wheelchair rugby players was and identified the intersection of athletic identity, self-esteem, and athletes' rugby involvement. Additionally, whether the athletes' disability was congenital (e.g., born with the disability) or acquired (e.g., something happened and the person became disabled later in life) is important to understanding identity. Many individuals that became disabled later in life suffer psychologically (Kennedy and Rogers 2000) and may experience lower self-esteem (Craig, Hancock, and Chang 1994) as they begin coping with their new life. Nagata (2014: 328) touched upon the interplay between sports, identity, and—potentially—coping with such impactful life experiences:

> [F]inding a sport that provides a sense of value and accomplishment is especially important and they gain resilience and an attitude of 'Don't tell us we can't.' The observed inverse relationship suggests that, as self-esteem is improved, their exclusivity decreases. . . . In the early stages, it appears that athletic identity supplemented the low self-esteem. The level of exclusivity early on suggests a high reliance on sport as a source of self-esteem.

A person's "self" is made up of many identities that are negotiated throughout the day based upon our social environments. Within sports, the social environments have expectations and athletes learn—through socialization processes—not only their sport, but also how important their sport is to defining them as a person. Society, then seeing how important the athlete sees the sport to them, reacts to that person exclusively as an athlete. Thus, reinforcing the original identity of being an athlete. Now that we have waded through the waters of differentiating between the self, identity, and theories for understanding how we as individuals and social factors give meaning to our lives (e.g., symbolic interactionism), we can address specific sociological concepts useful for helping administrators, practitioners, and educators understand how athletes maintain their predominantly athletic identities.

Reactions to the End of an Athletic Career

The loss of an athletic identity is particularly problematic if it's the result of a career ending injury—And re-defining oneself (establishing a new identity) afterwards can be prove problematic. Consider the following example **tale from a former student-athlete:**

Dr. HB is an Assistant Professor in the Human Performance Studies Department at Wichita State University where she specializes in interdisciplinary research involving both clinical exercise physiology and orofacial performance. Her work involves working with medical, health, and fitness entities and networks within her local community. While growing up in a small rural community, HB was actively involved in basketball and track from an early age. Her passion and performance for physical activity and high-school varsity sport played a major role in her competing as an intercollegiate student-athlete.

Beginning her freshman year of college while battling for a rebound during a basketball game, her life as an intercollegiate student-athlete would forever begin to change. It was the perfect play. HB won the battle at the rim and returned to the wood with basketball in hand as she remained in a tucked defensive stance. The other nine players began repositioning on the court and the clock continued to count down;

however, something was very wrong. HB remained motionless, completely motionless. Her body, more specifically her back, would not allow her to move. In that split second, several vertebral discs in her lumbar spine shifted and were now impinging on her spinal cord and nerves. Over the course of the next few months her faithful commitment to physical therapy began to silence the fear of what if and her sheer determination dampened the emotional scares of doubt. She had dealt with a minor setback involving a temperamental knee in high school and knew what it would take to get back into the game. Just like in high school, she wasn't going to coward, quit or be benched. Instead she was going to push harder and overcome any obstacle thrown at her and before long HB was back finishing her freshman season on the court.

The following year HB had transitioned into a new university setting and was excited to begin her new journey. Track and Field preseason training was in full force and she was looking strong. Unfortunately, the injury she had sustained to her back the prior year during basketball season was still her weak link. While performing a loaded exercise known as "good mornings" she began to relive that frightful moment from one year earlier. The immobilizing pain radiated up her spine and down her legs as she felt her hips shift. The right hip angled forward and down while the left hip repositioned backward and high. The overwhelming emotions of why, the fear of what if, the concern of being a financial burden, and a sense of being a failure as an intercollegiate athlete were once again all consuming. Then came the hard work and sheer determination to overcome and prevail again, as a TRUE athlete should. Months of physical therapy, as indicated by the isokinetic system, were finally producing desired results and the news HB had so diligently been working toward had arrived. Only one more full week of physical therapy and then she would be cleared to engage in intercollegiate sport once again.

Forward 72 hours later. A visible sense of excitement was noticeable as HB attended her first morning class of the week. The anticipation of lacing up her shoes and engaging in sport by week's end was uncontainable. Then . . . those emotions were abruptly interrupted. An EXPOLSIVE pressure followed by intense pain and excessive heat began to radiate throughout HB's spine. It was a sensation beyond any prior recollection and for the next six days, HB would lay in a hospital bed with temporary paralysis. Those same four discs that had caused her so many setbacks and moments of disappointment in prior years would now inflict change upon every aspect of her future in ways she had never considered preparing for. Over the course of the next 12 years, HB would undergo a total of four spinal surgeries and ultimately say farewell to intercollegiate sports. The silver lining amongst this horrific endeavor was that her spinal cord was only compressed and not severed when those four discs failed. The fact that she was sitting and not engaged in activity further minimized the trauma. In the first year following this life-altering event HB felt it best to preserve her days of glory, overcome her disappointment, dampen the embarrassment and shame she carried in succumbing to injury and furthermore, silence the unknown by transferring to another university.

HB began the next chapter of her journey as a Student and no longer as an Intercollegiate Student-Athlete. Her deep passion of sports, however, was never suppressed. Today you will see HB enjoying a leisure run or casually shooting around on the court.

She has even welcomed new activities in to her life such as hiking14ers in Colorado; however, she has never engaged in another organized game of basketball since that horrific morning. When further probed as to why organized basketball was now absent from her routine, it quickly became apparent that an element of fear and the sense of "what if" continue to linger within her subconscious. HB appears to be okay with that and knows it's a part of her story but refuses to allow it to define her. She embraces each day with a sense of gratefulness. She strives to learn from each new moment in life. She shares what she has experienced in hopes of helping others. HB attributes her strong character and ability to overcome such physical, mental, and emotional hurdles in large to her powerful support system found in her family.

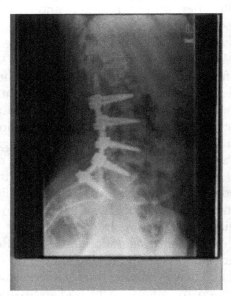 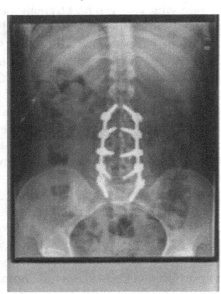

Courtesy Mark Vermillion.
X-Ray of HB's Spine

In conclusion, I'll leave you with this . . . in HB's office hang two images of her reconstructed spine. These images display extensive amounts of hardware (ten screws, four cages, two Herrington rods, and masses of bone grafting to stimulate bone fusion) that typically impose immediate impressions of grimace upon those who view it. What may be more inspiring though is the quote HB has hanging between these two images.

"I can be changed by what happens to me. I refuse to be reduced by it" by Maya Angelou.

Questions

What about you? Have you "retired" or transitioned from an athletic identity? What it a positive or negative transition? What do you think about needing to craft multiple identities throughout life?

Documentary Recommendation

Brian and The Boz (2014)

In *The Presentation of Self in Everyday Life* (1959) Erving Goffman uses theater references (known as dramaturgy or dramaturgical analyses), as a metaphor to describe and examine social interactions. Goffman speaks of life as being made up of actors, props, scripts, stages (both front and back stage), and performances as concepts to explain how people make or craft desired impressions of themselves in front of other people. Please note that "front stage" and "back stage" are concepts within sociology that refer to different modes of behavior that we engage in every day. The front stage is what we want others (the audience) the see. The back stage are aspects of our behavior (or modes of thinking) what we try to keep hidden from the audience. Known as impression management, Goffman (1959) hypothesized that we create roles and give performances to manage the impressions that other people have of us.. At its core, Goffman argues that one's belief in the role they are playing becomes their core identity- even if they are merely "acting."

Athletes oftentimes speak of adopting separate personas when getting ready for competitions or interactions with the public. And, the story of *Brian and the Boz* epitomizes both Goffman's views on impression management and sports figures' personas and self-marketing. In this ESPN 30 for 30 documentary, filmmakers tell the story of Brian Bosworth and his time both at the University of Oklahoma and (briefly) within in the NFL. In this documentary, filmmakers discuss not only the events that made Brian's career memorable, but also the persona he developed, known as the Boz, and how that persona began to impact the rest of his life.

John Leyba/Contributor/Getty Images

Ronald Martinez/Staff/Getty Images

The documentary follows Brian as he explains his football life—on and off the field—to his son, and attempts to come to terms with how he crafted/managed people's impressions of him back in the 1980s when he played football and then off the field when he was forced to retire due to injury. As an athlete, the Boz was a "larger than life" figure who gained fame and notoriety through his flamboyant personality. However, once his playing days ended, and he grew into middle-age, the public persona of the "Boz" became untenable and unrealistic, and "Brian" seemed lost in the word. In the end, the film asks: "Who was the Boz?" "Who is Brian?" "Which is the "real" person?

Interestingly, in 2014 and in 2016, Brian (or is it the Boz?) appeared in several commercials playfully pining for his glory days and wishing he could return to his youth in order to play football.

BECOMING AN ATHLETE. HOW ATHLETIC IDENTITY FORMS AND IS MAINTAINED

Oftentimes there is some confusion regarding the influence of sociology or psychology, especially when talking about issues of the self, identity, or internalization processes. Both disciplines offer useful theories and concepts. When we discuss identity development, though, we draw primarily from a sociologically inspired version of social psychology. While there are merits to both approaches, we feel the sociologically inspired view of social psychology allows us to explicitly connect how athletes develop a view of themselves and the powerful role society, culture, community, peer groups or family plays in this process. Sport is an institutional arrangement that has large and small scale impacts, and a sociological view allows for an explicit discussion of socialization processes, roles, statuses, and their importance in forming identities within a larger social environment.

Coakley (2015) stated that **socialization**—as a process—is based on a model of social learning, where individuals learn and develop within their cultures (or respective groups and communities) through social interaction; we develop by actively participating in social activities. For example, sport participation—as commonly viewed in American culture—aids in developing character. Or, as Nixon (2008: 168) discussed, youth sport athletes are socialized into certain sport roles that impact their time away from sport:

> Children and adolescents who participate in highly organized and competitive sports programs may have the common experience of being treated as 'little adults.' Much is expected of them as their parents and other adults invest a lot of time and money in their success. As a result, these youth sports stars find that they have little time to enjoy being children or adolescents, as they spend much of their lives in serious training or competition. The rewards and stresses of competing in youth or high school sports programs in the golden triangle thrust these young people into the limelight, where winning and losing are much more consequential for them than they are for others in their age group who play sports less intensely or who do not play sports at all.

As previously mentioned, sport is an institution that provides social structure for our daily lives. There are many characteristics of an institution that help examine identities of athletes. Social structure and how we learn it are parts of the cultural factors important for individual and social development. For example, sociologists, psychologists, and anthropologists have identified and defined the relatively simple, yet extremely powerful, concepts of roles and statuses for many decades. Within sport, these concepts help to better understand how culture sets expectations for athletes in terms of how to view both their identities and selves. Sage and Eitzen (2013: 8) noted quite succinctly: "Statuses and roles are social positions (statuses) and behavioral expectations (roles) for individuals." Or, as Linton (1936) stated, status is a person's position within a particular social system and the social honor associated with that position. When you think of the high-profile nature of a star, all-state quarterback on a high-school football team, you are examining that person's status in the high-school culture or surrounding community. On a related note, the role is a behavioral expectation associated with that position (e.g., status) in a social system. The person occupying the high-status position of the star, all-state quarterback may be expected to behave in certain ways—both in the classroom and outside of it.

Think of the classic movie, *Dazed and Confused*, when the one of the lead characters and quarterback of the football team dealt with status and role expectations. Randall "Pink" Floyd was the star of the football team and going into his senior year there were expectations from his coaches, teammates, and surrounding (Austin) Texas community. Pink was struggling with his decision to not only play football next year, but also whether to sign his coach's mandated pledge, which required him to abstain from certain elicit behaviors and stay away from "the wrong crowd," which would distract his focus from achieving a championship and being a good teammate. His status as the team's leader (and quarterback) also provided the expected roles and ways he would behave. The movie chronicles not only adolescent life in the late 1970s, but also the struggles between statuses, roles, expectations, and identities among some of these students and student-athletes.

A basic question associated with **statuses and roles**, then, is how does one acquire these in a social system or environment? How do you acquire status in sport? If a status is thought of as a position in a system or a form of social honor, then it can be either ascribed or achieved. Ascribed statuses are given to or placed upon persons or groups by culture or larger society. These are often associated with characteristics, such as sex/gender, age, race, ethnicity, socioeconomic status or family (background). Often times, depending on the culture, we are born into particular situations defined as more favorable or less favorable. This could include being born into a wealthy family that owns a professional sport franchise. As the individual grows up, they are associated with the prestige of being, potentially someday, a team owner. Or, perhaps, think of a young girl wanting to be an athlete when we know girls and women's sports are often less consumed by the general public in the United States.

Conversely, an achieved status is a position or social honor given to someone because they have earned it in some way, shape, or form. For many star athletes, they earn their status through their athletic accolades and exploits. Over time, their status goes from all-state to all-American to, perhaps, world champ or Olympic Gold medalist. These exploits are all, however, indicative of achieved statuses. It should be noted, though, that not all achieved statuses are positive. Being known as a cheater (e.g., Performance Enhancing Drugs and/or Substances) or someone that gets into trouble away from their sport, such as being academically ineligible or being arrested for various law violations, are also achieved statuses.

Another form of status that is important for our discussion is the master status. Master status is the dominant status a person is known for during interactions with other people or groups. Think of Michael Jordan. He is a successful business man, owner and chairman of the Charlotte Hornets NBA franchise, and billionaire associate of the Jordan brand with Nike. He also plays many roles including as a father, husband, community member, and philanthropist. However, to most people he is known as the basketball player. His master status (e.g., basketball player) dominates interactions with him and influence how many people see Michael Jordan, even today.

In addition to status, we spoke of roles, or behavioral expectations associated with certain statuses. A role set is the collection of roles that people fulfill or execute throughout the day. A student-athlete, by its name alone, involves the individual participating in social life as a student, an athlete, a representative of the school, a community member, or a member of other organizations or social groups. Adler and Adler (1991) penned a seminal work regarding roles and intercollegiate athletics, Backboards and Blackboards. The book follows a top-twenty NCAA men's, college basketball team and notes the myriad of roles, expectations, and other social dynamics associated with being a high-profile student-athlete in a popular sport. Throughout the course of their season, these (men's) basketball players would have to identify, adapt, and prioritize their role expectations, and their athletic, social, and academic roles. Ultimately, the concept of **role engulfment**, when a person's identity is based primarily on one role that becomes dominant over all others, is the theory used for examining and understanding both the struggles and the lives of these basketball players.

When you think about the popularity and excitement associated with, for example, men's NCAA (Division I) basketball, you can see how the expectations of these student-athletes lead to not only role engulfment, but also how their master status is set and comes to influence all other subsequent interactions with people on campus, in the community, and—for some people—around the country. Whether it is from peer groups, social media sites/posts, college boosters, sports fans, sports media members, or other forms of public scrutiny and adulation, reinforcement of these statuses and roles help to influence the individual's view of both their identities and, ultimately, selves.

IDENTITY, ROLE CONFLICTS, AND STUDENT-ATHLETES

Roles, statuses, and identities are important conceptual tools for examining retirement or disengagement problems for athletes from all levels. As previously discussed, roles often come into conflict and require the individual to let one role became the dominant (e.g., role engulfment) way people know an athlete (e.g., master status). For those in interscholastic or intercollegiate athletics, role conflict is often times heightened due to the additional role expectations, such as social roles, athletic roles, and academic roles.

For example, in 2008 and 2009 increased attention was paid to Myron Rolle, a standout defensive back on the Florida State University's football team. While completing his undergraduate degree in about five semesters, Myron also qualified as a Rhodes Scholar and had the opportunity to study at Oxford University for a year or enter the NFL draft. As Gordon (2016: paragraph 15) noted, "acceptance of the Rhodes scholarship, however, would mean he would skip his final year of college football and delay the start of his NFL career. When he was named a Rhodes Scholar for the 2009–10 academic year, Rolle had a decision to make."

What did he do? He temporarily said no to the N.F.L. draft, and become one of the most prominent athletes to accept a Rhodes scholarship. Despite the fact that a number of coaches said he abandoned his teammates by focusing on his education (*talk about role conflict!*), Rhodes eventually made it into the draft, played several seasons in the NFL, and eventually left to attend medical school and became a neurosurgeon (Maese 2017).

Erikson (1968) described the importance of identity development for adolescents and young adults. One of the things he identified was the crisis, or conflicts, sometimes occurring between differing identities. Reitzes and Burke (1980) examined the important time in an adolescent's life of college. They discovered that the college student identity, while decently impactful, was not the only dominant identity with only about one-third of their sample seeing that identity as extremely important and influential. What other identities, then, could be so impactful during this time in early adulthood? For us, we are examining sport and athletics. The athletic identity of student-athletes is one potential identity that could conflict, contradict, or exemplify the "crisis" Erikson and others theorized about regarding young people.

The **athlete identity** is a fairly recent concept. Brewer, Van Raalte, and Linder (1993: 237) defined the concept as the "degree to which an individual identifies with the athlete role." This recent research from sport psychology had examined and identified a separate athlete identity from non-athlete identities, thus making the concept important to a discussion centering on identity development and transition into and out of sport. Some research indicates athlete identity and sport participation have a negative impact upon student identity (e.g., Adler and Adler 1991), while the contrasting view is that sport participation does not hinder perceptions and opportunities for higher education (e.g., Potuto and O'Hanlon 2006).

Sturm, Feltz, and Gilson (2011) examined differences between Division I (i.e., athletic scholarships or grants-in-aid) and Division III (i.e., non-athletic scholarships or grants-in-aid) student-athletes regarding differences in student and athlete identities. Their research noted gender was the only significant factor regarding student and athlete identity; females, regardless of Division I or Division III status, had a higher student identity and lower athlete identity. Noting the unique experience of domestic, male athletes in traditional revenue generating sports, such as football and men's basketball, Harrison, Tranyowicz, Bukstein, McPherson-Botts, and Lawrence (2014) surveyed Division I football players using the "Baller Identity Measurement Scale." Their research reported that these Division I football players saw themselves as having high Baller identities and noted others probably viewed them in this way, regardless of the race of the respondent.

The aforementioned research conclusions and theoretical concepts bring together a larger discussion about not only the power of athlete identities, but also the influence larger society—those influences outside of the individual—has upon the salience of a particular identity. Women's sports are not as highly consumed here in the United States and one could surmise this structural reality impacts individual identity development. Various roles and statuses ascribed or achieved by individuals manifest themselves in how individuals "see" themselves. What happens, though, when the role you have played and the status you have been given for so long abruptly changes or ends?

TRANSITION AND IDENTITY: RETIREMENT ISN'T JUST FOR PROFESSIONALS

Transitioning from one important part of your life to the next is often a difficult thing, regardless of age or the sport played. We can think of many professional athletes that retire long after their athletic prime. Or, consider the story of professional boxer Sugar Ray Leonard. After a meteoric rise through the amateur ranks, which included an Olympic gold medal, Sugar Ray Leonard won his first 35 professional fights. As age and the toll taken on his body wore on, Sugar Ray Leonard would "retire" five to six times and eventually ended his career 36-3-1, according to Larry Schwartz (ND) whom was writing for ESPN. As a professional boxer, Sugar Ray won more than $100 million in prize purses. But, what kept him coming back for more? What kept him calling him to step into the ring for one more fight?

Vickers (2013) discussed how elite athletes often suffer from emotional and behavioral problems when trying to disengage from their sport. In fact, Vickers (2013) discussed Sugar Ray Leonard quoting him as saying, "Nothing could satisfy me outside the ring . . . there is nothing in life that can compare to becoming a world champion, having your hand raised in that moment of glory, with thousands, millions of people cheering you on." She went on to note, "Leonard's struggles with retirement were well documented, leading him to suffer from extreme bouts of depression and eventually making repeated comebacks." (Vickers 2013: paragraph 6).

Leonard and Schimmel (2016:63) provided an important and succinct commentary regarding the distinction of retirement, work transition, and when it occurs in a person's life:

> Transitions are universal events that occur in any stage of life. They are complex processes that are made up of a variety of factors, including psychosocial and situational factors . . . Transitions out of a chosen field, or retirement, occur at any age, not just in latter stages of life. It is considered a point of transition from an activity in which there has been a commitment of time and energy and role identification.

We often see retirement as the final step in a professional career. But, as indicated earlier, retirement—for our purposes—is part of the identity transition process involving a person's life and how they see themselves. The often cited or quoted statistic of less than 2 percent of NCAA FBS football players become professional NFL football players is a great example of how "retirement" is conceived within this chapter. Those players no longer playing NCAA football and not playing in the NFL do not have an official retirement ceremony, but they are confronted with the same type of transition and identity issues as those retiring from a long professional sporting career.

As previously discussed, role exclusivity and engulfment (Adler and Adler 1991) is the result of athletes (or any identity, for that matter) having a few of themselves as athletes first and only. This view is often supported or enabled by fans, members or a college or university campus, and media members. Stryker (1980) posited that a dominant role identity, such as being an athlete first and foremost in our case with this chapter, can have negative impacts on overall self-concept later on in life. This hypothesis seems to be borne out in athlete transition/retirement research, which indicates loss of identity can lead to not only emotional and behavioral problems, but also depression, anxiety and distressful reactions to new life situations (Vickers 2013). Symes (2010) summarized research indicating that a total disengagement from their sport is not necessarily a healthy reaction or coping mechanism when transitioning away from an all-inclusive sport career, regardless of whether it was a professional career or not.

Coping skills or mechanisms are simply ways people react to stressful or anxious life situations. Not all coping mechanisms, however, are positive ones. And, we cans seem many anecdotal examples of athletes having difficulty in their post-playing careers. Many former athletes suffer from not only emotional issues, such as depression, lethargy and anxiety, but also turn to negative coping mechanisms, such as the (ab)use of alcohol, drugs, or other forms of risk-taking behaviors, such as problematic gambling. Grove, Lavalee, and Gordon (1997) noted not only the social and emotional adjustments these athletes must endure, but also—in some professional athlete or elite amateur athlete situations—the financial and occupational adjustments that impact many relationships, including friends, coaches, peers, and family members.

While it may be difficult to do, Symes (2010) outlines some basic recommendations regarding how sport, educational, or athletic administrators can help with the oftentimes-difficult transition process. Specifically, she noted:

> 'Who am I?' most athletes know themselves pretty well on the pitch. . . . but what about when they are out of that environment? It is absolutely vital that we . . . encourage our athletes to consider who they are as a person as well as an athlete. Gaining a clear understanding of who they are 'off the pitch' will enable them to widen their sense of self, gain clarity over their other strengths and protect them from longer term psychological difficulties (Paragraph 9).

Other recommendations from Symes (2010), include holistic approaches emphasizing not only the further development of the person, but also a slow disengagement from their sport. Athletes, according to this view, have a "switch" in their athletic identity when they can slide into another part of themselves, namely the athlete and all the personalities and behaviors that entails. Athletes that are able to "switch on" and "get into the zone" have a better understanding of how to leave that persona behind first temporarily and then, over time, permanently (Symes 2010).

Book Recommendation

What Made Maddy Run: The Secret Struggles and Tragic Death of an All-American Teen.

In *What made Maddy Run*, the author Kate Fagan, details the life and death—by suicide—of 19-year-old runner Madison Holleran. The book is a powerful examination of role conflict, role engulfment, and the unique pressures that student-athletes face. Ultimately, Fagan argues that the depression and anxiety that often befalls student-athletes is a significant public health issue and she presents questions that force us to find possible ways to prevent similar tragedies.

In particular, she asks if athletes, teachers, and even coaches should encourage an athlete to quit a team or sporting activity if they seem unmistakably miserable.

Questions

*What do you think about this—Is "quitting" a dirty word in sport? When is the commitment to sport a detriment to one's own happiness?

*How do we create conservation about mental health and what strategies do you suggest to improve the mental health of student-athletes?

Reference

Fagan, Kate. 2017. *What Made Maddy Run: The Secret Struggles and Tragic Death of an All-American Teen*. Boston, MA: Little, Brown, and Company.

CHAPTER SUMMARY

The purpose of this chapter was to examine the processes and dynamics associated with retirement. In the course of the discussion, we posited that identity transition was a more encompassing way of talking and thinking about the issue at hand. To this end, we needed to develop a vocabulary that was specific enough to address the psychological and social aspects of the phenomenon. We started off by defining and delineating what is an identity and how that definition is associated with concepts of the "self" and roles. In order to discuss how identity forms within the socialization process, we review and apply Symbolic Interactionism to our chapter's topic.

Next, we moved to the larger and more social discussion of identity formation. Specifically, we highlighted the communities' or society's role in developing the multiple statuses (e.g., ascribed, achieved, and master statuses), roles and expectations that, ultimately, help to influence the individual's identity and how they see themselves. These many roles and expectations due, at times, come into conflict, which places individuals in unenviable positions of having to balance, maximize, prioritize, and manage social expectations.

Finally, we attempted to provide context to this wide-ranging issue and how the impacts are not simply upon individual athletes. Identity transition is a process that must be identified and supported by social entities if it is to have a measurable impact upon individuals across time, space, and place. We covered a lot of theoretical and scholarly ground; we discussed social theories that can be useful for delineating not only how to examine the problem, but also how these theories, concepts, and ideas can be used by practitioners and administrators to—potentially—address identity transition issues among a wide range of athletes, which includes former professional, collegiate, scholastic, or other competitive athletes. The practitioner or sport sociologist that understands how roles, identities, and statuses impact the thoughts and behaviors of not only athletes, but also spectators, coaches, or athletic administrators is the person best prepared to make impactful and holistic contributions to the lives of those involved in sports.

Discussion Questions

*There have been recent media campaigns attempting to broaden what it means to be an "athlete" in modern American life, which is in response to competitive fitness trends. Would you consider yourself an athlete? Why or why not?

*In your opinion, how important is a strong athlete identity for student-athletes wanting to compete and be successful in intercollegiate athletics?

Are there any differences between intercollegiate and professional athletes regarding the importance of a strong athlete identity?

*What obligations do athletic departments have to help develop student and other identities for student-athletes? What obligations to professional franchises or leagues have to develop or support other non-athlete identities within their athletes/employees?

Extra-Inning: Sport Case Study—Elder Bodybuilding

EVAN HURD PHOTOGRAPHY/Contributor/Getty Images
Senior bodybuilders pose before competition in Miami, Florida.

A small but growing number of 60- and 70-year-old bodybuilders have begun stripping down to Speedos, slathering on bronzer, and strutting their stuff onstage in amateur and pro-level competitions. Unlike weight lifting, which depends on brawn, bodybuilders train to look good in swimsuits that leave little to the imagination. They must perfect 8 to 10 poses and are judged on criteria such as grace, muscle symmetry, definition, and body shape. A choreographed routine to music is also required.

Why?

Some are retirees who were simply bored, others needed to increase bone density; still others refused to let the aging process zap their strength. Take Ernestine Shepherd who is best known for being, in her time, the oldest competitive female bodybuilder in the world, as declared by the Guinness Book of World Records in 2016 and 2017.

The Washington Post/Contributor/Getty Images

At 56, Shepher's sister asked her to join a gym. Sadly, her sister had an aneurysm and died shortly thereafter, but Shepherd followed through on her a dream. At 71, she competed in her first bodybuilding event and earned her Guinness title. She states, "Exercise keeps me happy and alive . . . I tell everybody that age is nothing but a number. And if there ever was an anti-aging pill, it would have to be exercise" (Mazziotta 2016: paragraphs 3, 9).

Questions

*How does this change your view of the health, physical activity, and the aging process?

*What about notions of beauty and the body—what are some of the positive and negative consequences regarding the pursuit of bodily perfection, even at an advanced age?

*How would you react to seeing your grandmother or grandfather in a bikini, competing in a body fitness challenge?

Reference

Mazziotta, Julie. 2016. "Oldest Female Bodybuilder Turns 80, Still Wakes Up at 2:30 a.m. to Train: 'It's My Joy.'" *People*, Jule 27. Retrieved July 4, 2017 (http://people.com/bodies/oldest-female-bodybuilder-celebrates-her-80th-birthday/).

CHAPTER REFERENCES

Adler, Patricia A. and Peter Adler. 1991. *Backboards and Blackboards: College Athletics and Role Engulfment.* New York: Columbia University Press.

Brewer, Britton W., Judy Van Raalte, and Darwyn Linder. 1993. "Athletic Identity: Hercules' Muscles or Achilles' Heel?" *International Journal of Sport Psychology.* 24:237–254.

Chadiha, Jeffri. 2012. "Life After NFL a Challenge for Many." *ESPN,* May 31. Retrieved July 4, 2017 (http://www.espn.com/nfl/story/_/id/7983790/life-nfl-struggle-many-former-players).

Coakley, Jay. 2015. *Sports in Society: Issues and Controversies* 11th ed. Boston, MA: McGaw.

Craig, Ashley, Karen Hancock, and E. Chang. 1994. "The Influence of Spinal Cord Injury on Coping Styles and Self-perceptions Two Years after the Injury." *Australian and New Zealand Journal of Psychiatry.* 28:307–312.

Cunningham, George B. 2007. "Diversity in Sport Organizations." Scottsdale, AZ: Holcomb Hathaway Publishers.

Ericsson, K. Anders, Ralf Th. Krampe, and Clemens Tesch-Römer. 1993. "The Role of Deliberate Practice in the Acquisition of Expert Performance." *Psychological Review.* 100 (3): 363–406.

Erikson, Erik H. 1968. *Identity: Youth and Crisis.* New York: W.W. Norton and Company Inc.

Gecas, Viktor and Peter J. Burke. 1993. "Self and Identity" Pp. 41–67 in *Sociological Perspectives on Social Psychology,* edited by Karen S. Cook, Gary Alan Fine, and James S. House. Boston, MA: Allyn and Bacon.

Gordon, Aaron. 2016. "The rejection of Myron Rolle." *SB Nation,* February 12. Retrieved November 17, 2017 (https://www.sbnation.com/longform/2014/2/12/5401774/myron-rolle-profile-florida-state-football-nfl-rhodes-scholar).

Grove, J. Robert, David Lavallee, and Sandy, Gordon. 1997. "Coping with Retirement from Sport: The Influence of Athletic Identity." *Journal of Applied Sport Psychology,* 9:191–203.

Harrison, C. Keith, Suzanne Malia Lawrence, Scott Bukstein, Neza K. Janson, and Keshia Woodie. 2010. "Myron Rolle's ESPN Page 2 Story: A Qualitative Approach to Blog Comments." *Journal for the Study of Sports and Athletes in Education.* 4 (3):231–241.

Harrison, C. Keith, Laurel Tranyowicz, Scott Bukstein, Ginny McPherson-Botts, and Suzanne Malia Lawrence. 2014. "I am what I am? The Baller Identity Measurement Scale (BIMS) with a Division I Football Team in American Higher Education." *Sport Sciences for Health.* 10:53–58.

Kennedy, Paul and Ben A. Rogers. 2000. "Anxiety and Depression after Spinal Cord Injury: A Longitudinal Analysis." *Archives of Physical Medicine and Rehabilitation.* 81(7):932–937.

Lally, Patricia S. and Gretchen A. Kerr. 2005. "The Career Planning, Athletic Identity and Student Role Identity of Intercollegiate Student Athletes." *Research Quarterly for Exercise and Sport.* 76:275–285.

Leonard, Jessica M., and Christine J. Schimmel. 2016. "Theory of Work Adjustment and Student-Athletes' Transition out of Sport." *Journal of Issues in Intercollegiate Athletics.* 9:62–85.

Linton, Ralph. 1936. *The Study of Man: An Introduction.* New York: Appleton-Century-Crofts, Inc.

Maese, Rick. 2017. "This Rhodes Scholar made the NFL. He's about to achieve his other dream: neurosurgeon." *The Washington Post*, March 21. Retrieved November 17 (https://www.washingtonpost.com/sports/redskins/with-neurosurgery-every-day-feels-like-a-football-game-for-myron-rolle/2017/03/21/40c4e1cc-0da1-11e7-9b0d-d27c98455440_story.html?utm_term=.a97ee6984e8d).

McCall, George J. and J. L. Simmons. 1966. *Identities and Interactions,* rev. ed. New York: Free Press.

Nagata, Shinichi. 2014. "A Pilot Study of Exclusivity of Athletic Identity among Wheelchair Rugby Players: Implications for Therapeutic Recreation." *Therapeutic Recreation Journal.* XLVIII (4):320–331.

Nixon, Howard L. II. 2008. *Sport in a Changing World.* 2nd ed. New York: Routledge.

Potuto, Josephine R. and James O'Hanlon. 2006. "National Study of Student Athletes Regarding Their Experiences as College Students." Available: http://www.ncaapublications.com/productdownloads/SARE06.pdf.

Reitzes, Donald C. and Peter L. Burke. 1980. "College Student Identity: Measurement and Implications." *Pacific Sociological Review.* 23 (1):45–66.

Sage, George H. and D. Stanley Eitzen. 2013. *Sociology of North American Sport* 9th ed. New York: Oxford University Press.

Schwartz, Larry. ND. "Sugar Ray was Ring Artist." http://www.espn.com/classic/biography/s/Leonard_Sugar_Ray.html.

Stryker, Sheldon. 1978. "Status Inconsistency and Role Conflict." Annual Review of Sociology 4:57–90.

Stryker, Sheldon. [1980] 2002. *Symbolic Interactionism: A Social Structural Version.* Caldwell, NJ: The Blackburn Press.

Sturm, Jennifer E., Deborah L. Feltz, and Todd A. Gibson. 2011. "A Comparison of Athlete and Student Identity for Division I and Division III Athletes." *Journal of Sport Behavior.* 34 (3):295–306.

Symes, Rebecca. 2010. "Understanding Athletic Identity: 'Who am I?'" Podium *Sports Journal,* May 24. Retrieved July 4, 2017 (http://www.podiumsportsjournal.com/2010/05/24/understanding-athletic-identity-who-am-i/).

Verducci, Tom. 2016 (October 3). "David Ortiz: The Exit Interview." *Sports Illustrated.* 125 (11):34–43.

Vermillion, Mark. 2010. "College Choice Factors Influencing Community College Softball Players." *Journal of Coaching Education.* 3 (1):1–20.

Vickers, Emma. 2013. Life after "Sport: Depression and the Retired Athlete." *BelievePerform.com.* Retrieved November 4, 2017 (http://believeperform.com/wellbeing/life-after-sport-depression-in-retired-athletes/).

Wininger, Steve and Tiffany White. 2008. "The Dumb Jock Stereotype: To What Extent do Student-athletes feel the Stereotype?" *Journal for the Study of Sports and Athletes in Education.* 2 (2):227–238.

Woods, Ronald B. 2014. *Social Issues in Sport.* 2nd ed. Champaign, IL: Human Kinetics.

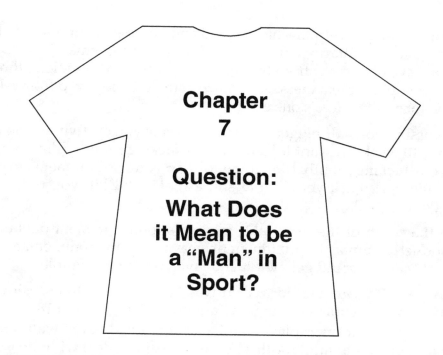

Chapter 7

Question:

What Does it Mean to be a "Man" in Sport?

Student Outcomes

After reading this chapter, you will be able to do the following:
- Define and discuss the existence (and impact) of masculinity and hyper-masculinity in sport.
- Understand how a "sporting masculinity" is intertwined with socialization and social class.
- Discuss how injury and pain (along with efforts to conceal these realities) are tied to sporting culture.
- Detail the history (and recent changes) of homophobia in male sport.

Be A Man! "It's rare that a man makes it through life without being told, at least once, 'Be a man,'" says Joe Ehrmann, a former NFL defensive lineman. "Those are the three scariest words that a boy can hear" (NPR staff 2014: paragraph 2).

> [Through my father and sport] I learned that . . . to be a man in this world, you better learn how to dominate and control people and circumstances . . . I ended up asking the question: What does it mean to be a man [in and out of sport]? (NPR Staff 2014: paragraphs 4, 6).

In 2013, the National Football League, sports fans and non-sports fans alike engaged in a collective conservation on what it means to be a man and to "man up" in sport. In October of that year, a story surfaced revealing that various members of the Miami Dolphins had bullied and harassed teammates to the point where one player voluntarily left the team. Specifically, lineman Jonathan Martin had taken a leave of absence from the squad and turned over violent, threatening, racist, and homophobic text messages and voicemails he received from fellow lineman, Richie Incognito. Here's one example:

> Hey, wassup, you half-nigger piece of shit. I saw you on Twitter, you been training 10 weeks. [I want to] shit in your fucking mouth. [I'm going to] slap your fucking mouth. [I'm going to] slap your real mother across the face [laughter]. Fuck you, you're still a rookie. I'll kill you (Petchesky 2014: Paragraph 32).

Though the coach of the team later made a strong statement denouncing the alleged conduct, a number of prominent players and sports commentators, said, in essence, that Martin should get over it and "man up." For example:

- Sportblogger J.R. Gamble said Martin was "too soft and too sensitive to deal with Incognito's relentless ribbing" (Gramble 2013: paragraph 18).
- Darren Woodson, former player and current broadcaster with ESPN, said "Jonathan Martin is at fault for this because he didn't deal with the issue in the locker-room . . . he let it get out . . . he should have handled his business without the help of the media" (Goldschein 2014: paragraph 5).

Grant Halverson/Contributor/Getty Images

Frank Alexander #90 of the Carolina Panthers rushes against Jonathan Martin #71 of the Miami Dolphins

Indeed, it is common in athletic hazing cases to blame the victim. Hank Nuwer, associate professor of journalism ethics at Franklin College, states: "Either he doesn't measure up or he's a sissy for reporting it . . . Or he doesn't understand that Incognito was just trying to toughen him up. It's always put that way" and the broader issue of bullying is ignored (Brady, Corbett, and Jones 2013: paragraph 9).

Ultimately, many argue that Martian was bullied because he didn't fit the traditional image of **hyper-masculinity**. Martin, a classic major at Stanford, and the son of two lawyers, was called "big weirdo" by several of his teammates. Investigations into the incident revealed that assistant coaches encouraged the behavior because they assumed Martin was "soft" due to his social, economic, and educational background and that he needed to be "hardened" (Brown 2013) in order to be an effective player in the NFL (this, despite the fact that he was drafted in the second round and had played football for the entirety of his youth and adult life).

After Martin left the team, he was briefly hospitalized and then joined his family in California where he underwent counseling for emotional issues (Martin later returned to the NFL, playing for several additional teams in his career). To the media, Incognito expressed regrets about the language he used with Martin but said it stemmed from a culture of locker-room "brotherhood," not bullying (although immediately after Martin left the team, Incognito boasted to fellow players about "breaking" him).

In male sport, it is common for athletes to use expressions of violence and aggression (as illustrated by Mel Bochner's Win, 2009) to bond and to "motivate" self and others—but athletes (as well as coaches and fans) often use sexual and gendered language of fem-phobia or homophobia to control behavior. Considerable research on masculinity documents the multitude of ways boys and men regulate gender conformity through discourse (Burstyn 1999). Much of this comes by threatening to unveil others as "sissies," "fags," and through the use of other emasculating and homo-sexualizing language. In sport, players who do not live up to the expected orthodox scripts of masculinity are often subordinated through ridicule.

Documentary Recommendation

Football High (2011)

High-school football has become an increasingly competitive sport in recent years—games are more intense, the practices are more strenuous, and the players themselves are bigger and stronger. Further, the culture of the game often promotes a type of masculinity and a desire to win that is often at odds with the health and well-being of the athletes.

As several of the high-school players state:

The game is about toughness . . . Whenever you start playing the game, you know that there's a chance you could get a concussion. Even if you do, it's—usually, it's not life-threatening or anything like that. It says it can shorten your life, but it won't shorten it, like, that much. And you only live once, so you might as well have fun while you're living.

You're only 17 once. I mean, I have the rest of my life to worry about pain and stuff like that. I can only, you know, play football for so long. I might as well, you know, use the time I have and worry about the effects later.

This documentary examines the various factors that increase the profound risk of injury in high-school football.

That men compete for dominance by using linguistic prowess to associate others with femininity or homosexuality is unfortunately nothing new in sport. Consider:

- While coaching at Indiana, Bob Kight once called a player a "pussy" and told a manager to line his dorm room with pictures of vaginas (Martin 2016:3). Knight apparently also put tampons in the lockers of players he considered soft (Wertheim 2017:22).

- In 2013, Rutgers men's basketball coach Mike Rice was fired after a video aired showing him assaulting his players and spewing homophobic slurs at them. In particular, the video (a compilation of Rutgers men's basketball practices from 2010–2013) showed Rice grabbing players, throwing basketballs at them from close range. In one instance, Rice fires a ball at a player's head. The tape also shows Rice kicking a player and screaming anti-gay slurs (Prunty 2013).

- In 2015, the head football coach of Sayreville War Memorial High School, was fired for allowing a culture of hazing to flourish in his locker room. In scandal that stunned the North Jersey town, a group of 15- to 17-year-old football players were accused of attacking members of the school's freshman football team in a locker-room ritual that involved flicking off lights, jumping the smaller players and, at times, allegedly groping their genitals or penetrating them from behind, using fingers poked through their pants. Some victims, played down the actions calling it "horsing around" (Fitzsimmons and Schweber 2014).

Why is this so common in male sport? Linguistic and physical violence, anti-feminine rhetoric, and same-sex sexual behaviors serve the purpose of humiliating, feminizing, and homo-sexualizing male recruits, in order to establish and reaffirm their position at the bottom of the teams' hetero-masculine hierarchy. Further, this hazing serves as a "test" designed by coaches and more senior students, to examine an individual's willingness to adapt to a near powerless state and give deference to authority. But again, why is this the case?

Sport Case Study

The Sport (and Ritual) of Stick Fighting: Becoming a "Man"

The Donga, or stick fight, is practiced by Suri tribesmen (in southern Ethiopia) at the end of each harvest season. It combines combat with ritual and sport and aims to get young men used to bloodshed—which village elders believe acts as necessary training for battle should they have to clash with other tribes.

The one-on-one battles take place between different Suri villages with around 20 to 30 fighters on each side. A fighter can challenge anyone he wants and hit any part of his opponent's body and they always fight naked to prove that they're tough. In accordance with tribal custom the men attempt to hide any pain they experience (and often drink beer throughout the contest as an attempt to mask injury).

The fights can be furious and may result in death, but there are also rules in place that are enforced by a referee (e.g., it is strictly prohibited to hit a contestant when he is on the ground). If a fighter dies during battle his family will be compensated (with around 20 cows or one girl).

CARL DE SOUZA/Staff/Getty Images

A male who wins the fights is allowed to choose their pick of a girl from the tribe for a date (and potential wife). The woman can refuse a warrior but being chosen by a champion is considered a great honor. Men who triumph in brutal and bloody Donga fights are considered heroes by the rest of the village and wider tribe. At the end of the fight, the winner, in a symbolic gesture of "sexual play," will point their sticks (mimicking a phallus) in the direction of the girl they want to date. If the girl puts a necklace around the stick, it means she is willing to date the champion.

In 1994, the Ethiopian government passed laws banning stick fighting but the tradition nevertheless lives on.

Question

Are there examples of similar "rituals of masculinity" in our (sporting) culture?

HISTORIC FRAMEWORKS AND THE EMERGENCE OF HEGEMONIC MASCULINITY

Organized sport in America has often been about power and obedience to authority. In fact, many 19th-century Americans saw a deep connection between industry and the athletic field, believing that organized athletics could create bodies able to sustain physical punishment and the violence of manly work. As Anderson (2010) states:

> Sport maintained little cultural value prior to the Industrial Revolution . . . However by the second decade of the next century these sentiments had been reversed. Sport became a tool of the Industrial class to socialize boys into the values necessary to be successful and this new economy, to instill the qualities of discipline and obedience, and to honor the hard work that was necessary in the dangerous occupations of industrial labor . . . In sport young boys were socialized into this value of sacrifice (for the team), so that they would later sacrifice health and wellbeing for family at work. Most important however to the owners and rulers of industry, was that future workers learned obedience to authority—and sport taught these boys docility (26-27).

As a result of these historical, cultural, and institutional forces, one of the core masculine scripts that has emerged from sport is the idea of sacrificing one's body for the sake of "team" (to this end, sport was also used as a training ground for war, with athletics teaching men "to own their duties as citizens of the Republic" and train them to manage "the burden of carrying on this country in the best way"). This historic shift to industry had other gendered effects too. Anderson continues:

> Factory work shifted revenue generation from inside the home to outside. Women's physical labor no longer directly benefited the family as it once did, and much of women's labor therefore became unseen and unpaid. Conversely, men's working spaces became dangerous and hard. Many removed rocks, welded iron, swung picks axes, and operated steam

giants. These environments necessitated that men be tough and unemotional. Men grew more instrumental not only in their labor and purpose, also in their personalities (2010: 27).

To this end, industry (and the sports that reflected it) created and maintained a culture of masculine hegemonic ideology—a culture of bodily sacrifice, and an emphasis on male stoicism and dominance with the oppression (negation) of females and femininities.

Historic Frameworks Continued: Male Sports as Symbolic "Cock Fights"

Sports scholar Dave Zirin further notes that while the era of industrialization produced gender segregation, it also produced a profound separation between the industrial elites and the working class—and sport became a brutal way of "measuring up" and gaining status over peers whom were denied status in the economic arena. "With the industrial push, and the dramatic polarization between the haves and the have nots, the games played by the working class became more brutal than and more segregated from those of their wealthier counterparts" (2008:8).

But masculinity has also been linked with the display of animal aggression and became the basic ingredients of the sport rituals of the era. Bull fighting, cock fighting, and dog fighting (all popular sports of the era's rural and urban poor), were activities for male members of an oppressed group to express masculine identity and aggression. Scholars have symbolically described these sports as "cock fights" and as a "thinly disguised symbolic homoerotic masturbatory phallic duel, with the winner emasculating the loser through castration or feminization" (Dundes as cited in Kalof and Taylor 2007:321). In his classic essay on cock fighting in a Balinese village, Clifford Geertz (1973) argued that while it appears that cocks are the ones fighting in the ring, actually it is the men. In Bali, men have a close identification with their cocks (same pun in Balinese as in English), who are symbolic exaggerations of the male ego. Other ethnographic studies of cock fighting document that the sport is a male event. The bird owners, the audience, and the birds are all male, and the attributes valued in the ring are masculine virtues (Marvin 1984).

The same is true of dog fighting (which continues to be a sport primarily practiced by the urban and rural poor) and is similarly centered on masculine values and the deployment of animals as symbols of macho aggression and menacing violence. In an extreme example of animal fighting, rites of masculinity, and professional sport, let us reflect upon the parable of Michael Vick. In 2001, quarterback and fan favorite Michael Vick, then 21, began his rookie year as a professional football player. The same year he and three associates began a dog fighting operation named "Bad Newz Kennels" on a 15-acre property he owned in rural southeastern Virginia. Michael Vick became a registered dog breeder and his co-conspirators set up the property for a dog fighting venture. They hosted fights at the Virginia property and transported dogs to other states to participate in fights (Macur 2007).

By 2004, Vick was one of the most popular players in the league and had a 10-year, $130 million contract with the NFL. By 2006, he was the NFL's highest-paid player. However, fan support would wane dramatically by 2007. Acting on testimony provided by federal witnesses, the U.S. Department of Agriculture executed a search warrant of Vick's property finding the remains of 6-8 dogs in two mass graves. Vick was accused of sponsoring dog fighting and authorizing acts of cruelty against dogs. Vick later acknowledged that he bankrolled the Bad Newz Kennels dog fighting enterprise. He also gave his associates money to bet on fights, and admitted to strangling, shooting, and electrocuting dogs that did not perform well in the fighting sessions. Ultimately, he served a 23-month prison sentence for bankrolling the dog fighting ring and for sponsoring illegal interstate commerce. But given the fact the Vick was one of the most popular and finically successful athletes in the United States, **why would he participate in dog fighting? Please discuss as a class.**

According to the Sociologist Lisa Wade, Michael Vick's participation in dog fighting was an effort to bolster his own sense of masculinity. She writes:

When the dogs win, it reflects on the men who trained them . . . You're tough because it's tough [but] when dogs lose, they threaten their owners' own sense of masculinity. . . . So the dogs are brutally punished for failing to be the hardest, meanest, and most vicious (Wade 2011).

The Washington Post/Contributor/Getty Images

Best Friends Animal Society provided shelter for 22 of Michael Vick's former pit bulls rescued from his dog fighting ring. They called them the 'Vicktory Dogs.' In the photo above is Lucas, covered in scars and believed to be Vick's champion fighting dog. Ironically, he was the most friendly of all. The court ordered that he must live out his days at the sanctuary with no hope of adoption.

THE SISSIFICATION OF SPORT: MASCULINITY UNDER ATTACK

A few years ago, most parents had few worries about sending their children out on the football field to play. Football, and especially youth football, was thought to be generally safe. However, Debra Pyka is convinced that playing youth and "pee wee" football caused her son's Chronic Traumatic Encephalopathy (CTE—a progressive degenerative disease of the brain found in athletes with a history of repetitive brain trauma, including repetitive concussions as well as sub-concussive hits to the head). She sued Pop Warner football (the program her son, Joseph, played with from age 11 to 14) for five million dollars, claiming the nonprofit failed to protect its youngest players and warn them and their parents about the permanent dangers of head trauma. Jones (2015) writes:

> [Joseph Chernach] would be dead at 25. Joseph hung himself . . . His brain was later found to have severe CTE . . . My son was the class comedian, loved school, always fun to be around . . . But we noticed after high school Joseph changed. He got depressed, angry, paranoid and withdrew from sports and his friends . . . I knew he had it even before we got the results. (Paragraphs 7-8)

The Pop Warner youth football organization settled the lawsuit in 2016. The terms of the settlement weren't disclosed, but Brian Heffron, a spokesman for Pop Warner said the organization would continue to be "a leader in addressing player safety, including around the concussion issues" and provide education for parents, coaches, and players (Johnson 2016: paragraph 3). NFL veteran turned safety-and-awareness advocate, Kyle Turley, argues that pee-wee football should be outlawed and banned.

> There can be serious disruption when those kids who are still developing are hurt. . . . do we really know what the bad effects of young boys playing tackle football really are? Many doctors I've talked to have said that the real problem is cumulative, that you can't really know how bad it is until you measure the effects of these kind of hits 10 or 20 years later. (Barra, 2013: paragraphs 14–15)

Indeed, many pediatricians are now recommending that children abstain from tackle football until high school (Meehan III and Landary 2015), and replace it with flag and other non-violent actions (Bachman 2015).

Documentary Recommendation

League of Denial (2013)

Thousands of former professional football players have claimed the league tried to cover up how football inflicted long-term brain injuries on many players. What did the National Football League know, and when did it know it? This documentary seeks to reveal the hidden story of the NFL and brain injuries.

In terms of a human face, the documentary chronicles the tragic fates of players like Hall of Fame Pittsburgh Steelers center Mike Webster, who was so disturbed at the time of his death he fantasized about shooting NFL executives and former Chargers great Junior Seau, whose diseased brain became the target of an unseemly scientific battle between researchers and the NFL.

Video Recommendation

Concussion (2015)

Mike Webster is a member of the Pro Football Hall of Fame class of 1997. Nicknamed "Iron Mike," Webster anchored the Steelers' offensive line during much of their run of four Super Bowl victories from 1974 to 1979 and is considered by some as the best center in NFL history. In 2002, he dies of a heart attack at the age of 50 (though he looks much older than is age suggests).

Bennet Omalu is a pathologist who handled his autopsy. Omalu questions how an otherwise healthy, and fairly young man could have degenerated so quickly. Upon examination of his brain, discovers that he had severe brain damage. He ultimately determines that Webster died as a result of the long-term effects of repeated blows to the head, a disorder he later calls chronic traumatic encephalopathy (CTE). The film stars Will Smith as Dr. Bennet Omalu and chronicles his fights against the National Football League who tries to suppress his research on CTE brain degeneration suffered by professional football players.

Who was Mike Webster?

From Pam Webster, Mike's Wife:

> Mike played center . . . It's the toughest position probably on the field. He's one of the smartest guys on the field. He was incredibly smart. And to see his brain declining years later was such a sad thing, because he was incredibly smart . . . You know, he never complained about injuries. . . . But at some point, he wasn't

experiencing feelings anymore of joy. Mike wasn't Mike . . . His anger was inappropriate to what the consequence—or the action was inappropriate to the consequence. His anger was out of control. And then at the same point 20 minutes later it would be like he's forgotten it and he's feeling really sad about it all. I came home, and he was angry about something; I don't even remember at this point what it was. But he took a knife and slashed all his football pictures. They were all destroyed and gone, and broken glass. And they were all down. And it wasn't Mike. Mike would have never done this. I mean, he was never one to boast about who he was or what he did or anything like that. He'd rather have pictures of his kids on the wall than his playing days. But I think he was so angry at himself and what had become of him, and in terms of being a football player and who he was and what had happened to the family that he just destroyed that part (The Frontline Interviews, 2013: Mike Webster's Legacy).

Sporting News Archive/Contributor/Getty Images

Reference

The Frontline Interviews. 2013. "The Legacy of Mike Webster." *PBS*. Retrieved November 4, 2017 (http://www.pbs.org/wgbh/pages/frontline/oral-history/league-of-denial/mike-webster-s-legacy/).

As far back as the 1920s, CTE has been known to affect boxers. However, recent scholarship has since confirmed CTE in retired professional football players and other athletes who have a history of repetitive brain trauma. This trauma "triggers progressive degeneration of the brain tissue . . . [and] the brain degeneration is associated with . . . memory loss, confusion, impaired judgment, impulse control problems, aggression, depression, suicidality, parkinsonism, and eventually progressive dementia (BU CTE Center 2016: paragraph 3).

PATRIK STOLLARZ/Staff/Getty Images

The sculpture, "Football Vignette" from American artist Duane Hanson showing the bodily violence experienced while playing the game.

Indeed, much of the iconic imagery of the American football player is derived from this willingness and ability to play through pain and use one's own body as a weapon of athletic war. To issue violence against self and others—has placed this athlete at the top of a masculine hierarchy of men. With growing medical evidence showing the enormous debilitative toll that comes from playing football, an increasing number of current and former professional football players are reconsidering letting their kids play tackle football. Consider:

- Troy Aikman, the Hall of Fame Cowboys quarterback, and current sports broadcaster, told HBO Real Sports, "If I had a 10-year-old boy, I don't know that I'd be real inclined to encourage him to go play football, in light of what we are learning from head injury" (DeLassio 2014: paragraph 2).
- Terry Bradshaw, former Steeler great and FOX sports broadcaster: "If I had a son today, and I would say this to all our audience and our viewers out there, I would not let him play football" (McIntyre 2012: paragraph 2).
- Brett Favre, another Hall-of-Famer, said "I'm almost glad I don't have a son because of the pressures he would face . . . But more the physical toll that it could take" (Wilson, 2014: paragraph 3).

However, not everyone feels that football should be avoided, nor should there rule changes that punish blows to the head in an effort to curtail concussions. For example:

- Former NFL linebacker, LaVar Arrington said, "To me its sissiification. That's the only way to put it. I won't live life scared and I don't want my boys to live life scarred" (Bossip Staff 2012: paragraph 2).
- Josh Bernstein of Right Wing News writes: New rules have slowly started to take over the game and have made it less violent and more cautious in the process. No longer can you hit a quarterback above the shoulders or below the knees. No longer can you hit a defenseless receiver coming over the middle to grab a leaping catch. No longer can a running back lower his head and flatten a would-be tackler. The rules have gotten so bad many fans and even players are wondering if they should just put on mini-skirts and play two hand touch (Bernstein 2013: paragraph 4).

In the end, one of the reasoned and enlightened voices of this controversy comes from ESPN journalist Howard Bryant who states:

> It's been a difficult time for every, every sport, especially the contact sports. You've got the CTE issues, the head trauma issues . . . whether it's the suicides of NHL players, the suicides of NFL players who all showed signs of CTE. We're starting to find out that this head trauma issue is not a joke and I think that people talk about it being the year of safety.

It really hasn't been the time of safety, in my opinion. I think it's really been the time of masculinity in sports because you've got this collision course, you've got the limits of what the human body can do, but you also have this macho culture where every single time you have sports bodies or governing bodies coming out saying, look, we have to make these games more safe for the players, then you've got this other group of the macho culture saying, hey, well, why don't these guys just wear dresses and why don't they, you know, why don't they wear high heels now? (in Wertheimer 2013: paragraph 13–15).

HYPER-HETEROSEXUALITY AND HOMOPHOBIA

Along with themes of hyper-masculinity, sport also teaches boys and young men about masculine sexuality. Historically, one of the most profound things they learn about masculine sexuality through the sport culture is **homophobic homosociability**—that is, the celebration of sport as a rare arena where men are permitted to be physically and emotionally intimate, and where homosexuality must be rejected in order to demonstrate that such intimacy is not sexually motivated (Burstyn 1999; Vaccaro ad Swauger 2016).

Throughout the 1990s and early 2000s, men's team-sports were characterized by high levels of homophobia. Researchers who examined the relationship between gay men and sport largely agreed that organized sport existed as a hostile environment for gay men (Bush, Anderson, and Carr 2012). In 1992, Messner stated, "The extent of homophobia in the sports world is staggering. Boys [in sports] learn early that to be gay, to be suspected of being gay, or even to be unable to prove one's heterosexual status is not acceptable" (34). Hekma (1998:2) further noted, "Gay men who are seen as queer and effeminate [were] granted no space whatsoever in what is generally considered to be a masculine preserve and a macho enterprise." Thus, men's sports have historically been defined as a place where homophobia and hegemonic masculinity is reproduced and defined, "since such athletes represent the ideal in contemporary masculinity—a definition which traditionally contrasts with what it means to be gay" (Bush, Anderson, and Carr 2012:108). Indeed, athletic masculinity has traditionally been portrayed as a hyper version of everything, "including exaggerated and extreme masculine behavior and a hyper sexual persona, which is understood as to connote an insatiable appetite that is satisfied with sexual conquest (and often) harm to women . . . and an intolerance known as homophobia" (Slatton and Spates 2014:170).

"Coming Out" and Backlash

In 2014 the NFL Network aired *A Football Life: Jerry Smith* (NFL Network 2014), a documentary about a same-sex sexual relationship that developed between two men who played together on the Washington Redskins in the late '60s and early '70s.

It profiled player Jerry Smith, who remained publicly closeted for his entire life and his former lover and teammate David Kopay. Kopay came out after his career ended in 1972 and wrote an autobiography in which he noted his sexual relationship with Smith. Though Kopay used an alias for his ex-teammate, Smith, who as noted was extremely guarded his private life, would never speak to Kopay again (unfortunately Smith died of AIDS in 1986). Kopay notes:

> I thought this [relationship with Smith] was really good . . . At least I was sharing something of myself with someone who's close and understood all that I had been through and understood so much of what we hoped for would come. And that's where we left it. (Gallahger 2014: paragraph 4)

Also included in the video is a review and reflection of the degree of homophobia in the NFL back then, and an account of Redskins head coach Vince Lombardi's outspoken intolerance for homophobia. Lombardi, who had a gay brother, "made it clear to the team that he would not tolerate any homophobic outburst directed at gay players" (Gallahger 2014: paragraph 2). But Smith's friend, David Mixner, "says it wasn't that simple, especially in that era. He contends that though some players might not have cared about Smith's private life, others would have oppressed him and ensured he lost his job had he come out" (Davis 2014: paragraph 15).

Consider how former NFL player David Kopay notes the ironic use of erotic language in sport:

> The whole language of football is involved in sexual allusions. We were told to go out and 'fuck those guys'; to take that ball and 'stick it up their asses' or 'down their throats.' The coaches would yell, 'knock their dicks off,' or more often than that, 'knock their jocks off.' They'd say, 'Go out there and give it all you've got, a hundred and ten percent, shoot your wad.' You controlled their line and 'knocked' 'em into submission. Over the years I've seen many a coach get emotionally aroused while he was diagramming a particular play into an imaginary hole on the blackboard. His face red, his voice rising, he would show the ball carrier how he wanted him to 'stick it in the hole' (Kopay and Young 1977:53–54).

The aggressive and homoerotic overtones of sport are also noted by famed anthropologist and folklorist, Alan Dundes (1978), who writes:

> The object of the game, simply stated, is to get into the opponent's end zone while preventing the opponent from getting into one's own end zone. . . . We can now better understand the appropriateness of the 'bottom patting' so often observed among football players. A good offensive or defensive play deserves a pat on the rear end. The recipient has held up his end and has thereby helped protect the collective "end" of

the entire team. One pats one's teammates' ends, but one seeks to violate the end zone of one's opponents. . . . I think it is highly likely that the ritual aspect of football, providing as it does a socially sanctioned framework for male body contact. . . . is a form of homosexual behavior. The unequivocal sexual symbolism of the game, as plainly evidenced in folk speech coupled with the fact that all of the participants are male, make it difficult to draw any other conclusion. Sexual acts carried out in thinly disguised symbolic form by, and directed towards, males and males only, would seem to constitute ritual homosexuality. . . . Thus in the beginning of the football game, we have two sets or teams of males. By the end of the game, one of the teams is 'on top,' namely the one which has 'scored' most by getting into the other team's 'end zone.' The losing team, if the scoring differential is great, may be said to have been 'creamed.' (75-88).

It should be noted that Dundes received death after the publication of his impish article (Buzinski 2012). Indeed, despite select examples, the history of the NFL is replete with homophobia. As a more recent example please consider the tale of former NFL punter Chris Kluwe who alleges that homophobia led to his firing. In his words:

Hello. My name is Chris Kluwe, and for eight years I was the punter for the Minnesota Vikings. In May 2013, the Vikings released me from the team. At the time, quite a few people asked me if I thought it was because of my recent activism for same-sex marriage rights. . . . The [then] head coach of the Vikings, Leslie Frazier, called me into his office [and] told me that I 'needed to be quiet, and stop speaking out on this stuff' (referring to my support for same-sex marriage rights). . . . Throughout the months of September, October, and November, Minnesota Vikings special-teams coordinator Mike Priefer would use homophobic language in my presence. . . . He would ask me if I had written any letters defending 'the gays' recently and denounce as disgusting the idea that two men would kiss. . . . and later said: "We should round up all the gays, send them to an island, and then nuke it until it glows". . . . [Afterward], I was frequently marked for negative scores by Mike Priefer. . . . So there you have it. It's my belief, based on everything that happened over the course of 2012, that I was fired by Mike Priefer, a bigot who didn't agree with the cause I was working for. . . . All we can do is try to expose their behavior when we see it and call them to account for their actions (Kluwe 2014: paragraphs 1, 9, 13, 15, 19, 28, 33).

Regardless of Kluwe's assertion that he does not believe the NFL has an institutionalized problem with homophobia, NFL scouting teams do seem to be obsessed with grilling prospects about their sexual orientation. For example, during the

2013 scouting combine in Indianapolis, University of Colorado player Nick Kasa was asked: Do you have a girlfriend? Are you married? Do you like girls? (Rosenthal 2013). Further, at the 2016 combine an assistant coach with the Atlanta Falcons asked prospect Eli Apple if he liked men. Apple stated:

> The Falcons coach, one of the coaches, was like, 'So do you like men?' It was like the first thing he asked me. It was weird. I was just like, 'no.' He was like, 'if you're going to come to Atlanta, sometimes that's how it is around here, you're going to have to get used to it.' (Jhaveri 2016: paragraph 2)

Unfortunately, during the same month that this occurred, two Atlanta men were scalded in an act of homophobia. Marquez Tolbert and his boyfriend Anthony Gooden Jr., were:

> jolted out of sleep by the feeling of boiling water splashing across their torsos, faces and limbs. Gooden's mother's boyfriend, Martin Blackwell, stood over them, pouring the water ... Then Blackwell ... yelled, 'Get out of my house with all that gay' (Kaplan 2016: Paragraphs 6–7).

Sport Case Study

The Gay Games

The Gay Games is the world's largest sporting and cultural event specifically for lesbian, gay, bisexual, transgender, and allied (LGBTA) athletes. Held every 4 years the games invite participation from all athletes—regardless of sexual orientation, race, gender identity, sex, religion, nationality, ethnic origin, political beliefs, athletic or artistic ability, age, physical challenge or health status. The Games offer a safe environment for LGBTA competitors and are open to anyone 18 years or older. Typically, about 10 percent of participants are non-LGBT, often friends and family who participate to show their support.

Founded as the Gay Olympics, it was started in San Francisco, in 1982, as the brainchild of Olympic decathlete and medical doctor Tom Waddell. His desire was to promote a spirit of inclusion and participation for persons marginalized and stigmatized because of their sexual orientation, as well as to promote the pursuit of personal growth via sport participation and competition.

The original sports that were offered at the first Gay Games were basketball, billiards, bowling, cycling, diving, golf, marathon, bodybuilding, power lifting, soccer, softball, swimming, tennis, track and field, volleyball and wrestling. 1,350 competitors whose origins ranged from over 170 cities worldwide competed in the first Gay Games. Currently, the game now hosts 35 sports and cultural events. Sports are as varied as softball, track & field, soccer and swimming to rodeo, bowling, volleyball and rowing. Cultural competitions have also been added to include choral and band performances (fun fact: the Olympics used to hold art and music competitions and give out medals for winners. See: Stromberg 2012).

The Federation of Gay Games (FGG) is the umbrella organization responsible for managing the Gay Games and works in collaboration with the staff and board of 2014 Gay Games. The FGG, an all-volunteer organization, safeguards the founding principles of the Gay Games: "Participation, Inclusion, and Personal Best." The FGG's assembly members include sports and culture organizations from around the world.

Question

In the last several years, The National Football League, National Basketball Association, Women's National Basketball Association, World Wrestling Entertainment, Ultimate Fighting Championship, and the Ladies Professional Golf Association, and collegiate football, baseball, and basketball have all had open LGBT players. Athletes have been coming out in high school, college, and professional sports around the world. This prompts some to ask why there is a need for the Gay Games. If LGBT people are making their way into the wider world of sports, then why create a separate event? What are your thoughts? Are the gay games still needed? Please take some time to debate.

Duane Prokop/Contributor/Getty Images

Gay Games Opining Ceremony 2014

Our opinion?

Those who participate in the Gay Games may not be the best athletes in the world, but they are people who enjoy the health and social benefits that come with participation in athletics. They know that a little competition is good for the soul. They know that they can push themselves to their personal best, and that they are in a supportive and affirming environment to achieve that personal best. Further, LGBT persons are still persecuted worldwide, so an event like this can foster both social support and "community" both locally and worldwide.

Slow Acceptance and the Growth of Alternative Masculinities

Despite decades of overt homophobia and misogyny, there is also select evidence that more progressive attitudes are starting to be embraced in various sport settings. For example, in research on openly gay high school and university athletes, Anderson (2011) shows that more team-sport athletes (as compared to individual sport athletes) are "coming out" in greater numbers than what was found a decade previously (Anderson 2002).

Beyond the high school and college level, several professional athletes (outside of the NFL) are also reporting that teammates are more accepting of their sexuality. For an example of this growth consider the following reactions to John Amaechi and Jason Collins. In 2007, NBA player John Amaechi came out and publicly announced that he was gay. His admission occurred 3 years after his playing career ended and then NBA player Tim Hardaway responded, "I hate gays. I don't like gay people and I don't like to be around gay people . . . I am homophobic. I don't like it. It shouldn't be in the world or in the United States" (Roth 2013: paragraph 3). He said further:

> I wouldn't want him on my team . . . I don't think that he should be in the locker room . . . There's a lot of other people . . . still in the closet and don't want to come out of the closet, but you know I just leave that alone . . . (Zeigler 2013: paragraph 9)

Hardaway later apologized and made repentance by becoming an activist on behalf of basic gay civil rights and, more recently, marriage equality (Roth 2013).

In 2013 NBA athlete Jason Collins, then an active player, publicly disclosed that he was gay. In contrast to the public's reaction to Amaechi's coming out, social media was brimming with support. For example, the Wizards organization tweeted, "We are extremely proud of Jason and support his decision to live his life proudly and openly" (Talbot 2013: paragraph 3). Further, then Denver Nuggets forward, Kenneth Faried said, "With Jason Collins . . . I believe our world as professional athletes will open up and become less ignorant of gay male athletes playing and more accepting and embracing of the whole situation" (Harper 2014: paragraph 10).

Ben Walton/Contributor/Getty Images

College Football: Cotton Bowl Classic: Missouri Michael Sam (52) victorious, kissing trophy after winning game vs Oklahoma State at AT&T Stadium. Arlington, TX

Further, in 2014 when Michael Sam (a college football standout at the University of Missouri) announced that he was gay, he became the first openly gay male athlete to "come-out" in Division I football. He said he was welcomed by his teammates, and felt that coming out liberated him, allowing him play to the best of his abilities (earning co-defensive SEC player of the year award in 2013). As a co-defensive player of the year, it was expected that Sam would be drafted into the NFL. He was ultimately picked in the seventh round (the last round) by the (then) St. Louis Rams.

Why so low? Unfortunately, Sam was talked about as a burden to be overcome by elder generation coaches, general managers, and team owners. He was something teams "wouldn't want to deal with," said Hall of Fame coach Tony Dungy (Reilly 2014: paragraph 7). As the Daily Beast noted, "CBSSports.com dropped Sam 70 spots on its draft board" after these and many similar comments (Curtis 2014: paragraph 18). Nonetheless, his draft announcement as well as the act of kissing his boyfriend in celebration was captured live on television. The act provided an inspiring moment for many. Wade Davis, a former NFL cornerback who came out after retiring in 2003, for example, remembered the kiss this way: "I could imagine that masculinity just screamed . . . 'Ahhhhh! You betrayed me, football!' [laughing]. . . . I also thought about how no straight guy can ever say he didn't see two men kiss during a sporting event . . . And how beautiful was that?" (Curtis 2014: paragraphs 7–8).

While Sam is no longer playing in the NFL (he was cut by the Rams and later the Cowboys) and was not given a tryout by the other 30 NFL teams (and Sam himself argues that this was due to widespread bigotry among NFL "elders" (Meyer 2015)), his kiss remains "unmoored from a happy ending, a free-agent image floating through cyberspace" that challenges homophobia and confronts people with the reality that gay people love like straight people do (Curtis 2014: paragraph 48).

Why this growing change and slow movement toward acceptance? Anderson (2009) theorizes that a cultural shift brought forth from generational change (the old guard dying out), as well as more gay positive media depictions, and the success of gay and lesbian social politics, all have combined to make society and sport more inclusive of male homosexuality. Thus, while the 1980s were characterized by extreme homophobia, and the 1990s began to see a crack in this hegemonic stigmatization, evidence from the early to mid-2000s show that brave athletes and social and cultural activists are helping to dismantle long-held cultural notions that sports are only for hyper-macho, homophobic jocks.

Final Thoughts on Masculine Sports Violence and the Body: The Effect of Sport on the Life-Course

Sports may have many positive health benefits including slowing the effects of aging (Baker et al. 2016), and improve mental and social health (Marzorati 2016). Yet, the physical nature of sport can also create a negative relationship with aging, as there are sports-related injuries that impact one's ability to live a healthy existence after sport. In this final section, we explore some of the more pathological and exploitative realities of sport and aging.

According to Rosenbloom and Bahns (2005), "the age at which one becomes an 'Elder' athlete varies by sport, but generally women 35 years and older and men 40 years and older [are considered old]" (p. 268). Further, football players are most closely clustered around their mean age of 26.74 years. However, these average ages do vary immensely by the sport and position played. In football, place-kickers (M = 30.79 years) and punters (M = 29.14 years) are older while those in running back and safety positions are younger (M = 26.06 and 26.01 years, respectively). In baseball, designated hitters have an average age of 35.75 years, with the catchers (M = 29.97 years) and first basemen (M = 29.56 years) being the next oldest positions. All positions within basketball hover around the average age of 26, with the small forwards averaging 25.75 years of age (the youngest average) and point guards averaging 26.87 years of age (the oldest average). This is important when one considers that the average professional athlete's career is over by age 33

(Hadavi 2011). For physically-demanding sports, like American football, it's as young as 28. Further, the average career span for professional basketball, football, and baseball is a mere 4.5 years, 3.5 years, and under 5 years, respectively (Eitzen 2016).

And what happens after sport for these professionals? One example from The Survey of Retired NFL Football Players (Cottler, et al. 2011) sheds some light on the physical and mental health among former players. The study, conducted by researchers at Washington University's School of Medicine in St. Louis, examined a cohort of 644 former NFL players and their use (and misuse) of painkillers. Most significantly, the study found remarkable health deterioration among the former players—only 13 percent reported current excellent health compared to 88 percent with excellent health at the time they signed their first NFL contract. Further, pain from NFL injuries was significant. Specifically, 93 percent of the sample reported pain with 81 percent of the players perceiving their pain to be moderate to severe. This level of pain is over three times the rate of the general population.

Cottler et al. (2011) also found that, regarding drug use, over half (52 percent) of the players reported using prescription opioids during NFL play. The overall rate of misuse during NFL play was three times the rate of the general population. Further, the strongest predictors of opioid use during their playing career were undiagnosed concussions and reported rates of heavy drinking. Undiagnosed concussions, which were reported by 81 percent of the sample, were strongly associated with misuse of opioids. This association might have been due to the fact that those who choose not to report concussions are the same players who choose not to reveal their pain to a physician, thus, managing their pain on their own. They may believe that if they report a concussion, they will be pulled from active play. Additionally, opioid use was also correlated with having three or more injuries, and being an offensive lineman. Offensive linemen have also been shown to be the least healthy football players, since they are the heaviest, and have been found to have cardiovascular problems (the average age of death for all NFl players is 55 years of age and 52 for NFL linemen, see: Hyman 2010).

Additionally, anecdotal data suggest that many injured players are able to play football only because of their use of prescription pain medications—and since these players often do not have sufficient time off during the NFL season to heal their injuries, they re-injure themselves. A cycle of injury, pain, and re-injury could lead to subsequent pain pill use during their time in the NFL which in turn could result in disability, continued pain and misuse of prescription pain pills later in life (Cottler, et. al. 2011).

Beyond pain and drug use, recent health discussions in sport have also included concerns about chronic traumatic encephalopathy, or CTE (introduced earlier in this chapter). In 2016, Jeff Miller, the NFL's senior vice president for health and safety, told the House of Representatives' Committee on Energy and Commerce, "that football-related head trauma can lead to brain disease" (however, from 2003 to 2009 the NFL's now disbanded Mild Traumatic Brain Injury Committee concluded in a series of scientific papers that "'no NFL player' had ever suffered chronic brain damage as a result of repeat concussions [and that] professional football players do not sustain frequent repetitive blows to the brain on a regular basis") (Breslow 2016: paragraphs 2, 5).

In his testimony before the committee, Miller said "his assessment was based on the research of Dr. Ann McKee, a neuropathologist at Boston University who has diagnosed CTE in 90 out of the former 94 NFL players she's examined" (Breslow 2016: paragraph 4). To date she and her colleagues have also found CTE in 45 college football players as well as six high-school football players. Indeed, the medical research makes it clear that concussions have potentially severe long-term consequences (Breslow 2016).

There is no doubt that this information is having an impact on players.

> . . . on America's youth and high school football fields, participation has been declining slightly across the country during the past five years, according to data from a sports industry group and state high school athletic associations, and questions about safety may be why some athletes are turning away from the game. (O'Connell n.d.: paragraph 2)

Further, the NFL is dealing with a number of high profile cases of stars leaving the game due to these concerns. For example, in 2014, star rookie, Chris Borland, left professional football after less than a year. Prompted by concerns over the long-term risks to the brain that can come from football, he chose to retire. Borland's decision shocked the NFL establishment and led ESPN to call him "the most dangerous man in football." Fainaru and Fainaru-Wada (2015) write:

> Borland has consistently described his retirement as a pre-emptive strike to (hopefully) preserve his mental health. "If there were no possibility of brain damage, I'd still be playing," he says. But buried deeper in his message are ideas perhaps even more threatening to the NFL and our embattled national sport. It's not just that Borland won't play football anymore. He's reluctant to even watch it, he now says, so disturbed is he by its inherent violence, the extreme measures that are required to stay on the field at the highest levels and the physical destruction he has witnessed to people he loves and admires – especially to their brains. (Paragraph 4)

When the Boston University affiliated Sports Legacy Institute asked him to endorse its campaign to eliminate heading in youth soccer, he agreed (studies suggest that persons who head soccer balls before age 14 were more likely to struggle with fundamental cognitive function, Comstock, et al. 2015). Borland indicated that he "knows some people probably blame him for contributing to the 'pussification' of football. 'I think in the eyes of a lot of circles, especially within football, I'm the soft guy. . . . But I'm fine with being the soft, healthy guy'" (Fainaru and Fainaru-Wada 2015: paragraph 23).

In the end, sports sociologist Michael Messner (2009) notes the paradox of masculinity in sport: Athletes are viewed as the epitome of health and physical condition; yet sporting violence (for which they are celebrated) comprise their overall physical and mental well-being thus challenging masculine identity. Vaccaro and Swauger (2016:96–97) concur, writing, "Severely injured players, who upon realizing their bodies are destroyed, often feel a complete loss of importance, mastery, and self-esteem . . . and no longer consider themselves masculine."

CHAPTER SUMMARY

In this chapter, we have asked, "what does it mean to be a man in sport?" In so doing, we have detailed how sport-masculinity is both homosocial, homophobic, and ironically homoerotic (and have noted the damaging and destructive realities of such hyper-masculinity). To this end, sports that emphasize a language and a normative culture of aggression and domination often encourage lived actions that lead to: chronic injuries, a passive and distorted vision of the life course, an inability to relate intimately and emphatically with other men, homophobia, and a compulsive concern with comparing oneself with other men in terms of what might be called life success "scores" (Coakley 2009: 256). In ways that are both fair and foul, Kidd (1987:259) notes that, "through sports, men can learn to cooperate with, care for, and love other men . . . But we rarely learn to be intimate with each other or emotionally honest. . . . on the contrary we are often socialized to express fondness for each other via teasing and/or mock fighting."

However, in this chapter we also note examples of progressive actions by select athletes that challenge and expand the boundaries of gender conformity and gendered socialization. These actions both inspire and create a more inclusive version of sport with a rise and greater acceptance of gay athletes and alternative masculinities. But in the end, we know such actions also threaten the established sporting order and pushback is real—and as such, we offer our support to those who continue to question and provoke (rather than embrace traditional) gender notions and ideals about masculinity and sport.

Discussion Questions

*How have (team, player, and cultural) attitudes of homophobia in sport changed recently? Are athletes more willing "to come out?"

*How has sport been used to combat homophobia and champion gay rights?

*Does hazing and bullying exist in contemporary sport? Have you ever witnessed or experienced this? What do you believe are the root causes of this?

*Discuss how socialization and sporting institutions encourage boys and men to conceal injury and pain—How do we change this?

*What can we do to keep sports fun and challenging, but make it safer?

*What are some other documentaries and films that explore the themes discussed in this chapter? How do they address any of the questions noted above?

Extra-Inning: The Professor who became an MMA fighter

Jonathan Gottschall, an English professor at a small liberal arts college took up the combat sport of mixed martial arts (MMA), at the age of 40. Why? He said he wanted to experience sports and bloodlust; to know what men endure to be men.

In part, it was because of job frustration and lack of professional fulfillment. Yes, he was a college professor with a PhD. But he was an adjunct making only $16,000 per year teaching writing composition to "freshmen who couldn't care less." He writes:

> Did taking up MMA—a sport where the whole point is to violently incapacitate the other guy before he can violently incapacitate you—seem like fun? It didn't. Did I actually think that the cage could free me from the cubicle? Yes, I was just desperate enough to hope that it could. But there was more to it than that. I wanted to fight because I was simply fascinated by fighting, and I wanted to learn about it—and write about it—from the inside. I wanted to fight because I'd always admired physical courage, and yet I'd never done a brave thing. I wanted to fight, I suppose, for one of the main reasons men have always fought: to discover if I was a coward . . . but mostly I wanted to feel alive (Gottschall 2015: paragraph 17).

His book, *The Professor in the Cage: Why Men Fight* (2015) describes the 3 years he spent at a Mixed Martial Arts (MMA) gym.

What do you think? Was this a midlife crisis? Is violence in this context functional? Do men (and women) use and experience violence to give them purpose—to make them feel alive?

Reference

Gottschall, Jonathan. 2015. "My own personal Fight Club: How an English professor became a cage fighter." *Salon*, April 17. Retrieved November 4, 2017 (http://www.salon.com/2015/04/17/my_own_personal_fight_club_how_an_english_professor_became).

CHAPTER REFERENCES

Anderson, Eric. 2002. "Openly Gay Athletes : Contesting Hegemonic Masculinity in a Homophobic Environment." *Gender & Society* 16(6): 860–877.

Anderson, Eric 2009. *Inclusive Masculinities: The Changing Nature of Masculinities.* New York, NY: Routledge.

Anderson, Eric. 2010. *Sport, Theory, and Social Problems: A Critical Introduction.* New York, NY: Routledge.

Anderson, Eric. 2011. "Updating the Outcome: Gay Athletes, Straight Teams, and Coming Out in Educationally Based Sport Teams." *Gender & Society* 25(2): 250–268.

Bachman, Rachel. 2015. "Flag Football: The Alternative for Concerned Parents: Worries about concussions have sent children to teams that don't tackle; growth for NFL Flag." *The Wall Street Journal,* November 9. Retrieved July 4, 2017 (http://www.wsj.com/articles/flag-football-the-alternative-for-concerned-parents-1447093342#:nrLR6uCc2UcS3A).

Baker, Joe, Parissa Safai, and Jessica Fraser-Thomas. 2016. *Health and Elite Sport: Is High Performance Sport a Healthy Pursuit?* New York, NY: Taylor and Francis.

Barra, Allen. 2013. "America's Most Dangerous Football Is in the Pee-Wee Leagues, Not the NFL." *The Atlantic,* August 31. Retrieved August 3, 2017 (http://www.theatlantic.com/entertainment/archive/2013/08/americas-most-dangerous-football-is-in-the-pee-wee-leagues-not-the-nfl/279229/).

Bernstein, Josh. 2013. "The Feminization of The National Football League." *Conservative Daily News,* November 7. Retrieved July 4, 2017 (http://www.conservativedailynews.com/2013/11/the-feminization-of-the-national-football-league/).

Bossip Staff. 2012. "For Discussion: Lavar Arrington Says Parents Who Keep Their Kids Out Of Football Are Participating In "Sissification," Do You Agree?" *Bossip.com,* May 9. Retrieved August 5, 2017 (http://bossip.com/583252/for-discussion-lavar-arrington-says-parents-who-keep-their-kids-out-of-football-are-participating-in-sissification-do-you-agree/).

Brady, Erik, Jim Corbett, and Lindsay H. Jones. 2013. "Blame the victim? Some players criticize Jonathan Martin." *USA TODAY Sports,* November 5. Retrieved September 1, 2017 (http://www.usatoday.com/story/sports/nfl/2013/11/05/bullying-jonathan-martin-richie-incognito/3449621/).

Breslow, Jason M. 2016. "NFL Acknowledges a Link Between Football, CTE" *Frontline,* March 15. Retrieved July 4, 2017 (http://www.pbs.org/wgbh/frontline/article/nfl-acknowledges-a-link-between-football-cte/).

Brown, Oliver. 2013. "Richie Incognito's alleged bullying of Miami Dolphins team-mate Jonathan Martin exposes NFL culture: Allegations of bullying of Jonathan Martin by his Miami Dolphins team-mate Richie Incognito shine a light on the more sinister elements of sporting life." *The Telegraph,* November 6. Retrieved July 4, 2017 (http://www.telegraph.co.uk/sport/othersports/americanfootball/10431322/Richie-Incognitos-alleged-bullying-of-Miami-Dolphins-team-mate-JonathanMartin-exposes-NFL-culture.html).

BU CTE Center. 2016."What is CTE?" *Boston University CTE Center.* Retrieved November 4, 2017 (https://www.bu.edu/cte/about/frequently-asked-questions/).

Burstyn, Varda. 1999. *The Rites of Men: Manhood, Politics, and the Culture of Sport.* Toronto: University of Toronto Press.

Bush, Anthony, Eric Anderson, and Sam Carr. 2012. "The Declining Existence of Men's Homophobia in British Sport." *Journal for the Study of Sports and Athletes in Education 6(1): 107–120.*

Buzinski, Jim. 2012. "Football as a homoerotic ritual – are players really gay?" *SBNation*, February 1. Retrieved November 4, 2017 http://www.outsports.com/2012/2/1/4052496/football-as-a-homoerotic-ritual-are-players-really-gay.

Coakley, Jay. 2014. *Sports in Society: Issues and Controversies*, 11th ed. Boston, MA: McGaw.

Comstock, R. Dawn, Dustin W. Currie, Lauren A. Pierpoint, Joseph A. Grubenhoff, Sarah K. Fields. 2015. "An Evidence-Based Discussion of Heading the Ball and Concussions in High School Soccer." *JAMA Pediatrics* 169(9):830–837.

Cottler, Linda B. and Arbi Ben Abdallah, Simone M. Cummings, John Barr, Rayna Banks, Ronnie Forchheimer. 2011. "Injury, Pain, and Prescription Opioid Use Among Former National Football League (NFL) Players." *Drug Alcohol Dependency* 116(1–3): 188–194.

Curtis, Bryan. 2014. "The Kiss: Michael Sam got drafted, we all witnessed something special, and then . . . what happened?" *Grantland*, December 12. Retrieved November 4, 2017 (http://grantland.com/features/the-kiss-michael-sam-nfl-what-we-saw-dallas-cowboys-st-louis-rams/).

Davis, Nate. 2014. "Friend: Gay Redskins TE Jerry Smith coped with 'horrendous existence'" *USA Today*, January 22. Retrieved November 4, 2017 (http://www.usatoday.com/story/sports/nfl/redskins/2014/01/21/jerry-smith-redskins-nfl-films-network-a-football-life/4730903/).

DeLassio, Joe. 2014. "9 NFL Players Who Wouldn't Let Their Sons Play Football." *New York Magazine*, November 14. Retrieved November 4, 2017 (http://nymag.com/daily/intelligencer/2014/11/9-nflers-who-wont-let-their-sons-play-football.html).

Dundes, Alan. 1978. "Into the Endzone for a Touchdown: A Psychoanalytic Consideration of American Football." *Western Folklore* 37(2): 75–88.

Eitzen, D. Stanley. 2016. *Fair and Foul: Beyond the Myths and Paradoxes of Sport*, 6th ed. Boulder CO: Rowman & Littlefield.

Fainaru, Steve. 2016. "NFL acknowledges, for first time, link between football, brain disease." *ESPN*, March 15. Retrieved November 4, 2017 (http://espn.go.com/espn/otl/story/_/id/14972296/top-nfl-official-acknowledges-link-football-related-head-trauma-cte-first).

Fainaru, Steve and mark Fainaru-Wada. 2015. "Why former 49er Chris Borland is the most dangerous man in football." *ESPN*, August 20. Retrieved November 4, 2017 (http://www.espn.com/nfl/story/_/id/13463272/how-former-san-francisco-49ers-chris-borland-retirement-change-nfl-forever).

Fitzsimmons, Emma. G. and Nate Schweber. 2014. "Board Approves Sayreville Football Coaches' Suspensions in High School Hazing Case." *The New York Times*, October 21. Retrieved November 4, 2017 (https://www.nytimes.com/2014/10/22/nyregion/board-approves-sayreville-football-coaches-suspensions-in-high-school-hazing-case.html?_r=0).

Gallahger, John. 2014. "Sports Closet: Documentary Recounts the Heartbreaking Romance Between Two Gay pro-Football Players." *Query*, January 23. Retrieved November 4, 2017 (http://www.queerty.com/documentary-recounts-the-heartbreaking-romance-between-two-gay-pro-football-players-20140123).

Gamble, J.R. "Rich Incognito Is A Coward, Jonathan Martin Is Soft and The Miami Dolphins Are To Blame." *The Shadow League*, November 5. Retrieved November 4, 2017 (https://www.

theshadowleague.com/story/rich-incognito-is-a-coward-jonathan-martin-is-soft-and-the-miami-dolphins-are-to-blame).

Geertz, Clifford 1973. *The Interpretation of Cultures:* selected essays. New York: Basic Books.

Goldschein, Eric. 2014. ESPN Talking Heads Show They Don't Understand The Jonathan Martin Situation." *SportsGrid,* February 14. Retrieved November 4, 2017 (http://www.sportsgrid.com/real-sports/nfl/espn-talking-heads-showing-they-dont-understand-the-jonathan-martin-situation/).

Hadavi, Tala. 2011. "Professional Athletes Prepare for Life After Sports." *VOA-Voice of America,* March 20. Retrieved November 4, 2017 (http://www.voanews.com/content/professional-athletes-prepare-for-life-after-sports-118377659/163130.html).

Harper, Zach. 2014. "Jason Collins Makes NBA History." *CBS Sports,* February 23. Retrieved November 4, 2017(https://www.cbssports.com/nba/news/jason-collins-makes-nba-history-after-signing-with-nets/).

Hekma, Gert. 1998. "As long as they don't make an issue of it . . .: Gay men and lesbians in organized sports in the Netherlands'. *Journal of Homosexuality* 35 (1):1–23.

Hyman, Mark. 2010. *Until It Hurts: America's Obsession with Youth Sports and How It Harms Our Kids.* Boston, MA: Beacon Press.

Jackson II, Ronald L. and Jamie Moshin. 2012. *Communicating Marginalized Masculinities: Identity Politics in TV, Film, and New Media.* New York, NY: Routledge.

Jhaveri, Hemal. 2016."Atlanta Falcons apologize for asking NFL draft prospect if he is gay." FTW! *NFL,* March 4. Retrieved November 4, 2017 (http://ftw.usatoday.com/2016/03/atlanta-falcons-eli-apple-do-you-like-men).

Johnson, Alex. 2016. "Pop Warner Settles Major Lawsuit Over Youth Football Concussions." *NBC News,* March 9. Retrieved November 4, 2017 (http://www.nbcnews.com/news/us- news/pop-warner-settles-major-lawsuit-over-youth-football-concussions-n535446).

Jones, Roxanne. 2015. "Should you let your kids play football?" *CNN,* March 20. Retrieved November 4, 2017 (http://www.cnn.com/2015/03/20/opinions/jones-football-kids-concussions/).

Kaplan, Sarah. 2016. "We were just burning': Ga. Man poured boiling water over gay couple as they lay in bed, police say." *The Washington Post,* March 18. Retrieved November 4, 2017 (https://www.washingtonpost.com/news/morning-mix/wp/2016/03/18/we-were-just-burning-ga-man-poured-boiling-water-over-gay-couple-as-they-lay-November 4, 2017in-bed-police-say/).

Karlof, Linda and Carl Taylor. 2007. "The Discourse of Dog Fighting." *Humanity and Society.* 31 (November): 319–333.

Kidd, Bruce. 1987. "Sports and Masculinity." Pp. 250–265. *Beyond Patriarchy: Essays by Man on Pleasure, Power, and Change,* edited by M. Kaufman. Oxford University Press.

Kluwe, Chris. 2014. "I was An NFL Player Until I Was Fired By Two Cowards and A Bigot." *Deadspin,* January 2. Retrieved November 4, 2017 (http://deadspin.com/i-was-an-nfl-player-until-i-was-fired-by-two-cowards-an-1493208214).

Kopay, David and Perry Deane Young. 1977. Th*e David Kopay Story.* New York, NY: Advocate Books.

Macur, Juliet. 2007. "Vick Receives 23 Months and a Lecture." *New York Times,* December 11. Retrieved November 4, 2017 (http://www.nytimes.com/2007/12/11/sports/football/11vick.html).

Marvin, Garry. 1984. "The Cockfight in Andalusis, Spain: Images of the Truly Male." *Anthropological Quarterly* 57:60–70.

Martin, Nick. 2016. "Former Indiana Player Alleges Bobby Knight Punched Him In Head, Squeezed Players' Testicles." *Deadspin,* October 25. Retrieved November 4, 2017 (https://deadspin.com/former-indiana-player-alleges-bobby-knight-punched-him-1788206021).

Marzorati, Gerald. 2016. "Better Aging Through Practice, Practice, Practice I can't promise this will prolong your life. But it will improve it." *New York Times,* April 29. Retrieved November 4, 2017 (http://www.nytimes.com/2016/05/01/opinion/better-aging-through-practice-practice-practice.html).

McIntyre, Brian. 2012. "Terry Bradshaw Wouldn't Let Son Play Football Now." *NFL.com,* June 14. Retrieved November 4, 2017 (http://www.nfl.com/news/story/09000d5d829d33b9/printable/terry-bradshaw-wouldnt-let-son-play-football-now).

Meehan III, William P. and Gregory L. Landry. 2015. "Tackling in Youth Football:COUNCIL ON SPORTS MEDICINE AND FITNESS." *American Academy of Pediatrics* 136(5). Available: http://pediatrics.aappublications.org/content/136/5/e1419.

Messner, Michael. 1992. *Power at play: Sports and the problem of masculinity.* Boston, MA: Beacon.

Meyer, Ken. 2015. "Michael Sam: My NFL Career Would've Been Better If I Didn't Come Out." *Mediate,* September 25. Retrieved November 4, 2017 (http://www.mediaite.com/online/michael-sam-my-nfl-career-wouldve-been-better-if-i-didn't-come-out/).

NFL Network. 2014. "Jerry Smith." *A Football Life: NFL Productions* (Episode Aired January 21).

NPR staff. 2014. "The 3 Scariest Words A Boy Can Hear." *NPR,* July 14. Retrieved November 4, 2017 (http://www.npr.org/2014/07/14/330183987/the-3-scariest-words-a-boy-can-hear).

O'Connell, Patrick M. n.d. "Spiral in youth football? Safety, other factors lead to a decline in sport's participation as parents, schools weigh how to respond." *Chicago Tribune* (n.d.). Retrieved, November 4, 2017 http://digitaledition.chicagotribune.com/tribune/article_popover.aspx?guid=e89afdca-00a4-41c7-ae8d-562b3deacc9f.

Petchesky, Barry. 2014. "The Worst Stuff From The Miami Dolphins Investigation." *Deadspin,* February 14. Retrieved November 4, 2017 http://deadspin.com/the-worst-stuff-from-the-dolphins-investigation-updati-1522846626.

Prunty, Brendan. 2013. "Mike Rice Fired at Rutgers After Abusive Behavior on Practice Tapes Comes to Light." *NJ.com,* April 3. Retrieved November 4, 2017 http://www.nj.com/rutgersbasketball/index.ssf/2013/04/mike_rice_fired_at_rutgers_aft.html.

Reilly, Travis. 2014. "Ex-NFL Coach Tony Dungy Backtracks on Michael Sam Remarks: 'I Feel Badly.' *The Wrap,* July 22. Retrieved November 14, 2017 (https://www.thewrap.com/tony-dungy-backtracks-on-michael-sam-remarks-i-feel-badly/).

Rosenbloom, Christine and Michele Bahns. 2005. "What can we learn about diet and physical activity from Master Athletes?" *Nutrition Today* 40:267–272.

Rosenthal, Gregg. 2013. "NFL team asks Colorado's Nick Kasa: 'Do you like girls?'" *NFL: Around the NFL,* Feburary 28. Retrieved November 4, 2017 (http://www.nfl.com/news/story/0ap1000000145664/article/nfl-team-asks-colorados-nick-kasa-do-you-like-girls).

Roth, David. 2013. "Ex-player, ex-hater: Tim Hardaway's turnaround on gay rights." *SBNation,* July 3. Retrieved November 4, 2017 (http://www.sbnation.com/2013/7/3/4491588/tim-hardaway-marriage-equality-in-Florida).

Schwartz, Nick. 2014. "Jason Collins, the NBA's first openly gay player, retires." FTW! NBA - *USA Today*, November 19. Retrieved November 4, 2017 (http://ftw.usatoday.com/2014/11/jason-collins-retire-first-openly-gay-player-nets).

Slatton, Brttany and Kamesha Spates (Eds). 2014. Hyper Sexual, Hyper Masculine?: *Gender, Race and Sexuality in the Identities of Contemporary Black Men*. Burlington, VT: Ashgate.

Stromberg, Joseph. 2012. "When the Olympics Gave Out Medals for Art." *Smithsonian*, July 24. Retrieved November 4, 2017 (http://www.smithsonianmag.com/arts-culture/when-the-olympics-gave-out-medals-for-art-6878965/).

Talbot, Margaret. 2013. "Game Change." *The New Yorker*, May 13. Retrieved November 4, 2017 (https://www.newyorker.com/magazine/2013/05/13/game-change-2).

Vaccaro, Christian A. and Melissa L. Swauger, 2016. *Unleashing Manhood in the Cage: Masculinity and Mixed Martial Arts*. Boulder, CO: Lexington Books.

Wade, Lisa. 2011. "The Secret Brotherhood Between Dog Fighting and Football." *Huffiest Masculinity*, November 17. Retrieved November 4, 2017 (http://www.huffingtonpost.com/lisa-wade/the-secret-brotherhood-be_b_67225.html).

Wertheim, Jon. 2017. "Throwing in the Chair: The Increasingly Bizarre and Sad Legacy of Bob Knight and Indiana." *Sports Illustrated*, March 10. Retrieved November 4, 2017 (http://www.si.com/college-basketball/2017/03/10/bob-knight-indiana-hoosiers).

Wertheimer, Linda. 2013. "Injuries Tilt The Balance In NBA, NFL." *NPR*, December 28. Retrieved November 4, 2017 (http://www.npr.org/2013/12/28/257822192/injuries-tilt-the-balance-in-nba-nfl).

Wilson, Ryan. 2014. "Brett Favre Reiterates He Wouldn't Want Son To Play Football." *CBS Sports*, July 16. Retrieved November 4, 2017 (http://www.cbssports.com/nfl/news/brett-favre-reiterates-he-wouldnt-want-son-to-play-football/).

Zeigler, Cyd. 2013. "Tim Hardaway Says: 'I Hate Gay People'" *SBNation*, February 20. Retrieved November 4, 2017 (http://www.outsports.com/2013/2/20/4009780/tim-hardaway-says-i-hate-gay people).

Zirin, Dave. 2008. *People's History of Sports in the United States: 250 Years of Politics, Protest, People, and Play*. New York, NY: The New Press.

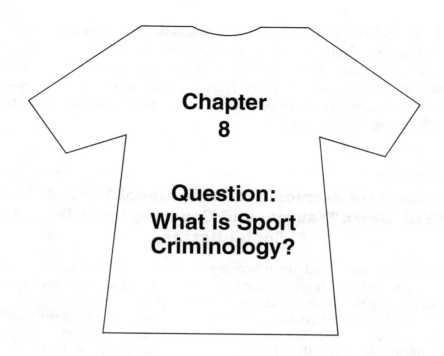

**Chapter
8**

**Question:
What is Sport
Criminology?**

Student Outcomes

After reading this chapter, you will be able to do the following:

- Understand the definition of criminology and the orientation of sport criminology.
- Know various theoretical frameworks and explanations for criminal behavior.
- Integrate theory to help explain the acts of crime in sport.
- Detail specific instances where sport has been used as "crime control."

SPORT CRIMINOLOGY: A DEFINITION

The following definition of criminology has been the standard for many years: Criminology is the (1) study of criminals (including the nature, extent, and cause of criminal offending); (2) the study of victims (including the study of harm and impact of crime and harm on the person(s) victimized), and (3) the study of punishment and crime control (i.e., what are the most effective forms/strategies of crime reduction) (Wolfgang 1963).

Thus, "sport criminology" is: (1) the study of athletes, sport managers (e.g., athletic directors, owners, trainers) and fans who have committed criminal offenses (on and off the field); (2) the academic and theoretical investigation into the causes and motivations for criminal offending, (3) the study of specific criminal offenses and sport-related crime such as illegitimate sporting violence, zemiology (the study of social harms), fraud, gambling, corruption, and other illegal acts—including athletes as victims, and (4) the examination of laws and punishments and the use of sport itself to combat these actions.

An example of Zemiology: The National Football League (NFL), Brain Trauma, and Covering Up or Denial of Social Harms

According to the book and documentary, League of Denial (2013), journalists, researchers, and former players argued that the NFL hid and covered up evidence linking head injury to chronic traumatic encephalopathy.

In a 2017 study, Dr. Ann McKee, a neuropathologist, examined the brains of 111 former NFL players—and 110 of those were found to have chronic traumatic encephalopathy, or CTE, the degenerative disease believed to be caused by repeated blows to the head (Mez, et al. 2017). One of the brains examined belonged to Ronnie Caveness—a linebacker for the Houston Oilers and Kansas City Chiefs. In college, he helped the Arkansas Razorbacks go undefeated in 1964. One of his teammates was Jerry Jones, now the owner of the Dallas Cowboys. Jones has rejected the belief that there is a link between football and CTE (Ward, Williams, and Manchester 2017).

Due in part to Dr. McKee's findings:

> More than 4,500 former athletes—some suffering from dementia, depression or Alzheimer's that they blamed on blows to the head—sued the league, accusing it of concealing the dangers of concussions and rushing injured players back onto the field while glorifying and profiting from the kind of bone-jarring hits that make for spectacular highlight-reel footage. (AP 2013: paragraph 3)

> In response, the NFL offered a $765 million. This settlement will affect 18,000 retired players and will "compensate victims, pay for medical exams and underwrite research" (AP 2013: paragraph 1).

Further, in the time following the release of the book and documentary, the NFL has since acknowledged a link between football and CTE, and has begun to steer children away from playing tackle football till later in adolescence, and encouraging safer tackling methods and promoting variations such as flag football.

Questions

What do you think about this? What are some other examples of sporting institutions denying or overlooking harm to athletes, fans, or society at large?

AN OVERVIEW OF SOCIOLOGICAL-CRIMINOLOGICAL THEORY

As detailed in Chapter 2, whenever we ask why our social world is the way it is (and why crime occurs) we are "theorizing" (hooks 1992). Again, in simple terms, a **theory** is a set of assumptions based on observations that help us to make sense of our experiences and to issue predictions about our human behavior. They are distinct lenses that help us to look at and focus in on particular aspects of human social life.

In criminology, there are various perspectives that help us ask and answer questions such as the following: Why do some people commit crimes while others obey the law? Why are some people targeted for victimization? How do social institutions create criminogenic situations (meaning a system, situation, or place causing or likely to cause criminal behavior)? A broad array of theories exist, ranging from neurological, biological, and social explanations—far too many that can be covered in this chapter. Thus, the following sections are meant as a representative sample of some of the more prominent examples that can help explain sport-related crimes.

Some theories are neurologically and biologically based and these argue that abnormalities in the brain can influence criminal actions (Raftner 2008).

Illustration of Theory: The Rabid Wolverine, Brain Trauma, and Crime—The Chris Benoit Tragedy

Christopher Michael Benoit (1967–2007) was a professional wrestler most famous for performing in the World Wrestling Federation/World Wrestling Entertainment industry (WWF/WWE). During his 22-year career, fans and wrestling historians have named him one of the all-time greats in the sport.

KMazur/Contributor/Getty Images

Benoit was a multiple time world champion and was often a main headliner, who wrestled under the moniker, "The Rabid Wolverine" (adopted due to his aggressive, attacking, and high-energy style). Unfortunately, on June 22, 2007, he murdered his wife and son, and later hanged himself. Subsequent research into this crime, suggests that brain damage from numerous concussions obtained during his wrestling career were likely contributing factors.

Tests conducted by neurosurgeon Julian Bailes, revealed that Benoit's brain "was so severely damaged it resembled the brain of an 85-year-old Alzheimer's patient" (ABC news 2007: paragraph 4). Further his brain was reported to have had an advanced form of dementia. Bailes and his colleagues concluded that "repeated concussions can lead to dementia, which can contribute to severe behavioral problems (ABC news 2007: paragraph 13).

Question

In an interview, neuropathologist Dr. Bennet Omalu (the scientist who first discovered CTE in athletes) said he would "bet his medical license" that O.J. Simpson suffers from the end effects of a life filled with head injuries—and that this explains his violent acts against others. Do you agree/disagree with this neurological/biological argument of criminal behavior? What other social/criminological explanations exist to explain his behavior?

Reference

ABC news. 2007. "Benoit's Brain Showed Severe Damage From Multiple Concussions, Doctor and Dad Say." *ABC* News, September 5. Retrieved November 4, 2017 (http://abcnews. go.com/GMA/story?id=3560015).

Documentary Recommendation

OJ Made in America (2016) is a five-part documentary that critically examines the role race and social status played in the ascension, climactic peak, and violent fall of OJ Simpson. The film's 2016 release was particularly timely in light of OJ's release from prison in 2017. OJ Simpson was granted parole and released from prison, which shortened his 30+ year sentence for kidnapping and armed robbery. His conviction in 2008 involved OJ Simpson, and multiple armed associates, violently confronting a sport memorabilia collector in 2007.

OJ: Made in America examines OJ Simpson's rise in popular culture. The documentary takes an in-depth look at the race relations in the 1950s and 1960s in Southern California and how that environment not only influenced, but also contextualized OJ's childhood and adolescence. Continuing with his famed collegiate football career with the USC Trojans, where he won a Heisman trophy in 1968, the documentary examines race relations, popular culture, and OJ's professional football career—on and off-the-field—in the NFL. Any documentary discussing OJ's life would not be complete without the allegations of domestic violence in the late 1980s and the penultimate allegations of murdering both Nicole Brown Simpson (his wife) and Ronald Goldman in 1994. Additionally, the high-profile media coverage of the subsequent trial—and acquittal—are discussed, examined, and placed into both historical and sociological context.

OJ: Made in America is an in-depth examination of race, class, police violence, domestic violence, and the criminal justice system's impact on individuals in American culture. These themes—told through the lens of OJ Simpson's life—help to understand how violence impacts not only sports, but also the lives and communities of people all across America.

Pool/Pool/Getty Images

*As noted, in 2017, Mr. Simpson was paroled from prison. His parole hearing was broadcast live on ESPN—thus giving the public a first-hand look into parole proceedings (probably, the first time the pubic-at-large has ever witnessed such an event). Indeed, a strange pairing of sport and criminal justice.

Beyond neurological/biological theories, most criminological theories are sociological in nature, emphasizing the influence of elements outside of a person's genetic nature. Here, these theories argue that criminal behavior is an "adaptive response to societal pressures such as social structures, culture, social institutions, and processes such as learning" (Rennison and Dodge 2018:67). Ultimately, sociological theories argue that criminals are not all that different from non-criminals, but they experience different pressures, strains, and limited opportunities.

For example, **learning theory and differential association theory** (Galliher 1988) maintains that criminal behavior is learned or "coached" by parents, teachers, and peer groups. Remember in Chapter 2, when two Texas high-school football players purposively slammed into the back of a referee? They said they were told to do so by their coach and given a moral justification to do so. Other socialization theories suggest that a considerable degree of sporting violence can be attributed to how boys and men are socialized to handle disagreements.

Illustration of Theory:
Learned Violence and the Death of a Hockey Dad

In 2002, a 44-year-old truck driver was convicted of involuntary manslaughter for beating another man to death during their sons' hockey practice in an incident that seemed to "epitomize the worst in parental fervor over youth sports" (AP 2002: paragraph 1).

"Thomas Junta claimed he killed Michael Costin, 40, in self-defense after they argued over rough play during the practice on July 5, 2000" (AP 2002: paragraph 2). But the jury of nine women and three men saw it differently. They found Junta guilty, and in so doing, put a spotlight on the problem of parental violence and toxic masculinity at youth sporting events.

The confrontation between the two men began when Junta became angry about the level of physical contact between the youth being allowed under the supervision of Costin at what was supposed to be a non-contact scrimmage. The specific incident that seemed to prompt Junta to act in violence was when he saw another player elbow his son in the face (AP 2002).

"Witnesses said that when Junta yelled at Costin for not controlling the rough play, he snapped: 'That's hockey.' The two men then got into a scuffle near the locker rooms, but it was quickly broken up by bystanders" (AP 2002: paragraph 14). However, Junta returned moments later, delivering multiple punches to Costin's face, killing him. During the trial, the prosecution repeatedly called attention to "Junta's size - 6-foot-1 and 270 pounds. Costin was 6 feet, 156 pounds" (AP 2002: paragraph 18).

This incident of violence even made it to an episode of the popular TV show, The Simpsons (Season 15, episode 4, "The Regina Monologues" 2003) where Bart is playing a video game, titled "Hockey Dad." The game begins when one child athlete scores against the goalie of the opposite team. In response, one father yells, "Your kid sucks!" Another father in the stand yells "bring it on." The parents then attempt to beat each other up with fists, kicks, even stomping on the opponent's face. Once one of the fathers has killed the other, the victor does a victory pose while two police officers handcuff him and an off-screen announcer shouts: "You're a big man! BIG MAN!!"

The jurors (and the *Simpson* writers) suggest that **toxic masculinity** (learned norms of masculinity that include dominance, especially dominance over women), pride in excelling at sports, the inability to deal with shame and loss, as well as an over reliance on physicality to deal with confrontations (Kupers 2005), was the core factor in the fight between Junta and Costin.

References

Associated Press. 2002. "Hockey Dad Convicted in Death." *Wired,* January 11. Retrieved November 4, 2017 (http://www.wired.com/2002/01/hockey-dad-convicted-in-death/).

Kupers, Terry A. 2005. "Toxic Masculinity as a Barrier to Mental Health." *Journal of Clinical Psychology* 61(6): 713–724.

Sport Case Study

Wife Carrying

Speaking of dominance over women, we introduce you to the sport of wife carrying.

Wife carrying is most known as a Finish sport that "plays with" and transposes a violent origin. Its history is based around the 19th century legend of Herkko Rosvo-Ronkainen, or "Ronkainen the Robber." Ronkainen and his thieves would raid and pillage villages, stealing food and abducting women (i.e., carrying these women on their backs) as they would flee back to the bandit's stronghold.

The modern sport is played with two contestants: a male carrier and a female "passenger" (the "wife" is either carried over the shoulder, or upside down with her arms holding her "husband's" waist and her legs wrapped around his shoulders and head). The husband and wife terminology can be symbolic as the persons do not have to be related to each other.

TIMO HARTIKAINEN/Stringer/Getty Images

Participants must be at least 17 years of age, and the "wife" must weigh at least 108 pounds (if she does not, she is weighted down with a rucksack containing the allotted necessary weight). With the wife in a carried position, the couple race along an obstacle course of approximately 770 feet that features sandy and rocky terrain, a submerged pool or water feature and a waist-high barrier than mast be crossed.

Historically, those with the fastest time would win their "wife's" weight in beer—but now prizes vary by competition. Today, prizes are also awarded for most entertaining couple, best costumed, and most fit or strongest carrier.

Overall the spirit of the completion is designed to be fun and whimsical. But one critique of the sport is that it reinforces stereotypical gender roles, as women as the passive /abducted participants of the event. Many participants argue against this, as they say it brings the couple closer together and fosters social relationships. Further, in some variations of the contest (practically as its spreading globally), there are now same-sex couples competing and in some cases, women will carry men.

*The Finns are also known for the sports of: swamp (mud pit) soccer, timed mosquito killing championships, and more recently, competitive hobby-horsing, wherein competitors trot and hurdle obstacles while riding the wooden toys. Why? Finland endures long, dark winters. Thus, as Hanna Vehmas, a sports sociologist in Finland states, "I think we go a little crazy in the summer, mix that with alcohol, and maybe we want to compete a little bit" (Keh 2007: paragraph 23).

Reference

Keh, Andrew. 2017. "Finland has a Sports Screw Loose." *New York Times,* July 27. Retrieved November 4, 2017 (http://www.nytimes.com/2017/07/27/sports/finland-has-a-sports-screw-loose.html?_r=0).

Another sociological theory, **social bond theory** (Hirschi 1969), holds that a person's lack of (or loss of) attachments to core or significant others makes one more likely to commit crime—simply because there is no one around to look out for them or to act as a moral compass for them.

Illustration of Theory:
The Saints, the Roughnecks, and Social Bonding

Much of the work of legendary sociologist William Chambliss revealed how lower-class individuals (and the crimes or acts of delinquency they committed) were made more visible by society than those of middle-class criminals. As a result, poor people were more likely to be targeted, resulting in much higher rates of surveillance, negative stereotyping, and criminalization.

This reality holds true in his classic study of small town high-school street gangs, *The Saints and the Roughnecks* (1973). In this research, Chambliss showed how the petty crimes committed by members of a middle-class gang (who he termed "the Saints") generally resulted in just "a slap on the wrist," while the same crimes committed by lower-class gang members (termed the "Roughnecks"), led to harmful sanctions, profiling and, in some cases, arrest and imprisonment.

As a result of this profiling, the high school youth known as the Roughnecks grew up with their teachers and other adult supervisors primarily viewing them as delinquents. Indeed, these adults were generally unwilling to offer mentorship or aid. In response, the boys internalized a feeling of rejection and adopted personas of defiance and generalized aggression.

However, two of the roughneck boys were able to find an escape from this through sport. The two were good at football and attracted the interest of collegiate scouts. These recruiters, as outsiders to the community, did not hold the same negative impressions of the young men and were willing to offer mentorship, friendship, and a chance to escape the detrimental labels that the community had placed on them.

Both of these football players received athletic scholarships to college, and for these two former "roughnecks," college enabled the development of new social relations, new social bonds, and new social identities that broke their old patterns of deviance. Both graduated college in four years, and became teachers and coaches—thus reflecting the power of sport to facilitate social relations and mentor-mentee bonds that supplanted their membership and bond with delinquent youth.

Reference

Chambliss, William J. 1973. "The Saints and the Roughnecks." *Society* 11(1): 24–31.

Criminogenic theories focus on the factors that produce crime or lead individuals to engage in criminal acts. One way that criminogenic theory can be used is to look at how organizations can support the production of crime. In this case, it holds that "organizations have distinctive cultures that are more or less tolerant of law violation for the benefit of the [organization]" (Apel and Paternoster 2009:15). So, in terms of sport, the organization would be an athletic department, a school or university, or a professional sports franchise that overlooks deviant and criminal action in order to win and excel in sport. Within this premise, some organizations turn a blind eye to ethical and legal infractions if it benefits the organization. When this happens, it creates a "culture of rule breaking which is learned just as any other business practice is learned" (Apel and Paternoster 2009:15). Additionally, an organization with a less than strict view toward ethical behavior may attract people with loose ethical boundaries, which itself leads to offending behavior (Apel and Paternoster 2009).

Illustration of Theory:
Corporate and Criminogenic Sport Institutions

Please consider the following examples:

UNC, Chapel Hill: Cheating, Academic Fraud. The University of North Carolina, Chapel Hill (UNC) is one of the most well-respected public universities in the United States. However, their athletic department was involved in one of the most egregious academic scandals in NCAA history. Internal investigations began back in 2010 with a focus on impermissible benefits to student-athletes. Years of investigation and testimony has uncovered a system based on "fake" or "sham" classes, which impacted thousands of student-athletes over the course of decades with much of the recent attention centering on the Men's Basketball team and their 2017 NCAA national championship.

A former academic tutor and employee of the athletic department levied allegations of academic fraud and misconduct in 2014 and additional investigations—including reports by the former North Carolina Governor, and one by a former official of the Department of Justice—revealed a systematic process of enrolling student-athletes in the African-American Studies department where a professor and administrator were complicit in providing student-athletes with grades they, in most cases, did not earn. It was widely reported, by a variety of outlets and investigations, that examples of the academic misconduct included "fake" classes, plagiarism, and allegations that a disproportionate number of student-athletes were literate on various grade-school levels. The scandal, which was corroborated by former UNC student-athletes, is thought to go back to the early 1990s.

University of Louisville: Sex, Escorts, and Men's Basketball. In 2016, the University of Louisville's Men's Basketball program was alleged to have used sex workers/

escorts to perform sexual acts and lure potential basketball recruits to the team (as well as "entertain" existing team members). Some, if not many, of the young men involved in this scandal were under the age of 18 at the time of the incident. In the investigation that followed, the former director of basketball operations was identified as the organizer of these sex-recruitment parties (he had since moved on to another university by the time allegations became public) (see: Powel and Cady 2015).

While the university self-imposed a 2015–2016 postseason ban, the NCAA—during the summer of 2017—disciplined the basketball program for unethical conduct and lack of program oversight. The punishments included suspending head coach, Rick Pitino, for five conference games during the beginning of the 2017–2018 season, vacating wins and records from December 2010–July 2014 (including their 2013 Men's Basketball National Championship), forfeiture of money received as part of conference revenue sharing agreements for 2012–2015 tournament appearances, and four years of probation, which includes scholarship reductions. At the time of this writing, Louisville was considering appealing the NCAA's sanctions.

Questions

What are some additional institutional criminogenic sporting examples? What solutions do you recommend to limit these types of "corporate" criminal subcultures?

Reference

Powel, Katrina and Dick Cady. 2015. *Breaking Cardinal Rules: Basketball and the Escort Queen.* Amazon Digital Services.

Feminist criminology is a set of theories that explore women and girls' specific and unique relationship to crime and victimization (Renzetti 2013). For example, feminist criminology theory argues that women hold less power in society and as such will have a greater likelihood of being victimized. How does this play out in sport?

Take the reality of domestic violence and sexual assault. For the most part, athletes have extremely low arrest rates relative to national averages. Yet, their relative arrest rate for domestic violence is much higher than for other crimes (Morris 2014). Further, because elite athletes are typically players that have high salaries or are the "money makers" for their respective sport organizations, organizations have attempted (for the most part) to "save" or cover for their athletes accused of domestic violence or sexual assault. As an elite athlete with prestige and status, many are seemingly given preferential treatment which results in athletes being convicted less frequently than non-athletes (Repetto 2016).

Illustration of Theory:
The Baylor Sex Scandal, Feminist
Criminology and Institutional Deviance

Baylor University, located in Texas, is a well-respected academic institution founded in the Christian (i.e., Baptist) tradition of religiously inspired higher education. However, the football team has been at the center of the scandal and various reports have identified a culture of sexual assault, silence, and violence against women was pervasive at the institution.

The scandal, which began with investigations and allegations surrounding a football player transferring to Baylor from another university, included a multitude of violations, crimes, and alleged criminal activities. Several victims have pursued or are currently pursuing legal action and allegations have singled out as many as 30–35 football players involved in rapes, gang rapes, sexual assault or forms of sexual battery. In the wake of this ongoing scandal, university officials failed to properly investigate or take the appropriate action in regards to allegations of rape, sexual assault, and other crimes or forms of violence against women. Several university employees and officials were either demoted, let go, or have since resigned, including the university's President, Athletic Director, head football coach, and Title IX coordinator.

Like all colleges and universities who must abide by the Title IX federal mandate, Baylor is required to thoroughly investigate allegations of sexual violence, and provide security, counseling services and academic help to victims—which Baylor apparently did not do. Further, reports indicate that the school's chief judicial officer, head coach, and several assistant coaches tried to talk women out of pursuing anything against the alleged offenders (Lavigne 2017).

A mother of one the victims stated: "Their football team is their priority. The money that comes to them from football is their priority . . . You cannot serve two masters. Theirs is money. They don't care about their students. They don't care about the victims" (Lavigne 2017: paragraph 65).

Questions

In 2016, University of Oklahoma football coach, Bob Stoops, discussed at a press conference the case of one of his players, Joe Mixon. Mr. Mixon punched a young woman in the face shattering multiple bones. The event occurred in 2014 during which time Coach Stoops offered to let Mixon leave, transfer or sit out the 2014 football season—a season he was able to redshirt, since the event happened before his freshman year. During the press conference, Coach Stoops spoke of the "different time" in 2014 as compared to a few years later where he said an incident like that now would result in the immediate dismissal of the player.

How do any of the concepts in this chapter help to explain or contextualize this case? Also, was the "punishment" worthy of the crime committed? Should athletes (and other individuals in society) be given a second chance when involved in a violent crime such as this one?

Reference

Lavigne, Paula. 2017. "Baylor Faces Accusations of Ignoring Sex Assault Victims." *ESPN*, July 13. Retrieved November 4, 2017 (http://www.espn.com/espn/otl/story/_/id/14675790/baylor-officials-accused-failing-investigate-sexual-assaults-fully-adequately-providing-support-alleged-victims).

One prominent study showed that male student-athletes make up only 3 percent of the student population on college campuses, however, they account for 19 percent of sexual assaults and 35 percent of domestic assaults on campuses (Crosset, Benedict and McDonald 1995). More recent reports have supported these findings (Siers-Poisson 2014; Ladika 2017).

What might explain this? The work of Brown, Sumner and Nocera (2002) provides some insight. They analyzed athletes' attitudes toward women and their levels of sexual aggression toward women. They found that elite athletes who were celebrated for their on-field aggression, who also held strongly traditional attitudes toward women (i.e., to view women as inferior to men), had highest levels of sexual aggression toward women. The argument they made is that elite athletes who are trained to be aggressive on the field, who also view women as inferior, are likely to view women as objects and, therefore, feel entitled to them as sexual objects. Simply stated: High levels of aggressiveness, mirrored with traditionalist attitudes toward women, can lead to higher rates of domestic violence and sexual assaults. Thus, it's not all male athletes who act this way, but a small subset who are socially celebrated for their on-field legitimate violence and who also apparently hold strongly enculturated negative attitudes toward women.

Documentary Recommendation

The Hunting Ground (2015) is a documentary about the incidence of sexual assault on college campuses and the failure of administors to deal with it in an adequate manner. The film presents interviews with students who allege they were sexually assaulted and that college officials were more concerned with minimizing rape statistics than with the welfare of the students who came forward to report an alleged assault.

In terms of sports, *The Hunting Ground* interviews campus officials and peace officers who criticized how sexual assault investigations were handled at their institutions. Specifically, an officer was told by university officials that he was not allowed to conduct any investigations of athletes while they were on athletic department property. Further, a significant section of the film is focuses on Jameis Winston the former star quarterback for the Florida State Seminoles team and the accusation of sexual assault against him (and the alleged flawed investigation by police and university officials) while at Florida State. His accuser, Erica Kinsman, who goes public in the documentary says Winston raped her; Winston says the sex was consensual.

But apart from this storyline, the documentary presents evidence that college athletic departments are often allowed to oversee sexual assault cases involving their own athletes, thereby seemingly violating the proper (legal) modes on investigation.

Question

Are "big-time" sport schools more apt to be criminogenic because of their desire to win championships and the fame and money that comes with it?

Feminist Criminological Critiques of Professional Sport and the Handling of Domestic Violence

Some of the male major professional sports leagues in the United States have specific detailed policies in place for the handling of domestic violence—Yet all have come relatively late to the table: The NFL (in 2014), MLB (in 2015), and the NBA (in 2017)—as of this writing the NHL mandates training in sexual assault and domestic violence awareness but the league does not have a formal personal conduct policy nor a policy specifically addressing domestic violence or sexual assault. Finally, Major League Soccer does not have a specific plan or disciplinary action for domestic abuse (it is noted in its constitution as a violation).

Policies related to Domestic Violence and Sexual Assault in Professional Sport

The policy of the NFL reads:

Violations of the Personal Conduct Policy regarding assault, battery, domestic violence or sexual assault that involve physical force will be subject to a suspension without pay of six games for a first offense, with consideration given to mitigating factors, as well as a longer suspension when circumstances warrant.

The policy of MLB reads:

The Commissioner's Office will investigate all allegations of domestic violence, sexual assault and child abuse involving members of the baseball community. The

Commissioner may place an accused player on paid administrative leave for up to seven days while allegations are investigated. Players may challenge any decision before the arbitration panel. Discipline: The Commissioner will decide on appropriate discipline, with no minimum or maximum penalty under the policy. Players may challenge such decisions to the arbitration panel.

The policy of NHL reads:

The National Hockey League does not have a formal personal conduct policy or one specifically addressing domestic violence or sexual assault. Currently however, all 30 teams must go through "hour-long educational sessions with outside professionals" on sexual assault and domestic violence.

The policy of the NBA reads:

The NBA's policy on domestic violence, sexual assault and child abuse addresses these acts by players in the following ways. First, players go to a policy committee made up of individuals representing the NBA, the players' union and independent experts in the field. Players can reach out to this committee on their own or be required to go if there is a criminal conviction or the commissioner makes a disciplinary determination against the player. This committee then oversees a treatment and accountability plan for the player. Punishment is doled out by the NBA commissioner who will determine the appropriate disciplinary action to be taken on a case-by-case basis. The commissioner has the power to punish anyone who violates the policy such as not following their treatment and accountability plan or someone convicted or who pleads guilty or no contest to charges.

The policy of MLS reads:

A Player shall be determined to violate [policy] as follows: (i) through receipt of a Verified Positive (as defined below), (ii) use or possession of any controlled substance without a prescription, (iii) abuse of a prescription drug, (iv) use of alcohol on work premises or reporting to work under the influence of alcohol or otherwise being affected at work by the consumption of alcohol, (iv) use or possession of Illegal Substances (as defined below), (v) use or possession of Performance Enhancing Substances (as defined below), (vi) violation of criminal law (other than traffic related misdemeanors, littering, jaywalking, and other similar offenses), (vii) domestic violence . . . The degree of discipline shall depend upon the nature and severity of the violation.

Questions

What do you think of these policies? Do they take the issue of domestic violence seriously enough? Does the flexibility of the rules of punishment give the commissioners too much power to be harsh (or lax) regarding punishment?

Indeed, multiple domestic violence and sexual assault cases have rocked the professional sports world in the last few years. Please consider some recent examples of domestic violence in professional sport:

- In 2014, Former Ravens running back Ray Rice was captured on video punching and knocking out his then-fiancée (now wife) Janay Palmer. Since Rice's dismissal from the Baltimore Ravens and his indefinite suspension from the NFL, he has since become an advocate for domestic violence awareness and prevention. Further, his case forced the NFL to strengthen its policies of punishment for those found guilty of acts of domestic violence (Hill 2014).
- In 2014, Kansas City Chiefs linebacker Jovan Belcher shot his girlfriend Kasandra Perkins to death in an extreme case of domestic violence. After this, he drove to the Chiefs' training facility, where, after thanking several of his coaches for all they had done for him, he shot himself in the head. The NFL decided that the next game to be played would proceed as normal with the exception of a moment of silence for victims of domestic violence. An aautopsy showed that Belcher had chronic traumatic encephalopathy (CTE), the degenerative brain disease found in persons with a history of repetitive brain trauma (Crime Insider, Staff 2014).
- Floyd Mayweather, Jr, the famous boxer and the world's highest-paid athlete has been charged with domestic violence on more than one occasion. In 2015, during his bout with Manny Pacquiao, several female reports (Michelle Beadle and Rachel Nichols), who covered Mayweather's history of domestic violence, tweeted that Mayweather's camp had "banned" them from the MGM Grand Arena, preventing them from covering the fight (Schwartz 2015).
- In 2017 Former MMA fighter War Machine (Jon Koppenhaver) was sentenced to life in prison for the brutal beating of his ex-girlfriend Christy Mack. The jury found him guilty on the charges of: domestic violence, sexual assault, and preventing a victim from reporting a crime. War Machine was accused of stalking and holding Mack, at her home, against her will. Prosecutors told the jury that War Machine broke in and beat her until she was unconsciousness, then sexualyl assaulted her. Afterwards, he apparently told her that "this is it. I've got to kill you now." Mack said she escaped when War Machine went looking for a knife in the house. After the attack, she tweeted photos of her eyes swollen shut with bruising, along with other injuries, including broken teeth, a broken nose (and other facial bones), organ damage, and a fractured ribs (Kaye 2017).
- Giants Kicker Josh Brown Brown was arrested in 2015 and was charged with assaulting his wife. Various police and court records noted that Brown had assaulted her nearly two dozen times, including at least once, when she was pregnant. The league investigated the matter for nearly a year—In the end, Brown was suspended for one game (Reimer 2016).

Feminist criminologists contend that such tragedies (and the tendencies of lax punishment) are the result of a historic, yet pervasive violent gender hierarchy that privileges male entitlement and maintains a deep societal contempt for the lives of girls and women. As Delaney and Madigan 2015:220) write:

> As a microcosm of society, we are not surprised that there are some athletes involved in domestic violence as this violent and unethical behavior exists throughout society. Sports leagues are not the only organizations that need to address the serious nature of domestic violence, as any civil society that tolerates or turns a blind eye to domestic violence should be ashamed of itself.

***

In the remaining portions of this chapter, we turn to other prominent sporting criminological concerns. We begin with illegitimate vs legitimate on-the-field sporting violence.

Prominent Criminological Concerns in Sport: Illegitimate vs Legitimate on-the-field Sporting Violence

In sports, such as boxing, football, hockey, MMA, aggressive physical contact is an expected part of the contest. The law recognizes this as the "implied consent doctrine: that is, participants voluntarily assume certain risks of injury or violence during a sport activity" (Epstein 2009: paragraph 6). Howevever, at what point does aggressive sporting play become an intentional and excessive use of force that will subject an athlete to criminal liability?

Examples of illegitimate violence include:

- In 2004, Todd Bertuzzi (then a forward for the Vancouver Canucks) maliciously struck his sporting opponent, Steve Moore, in the back of the head rendering him unconscious and permanently disabled. Criminal charges filed against Bertuzzi which resulted in a guilty plea of criminal assault causing bodily harm and a sentence of one year's probation plus 80 hours of community service. He also forfeited $501,926.39 US in salary and hundreds of thousands more in endorsements. Various players for Vancouver said there was a "bounty" on Moore's head in an attempt to negate his hard, aggressive (but legal) playing style (Vancouver Sun 2014).
- Also in 2004, several members of the Indiana Pacers and the Detroit Pistons of the National Basketball Association (NBA) started a fight that spread into the stands and involved multiple players, coaches, and spectators. The league suspended nine players (one of them for 73 games, which cost the player almost $5 million in salary loss) and five players pled no contest to misdemeanor assault charges. Five players were also charged with assault, and all five of them were eventually sentenced to a year on probation and community service. Additionally, five fans also faced criminal charges and were banned from attending Pistons home games for life. The fight also led the NBA to increase security presence between players and fans, and to limit the sale of alcohol (Price, 2014).

- On January 6, 1994, figure skater Nancy Kerrigan was attacked while training for the U.S. Figure Skating Championships. She was struck with a metal baton to her knee leaving unable to compete. The police eventually arrested Jeff Gillooly (the ex-husband of one of Nancy's chief rivals, Tonya Harding). With Kerrigan out, Tonya Harding won a place on the Olympic team. However, since Kerrigan's injuries were the result of a criminal assault, rather than a skating accident U.S. figure skating decided to make her part of the team and allowed her to compete at the Winter Olympics in Lillehammer, Norway. Ultimately Kerrigan won a silver medal, and Harding returned facing charges of conspiracy and interference with the investigation of the assault on Kerrigan. Harding eventually pled guilty to being involved in the attack, and was banned her for life from competition (Kerrigan 1996).

- In 1977, Kermit Washington (of the LA Lakers) punched Rudy Tomjanovich (of the Houston Rockets) during an NBA game. Washington's punch fractured Tomjanovich's skull, nearly killing him. Washington was fined $10, 000 and suspended for 60 days. Cobbs (1985) writes, "A lawsuit growing out of the incident was settled out of court in 1979. The Rockets filed a $1.8 million suit against the Lakers for the loss of Tomjanovich's services" (paragraph 39). Cobbs (1985) goes on to note that the punch had a positive effect on the game of basketball as league officials stepped up their policing and punishment of fighting within the game.

- In 1996, a player from St. Pius high school in Albuquerque, NM—with his father's help—shaved down his helmet buckles to a razors edge in order to cut several players from the opposing team. At least five players suffered cuts and one had to be taken to the hospital for stiches. The student was banned from expelled and banned from competition. The father was sentenced to several days in jail and was charged with conspiring to commit aggravated assault with a deadly weapon (Associated Press 1996).

- On December 29, 1978—Woody Hayes, the famed 65-year-old coach of the Ohio State Buckeyes punched an opposing player. When the player, Charlie Bauman, of Clemson University, intercepted a pass, Coach Hayes ran over to him and threw a punch at Bauman and grabbed at the players neck. Hayes apparently yelled yell at Bauman, "You SOB, I just lost my job!"(Bennett 2013: Paragraph 10).The next morning, Hayes was fired. Though no criminal charges were ever filed, Hayes never coached again.

- In 2012, the coaching staff of the Orleans Saints, were found to have institutionalized a "bounty system" (at least for a period of 3 years) whereby players were rewarded with cash to players who deliberately injured an opponent. NFL Commissioner Roger Goodell responded with some of the most severe sanctions in the league's history. Defensive coordinator Gregg Williams was suspended indefinitely, though this would be overturned the following year. Head coach Sean Payton was suspended for the entire 2012 season—the first time in modern NFL history that a head coach has been suspended for any reason (Schefter, ESPN Chicago, and Associated Press 2012).

Assignment

After reading these case examples, what theories do you think best apply to explaining why the acts occurred? Is it a combination, or none? Please apply your own sociological and criminological imaginations to offer explanations.

Sport Case Study

Calcio Storico and Legitimate Sport Violence

Violent fighting is normally considered a crime—but in the sport of Calcio Storico, it is the essence of the game itself and is totally legitimated. Calcio storico ("foot-game," now meaning "historic football") is an Italian sport created during the Italian Renaissance. According to several (Borden 2015, Stone 2017) it is the "original goal game," where two teams defend their side and attempt to penetrate their opponent's goal. Soccer, hockey, lacrosse, rugby, and American football are all iterations on the of this game. But in this sport, the violence and fighting is purposive and not a byproduct of frustrated gameplay.

The rules: two teams of 27 players each start the game on different sides of a sandy field (approximately 262 x 131 feet). A ball is placed in the middle. For 50 minutes, the male players/fighters do whatever it takes to get the ball into the opposing team's net—including hand-to-hand and mixed martial art combat. Head-butting, punching, elbowing, and choking are allowed. However, kicks to the head are banned. Further, it is also prohibited for more than one player to "gang-up" on an opponent. Such violations will lead to an expulsion. No substitutions are allowed for injured or expelled players. Additionally, players over 40 and those with serious criminal convictions, as well as non-Florentines are banned from the game.

AFP Contributor/Contributor/Getty Images

In gameplay, "forwards" will try to pin down their opposite numbers so their team-mates can attack with the ball and head for goal. Every time a player throws or kicks the ball above the net, the opposing team is awarded with a half point. A full point is awarded for successfully running or kicking it in.

Why?

As Stone (2017: paragraph 5) writes, "Men routinely leave the field with bloody faces and broken limbs . . . And for what?. . . .the glory. One can't put a price on being a neighborhood legend." While Bordon (2015: paragraph 9) states, players argue that it's "the sensation of [proving yourself] truly being a man".

What is the origin of the game?

Around the 13th or 14th century, noblemen in Florence developed this as a way to test their bravery, to train for war, and to honor their Christian heritage with a blood sacrifice for Lent (Williams 2013, Cathcart 2016).

What similarities do you find in this sport and the others examined thus far?

References

Borden, Sam. 2017. "A Most Dangerous Game." *New York Times*, June 30. Retrieved November 4, 2017 (https://www.nytimes.com/2015/07/01/sports/the-most-dangerous-game.html).

Cathcart, Will. 2016. "The Village Where People Celebrate Easter by Beating the Hell Out of Each Other." *Vice*, May 13. Retrieved November 4, 2017 (https://www.vice.com/en_us/article/kwka79/georgias-easter-bloodsport-lelo).

Stone, Daniel. 2017. "See the Violent Italian Sport that Inspired Modern Football." *National Geographic*, July 23. Retrieved November 4, 2017 (http://www.nationalgeographic.com/photography/proof/2017/07/italy-sport-calcio-storico-sport-photos/).

Williams, Victoria. 2013. *Weird Sports and Wacky Games*. Santa Barbara, CA: Greenwood.

Specific Sport Criminological Concerns: Gambling and Doping (Fan violence is also a major part of sporting criminology, but we are saving this discussion for the final chapter).

We start with gambling. In 1992, Congress outlawed most sports gambling with the exception of Nevada and Atlantic City (for a history of why this is, please read Barker and Britz 2000). Numerous states, have recently pushed bills to legalize sports betting—and the outcome of these efforts are still undecided as of this writing). In legal transactions, gamblers can bet on the outcome of any professional or collegiate sport, but professional and collegiate athletes however are banned from sports betting in an attempt to preserve the integrity of the game and prevent athletes from being targeted with harm or incentivized to "throw" a game.

Examples of illegal sports gambling include:

- Perhaps the most infamous case of sports gambling—the Black Sox scandal of 1919. In the world series of that year, the Cincinnati Reds beat the Chicago White Sox.

However, investigations revealed that eight players on the White Sox were guilty of underperforming in order to lose in return for a monetary payout—this is why the team is known today as the Black (darkened with scandal) Sox (Asinof 1977).

Movie Recommendation

Eight Men Out (1988) is a dramatization of the events surrounding the case against eight of the 1919 Chicago White Sox players (forever labeled by history as the "Black Sox") who were accused of accepting bribes to deliberately throw the World Series. The movie indicates that the players were particularly susceptible to this because of the deplorable way the White Sox owner, Charles Comiskey, treated them. For example, pitcher Eddie Cicotte was eligible for a $10,000 bonus if he won at least 30 games in a season, so after he won his 29th game of the year, Comiskey ordered the manager to bench him in order to prevent him from getting the bonus. Racketeers and gamblers take advantage of the situation to offer, and sometimes threaten, certain members of the team money in exchange for poor play that would guarantee a White Sox loss in the World Series. Eight players were charged with conspiracy, but all were found not guilty. Unfortunately, this did not prevent the baseball commissioner from banning the players from baseball for life.

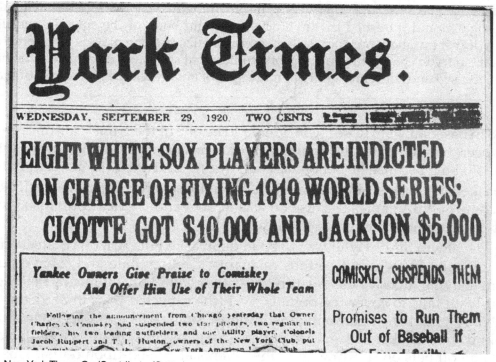

New York Times Co./Contributor/Getty Image

One of the themes in Eight Men Out is the concept of fair play. As the scandal broke, it shattered the trust of the fans and turned their heroes into criminals. While there is still debate as to who was or was not involved (and some players maintained their innocence until their deaths), the scandal mars their image to this day as all are banned from ever entering the Baseball Hall of Fame. Charles Comiskey, on the other hand, had the honor of his name being on the stadium, Comiskey Park, where the White Sox played for 80 years. This is not to suggest that treating people poorly or unfairly equates with cheating and conspiracy charges, but it highlights where bad behavior will and will not be tolerated in sports . . . and if it affects the outcome of a game to benefit or harm gamblers, it will not be tolerated.

While it has been approximately 100 years since the Black Sox scandal, it still engenders several questions. The movie implies that there were extenuating circumstances that contributed to some members of the 1919 White Sox team taking bribes (including threats made against their family and the way Comiskey treated them) and a jury found them not guilty of the charges against them.

Questions

Should the baseball commissioner have abided by the legal ruling and let the players continue to be a part of the league or was banning them from the game forever justified? Should cheating in sports (e.g., taking money to affect outcomes, taking performance enhancing drugs, altering/moving the ball to benefit one team/athlete over another, etc.) be a criminal offense or is it something that should solely be regulated, investigated and punished by the official oversight body of the sport in question? What does it say about our society that we criminalize and ban players who somehow "cheat" to try to change the outcome of a contest, but still cheer for athletes who have been accused and/or found guilty of crimes off of and unrelated to the field of play?

- Also in baseball, Pete Rose—considered to be one of the game's all-time greats—has been banned from the sports and thus far, has been denied entry into the Hall of Fame because he bet on baseball during his career (Rodenberg 2014).
- In basketball, former NBA referee Tim Donaghy said he purposively affected the outcome of NBA games because he was in debt and try to recoup his losses my betting on games he refereed (Branca 2015).
- In 1994, Stevin Smith, who was deep in debt, asked his Arizona State teammate Isaac Burton Jr. to miss free throws against Oregon State and "shave points." Point shaving, doesn't mean letting the other team win—it means making sure your team fails to cover the point spread (the expected margin of victory) projected by established gambling institutions. Smith was approached by "underground" bookmakers (illegal accountants for gambling organizations that accept and pay off bets on sporting and other events at agreed-upon odds). This act of point shaving by two members of the Arizona State basketball team became one of the nation's most notorious sports gambling scandals. In an agreement struck with federal prosecutors, Smith and Burton pleaded guilty to conspiracy charges.

The two former Sun Devils admitted taking bribes for fixing four games and Smith served time in prison (Associated Press 1997).

- What about fantasy sport? Are fantasy sports fixed? In fantasy sport, participants go online to online game where assemble imaginary or virtual teams of real players of a professional sport. These participant's teams compete (and bets may be made) based on the statistical performance of those players' players in actual games. This performance is converted into points that are compiled and totaled. Fantasy operators such as DraftKings and FanDuel have come under scrutiny recently as news broke that their employees were scoring among the top money-winners each week. After a DraftKings employee won a major jackpot on FanDuel's site in October 2015, the New York State attorney general began an inquiry into whether employees of the companies used inside information to prey on customers on each other's sites (Easterbrook 2015).

Problems Associated with Gambling

Delany and Madigan (2015: 196–197) write:

> On the one hand, most people bet low stakes and can absorb defeat if their bet loses. On the other hand, people who make large bets and cannot really afford to lose are bound to face harsh economic realities as it becomes easier to gamble one's fortune . . . to quote CEO of Las Vegas Sands Corp. Sheldon Adelson, 'click your mouse, lose your house.'

Beyond the potential for personal financial loss and debt, the NCAA opposes all forms of legal and illegal sports wagering, believing it makes student athletes susceptible to organized crime and targets for harm. Though, proponents of gambling have argued that legalizing it would lessen the influence of illegitimate **bookmakers** (an accountant that accepts and pays off bets on sporting and other events at agreed-upon odds) and allow the state to better police game fixing and the targeting of athletes because they could "see" the vast sums of money being wagered and investigate anything that seems extreme and suspicious (CBS 60 Minutes 2011)—as opposed to illegal gambling, where everything is under the radar and out of sight.

Should Sport Betting be Legalized?

Some argue that since sport betting is already occurring (law enforcement officials estimate that more than $150 billion is placed annually with illegal bookmakers and with offshore accounts), it would be best to legalize it and regulate it.

What is your perspective on this issue? List the pros and cons of the criminalization vs legalization debate.

Now we turn to a brief discussion of drugs and sporting criminology.

Another example of Zemiology and a Sports Entity as a Criminal Organization

Heidi Krieger and a body forever changed by steroids

Heidi Krieger, once an athlete of the steroid-fueled East German sports program, "did not ask questions when her coaches gave her daily 'vitamins' with her also daily extended weight-lifting sessions," which enabled her, at one point over a two-week stretch, to lift more "than 100 tons" in the weight room (Pells 2015: paragraph 1). Krieger, competed in the shot put for East Germany in 1987—but never made the Olympics. She did however win a gold medal at the 1986 European Championships.

Krieger, without her knowledge, or consent, was a test subject of "State Plan 1425"—a systematic plan of East Germany to build superior athletes (with then, undetectable) steroids. The plan ultimately grew her muscle mass, but stole away her womanhood.

Heidi Krieger is now Andreas Krieger.

AFP/Stringer/Getty Images

He (Andreas Krieger) says that the chemicals altered his female body so profoundly that he felt he had no choice but to transition male.

The decision to become Andreas alienated him from his biological family, but when the secret program was exposed, he met other athletes who were also part of the program and found both symbolic and newly chosen family members. One of those new family members was the former East German swimmer Ute Krause.

In 2002, they married and Ute says of their marriage: "With her husband, she has no need to explain herself and the similar pain she experiences as a result of the steroids, It's like the German proverb: Geklagtes Leid ist halbes Leid. Suffering shared is suffering halved" (Brown 2015: paragraph 19).

References

Brown, Oliver. 2015. "'The person who pays for everything is the athlete'" *The Guardian*, November 14. Retrieved November 4, 2017 (http://www.telegraph.co.uk/sport/others-ports/athletics/11996319/The-person-who-pays-for-everything-is-the-athlete.html?version=meter+at+null&module=meter-Links&pgtype=Blogs&contentId=&mediaId=&referrer=&priority=true&action=click&contentCollection=meter-links-click).

Pells. Eddie. 2015. "Former East German athlete testifies to the evils of doping." *The San Diego Union-Tribune*, November 12. Retrieved November 13, 2017 (http://www.sandiegouniontribune.com/sdut-former-east-german-athlete-testifies-to-the-evils-2015nov27-story.html).

A now infamous survey asked U.S. Olympians and aspiring Olympians the following questions: (1) if you were offered a banned performance enhancing drug, with the guarantee that you would win and not get caught, would you take the substance? (195 athletes said yes while three said no); and (2) would you take a banned substance that would ensure you would win every competition you entered for the next 5 years, with a guarantee that you not get caught, but also with the guarantee that you will die from the side effects? (more than half of the athlete said yes) (Conner and Mazanov 2009).

What does this tell us about American society and our willingness to win athletic fame and fortune at any cost?

Another example: In 2006, American Floyd Landis won the Tour de France that was stripped of this metal after a failed drug test. Despite claiming his innocence, he finally eventually came forward in 2010, admitting to drug use in charging former teammate Lance Armstrong with cheating as well. Landis said publicly that he saw Lance Armstrong receiving blood transfusions during races (the use of blood transfusions—or blood doping-increases one's red blood cell count thus enhancing their endurance).

Lance Armstrong was once one of America's most beloved athletes—he won seven Tour de France titles (now stripped) and is barred for life from all sports events under the auspices of the World Anti-Doping Agency. Armstrong is also a cancer survivor. In 1996, he received a diagnosis of testicular cancer that also went to his brain and stomach. With his chances of survival put at less than 50 percent, he underwent surgery and chemotherapy. But he recovered and formed a cancer charity that would bring in millions of dollars in contributions through the sale of yellow wristbands with the word "Livestrong." Several medical professionals have speculated that his drug use (including steroids, testosterone, cortisone, growth hormone and EPO—an illegal performance-enhancing drug) may have contributed to the growth and development of his cancer (Moisse 2012).

The prohibition around, and punishment of, the use of performance-enhancing substances has traditionally been dealt with by sport regulatory bodies. And yet, despite the work of regulatory bodies, doping continues to exist. It has been argued that doping is akin to defrauding fellow athletes from an income, and on this premise, they feel it should also be considered alongside criminal activities such as financial fraud—and maybe this is the only way to lessen doping—charge those found guilty with fraud (Nitz 2012).

We know that despite these well-publicized examples; despite the risk of being expelled and banned from one's sport; despite the possible negative impacts on one's health, athletes will continue to take performance-enhancing drugs for as long as the "winning is everything" culture is dominant in sport. Of concern are the symbolic, cultural, and institutional forces that encourage harm against one's self—especially as expressed in the context of drug use to achieve better performance. How do we change these realities? And can they be changed—What are your ideas?

Specific Criminological Concerns in Sport: Sport as Social Control

In this final section, we examine how sport has been used to prevent crime and enhance social control. Indeed, research suggests that sport may be used to provide life skills training, to build resilience, reduce anti-social behavior, increase adaptive and positive behavior and address risk factors related to violence (Armstrong and Hodges-Ramon 2015, Goombridge 2016).

For some, sport provides an antidote to deviance as it is believed to divert troubled individuals from the lure of crime, teach them to abide by societal norms and motivate them to pursue more positive futures (remember our "saints and roughnecks" discussion). One of the more well-known sport intervention programs in this mode was the Midnight Basketball League (MBL). The program, begun in the United States in 1986, was premised on the idea that basketball could reduce inner city crime by providing poor, young men (aged predominately between 17 and 25) with a safe and constructive activity between 10 p.m. and 2 a.m.—the time considered to be "high crime" hours. During its first 3 years, MBL was credited with a general drop in crime in the areas of its implementation. The reported benefits of participation included general enjoyment, reduced intergang violence, the forming new relationships, the acquisition of new skills, and purposive time management.

Other similar interventions include Hoops in the Hood, The Carroll Academy Sport program, and InnerCity Weightlifting:

The "Hoops in the Hood" program is a network of community-run basketball games in 14 Chicago neighborhoods. "Designed to literally take back the streets from gangs and violence, the program sets up in public safety 'hot spots' in parks and on blocks that most residents avoid on an average summer night" (Vogel 2016: paragraph 1). In addition to engaging young people during the summer months, Hoops is a structure for local residents to take back their streets from criminal elements. Those studying the program suggest that crime goes down on blocks that have been closed off for Hoops games (Vogel 2016).

In its inaugural year, "SC Featured" (a segment of ESPN's SportsCenter that reports on stories that fall outside of traditional sports news), produced two pieces that brought together sport and the criminal justice system. The first, *Losing to Win* tells the story of the Carroll Academy Lady Jags who had lost 213 straight basketball games. Carroll Academy is a school for grades 6-12 and is operated by the Carroll County Juvenile Court to keep the youth out of state custody. The youth are direct referrals from schools and the court system for things like disorderly conduct, aggravated assault, shoplifting, truancy, drugs and alcohol, etc. Carroll Academy maintains a basketball program where the students are often court ordered to play. Most of them have never played basketball before (or any sport for that matter), but they are given a crash course and taught the basic rules of the game. Crucial to the philosophy of their basketball program is that it is not at all about winning, but about learning how to overcome adversity and acquiring the tools necessary to "win" in the game of life, including: anger management, fighting through disappointment, working with others, and fortitude (Vimeo links: Losing to Win: https://vimeo.com/65832837).

A second piece from SC Featured, *Redefining Strength*, tells the story of InnerCity Weightlifting—which is a gym that works with traumatized and often criminalized youth. InnerCity Weightlifting was founded by Jon Feinman, who initially came into inner city Boston as an AmeriCorps member and was tasked with engaging at-risk kids via sports. He chose weightlifting as "that sport" and found that while weightlifting was the "hook," that brought kids to the gym, it was the ultimately the relationships formed within the that made the real difference in the lives of the participants. The piece profiles not only Feinman, but many of the youth who have benefited from the program. Again, these are youth who have not ony committed crimes (often violent crimes) but who have also been victims themselves. For these individuals, the program starts by being a safe place away from violence where they can build trust in each other and learn the discipline of weightlifting. Following this, the program helps members get their GEDs, and trains to become personal trainers (and works with them to build a clientele list and earn a legitimate living through weight loss and strength coaching/training.

One of the things that both of these pieces suggest is that: while engagement in sport does not guarantee that you will escape the things in the community that are hard or harmful; sport, and more so, the caring adult coach and mentor, can change how you will engage and respond to those negative situations. Both programs mention reductions in interpersonal conflicts, making better life choices and an increased ability to persevere when things get tough. As Randy Hatch, head coach of the Lady Jags tells his team after yet another loss:

> This is nothing compared to what you are going to face in your life. Twenty, twenty-five, thirty years from now, when I'm gone, and you come home and you find out your husband has lost his job, that's adversity . . . This is nothing. This will prepare you for that.

In the end, these sport programs serve as a method of crime reduction by giving persons the chance to take a different path, and break the cycle of poverty and/or engagement in illegal or violent activities.

Questions for Class Discussion: Within the context of this book, these pieces bring up several relevant questions. Social bonding theory basically argues that individuals who have stronger attachments to conventional society are less likely to engage in deviant or criminal behaviors . . . how does this relate to these two stories? In a previous chapter, we looked at the intersection between poverty and sport and there is an obvious connection to poverty in these pieces . . . how does the information you learned about in that chapter connect to these stories? These stories present interesting case studies on the power of sport to act as a crime deterrent for individuals by giving them skills and resources to avoid some of the behaviors and situations that might have previously gotten them in trouble . . . what are your thoughts about using sport in this way and does it say something about the social value of sport? (Redefining Strength: https://vimeo.com/88020831).

Sports in Correctional Institutions

In terms of enabling social control and positive time management, research on sport in jail and prison settings has some supportive findings. For example, yoga has been offered in correctional institutions as a way to occupy inmates' time in positive ways, teach mindfulness, and improve physical health (Prison Yoga Project 2017). And returning once again to a discussion of chess, the play of chess provides many of the above attributes, including increasing creative intelligence, patience, and cause-and-effect relational thinking (Sholtis and Nicotera 2016).

Other traditions have used dance (in all of its permutations, see Heckel 2015) and boxing (Meek 2014) to promote health, personal expression, aggression release in prosocial and regulated forms, and freedom (through movement).

But sport can also be harmful or at least mixed in its application and results in correctional facilities. Consider the two following examples:

Documentary Recommendation

Prison Fighters: 5 Rounds to Freedom (2017) examines a highly controversial practice in Thailand's criminal justice system whereby inmates can earn their freedom by winning a series of Muay Thai fights. In Muay Thai, competitors fight erect, like in boxing, but elbows, knees, and kicks are allowed. In terms of meaning, MUAY literally means "combat," while the word THAI is reflective of the Thai nation, Therefore, the word Muay Thai is translatable as "Thai boxing/combat," or the "nation's sport."

Under the law in Thailand, violent criminals, including those convicted of murder and sexual assault, have been freed and, in some cases, fully absolved of their crimes through their participation in prison fights. As Stephen Espinoza, Executive Vice President and General Manager, for SHOWTIME Sports says:

> Redemption is a common metaphor in sports stories, but this is a story about actual redemption and rehabilitation, with prisoners literally fighting for their release from prison. This film brings viewers inside a personal story of crime and punishment, set against a societal debate about the meaning of justice, rehabilitation and the opportunity for a second chance (SHOWTIME Press Release 2017).

Why is this the case?

Culturally, the sport its believed to foster discipline, focus and a way to tame anger and aggression. And prison officials say that a sentence reduction is not automatic especially if a prisoner behaves badly, no matter how skilled he is as a fighter. But, if a prisoner shows real commitment to improving himself then we are willing to offer incentives such as a sentence reduction. The documentary centers on Noy Khaopan, an incarcerated person convicted of murder, and American Cody Moberly of Wichita, Kansas, a professional fighter who serves as Noy's opponent in his final fight for freedom. The film also focuses on former fighters who have "earned" their way to freedom through the Prison Fight system.

Discussion

Granting convicted felons parole for sporting prowess is controversial—why should convicted murderers earn their freedom with the use of their fists and feet? Craft an argument that defends this unique tradition of criminal justice and sport—as well as an argument that critiques this tradition.

Reference

SHOWTIME Press Release. 2017. "Spring Programming Preview." *SHOWTIME,* February 3. Retrieved November 4, 2017 (http://www.cbspressexpress.com/showtime/releases/view?id=47009).

Prison rodeo: An interview with journalist Aviva Shen

Aviva Shen is a New Orleans-based journalist whose work focuses on criminal justice.

What is the Angola Prison Rodeo?

Aviva Shen: A 53-year-old tradition at the biggest and most notorious prison in Louisiana the incarceration capital of the world. . . . For $20 a ticket, thousands flood into the 18,000-acre prison each Sunday in October and one weekend in April to watch inmates battle bucking horses and angry bulls.

Is it dangerous?

Aviva Shen: Inmates receive no training before they go out to perform. Reports of serious injuries have resulted in helmets, mouth-guards and vests for participants. These precautions are about the only way the tradition has evolved since it began in the 1960s. Despite the danger, there's always a waiting list of inmates who want to risk their bodies . . .

Why?

Aviva Shen: Money. Inmates are awarded varying amounts of cash depending on the riskiness of the event. There's "convict poker," in which a bull is released on four inmates at a poker table. Whoever manages to stay in their chair the longest wins $250. The most dangerous event is "guts and glory," where inmates try to pluck a poker chip from between the horns of a charging bull for a chance at the grand prize: $500. That's a windfall compared with what he can earn the rest of the year, when inmates are required to work for wages of between 2 cents and 75 cents an hour.

William Widmer/Contributor/Getty Images

This sounds exploitative. Is it?

Aviva Shen: Prison officials are adamant that no one is forced to participate in the rodeo. But the economics of the prison system challenge the definition of choice. The rodeo is the only chance most Angola inmates get to make a livable income. Further, rodeo revenue props up virtually all of the programs that shape inmates' lives, including trade schools, activity clubs, an award-winning magazine, and the prison hospice. Many clubs set up rodeo concession stands, where they raise an estimated $80,000 a day. But, yes, this pay scale—coupled with the fact that more than 75 percent of its 6,300 inmates are black—is why Angola is frequently called a modern-day slave plantation. . . . this is a distinctly American spin on the Roman Colosseum.

Questions

What are your reactions to this? What are the positive and negative elements of prison rodeo as it is conducted at Angola?

Excerpted from: Shen, Aviva. 2016. "Angola prison rodeo offers risks and rewards for Louisiana's hard-knock lifers." *Guardian*, October 29. Retrieved November 4, 2017 (http://www.theguardian.com/us-news/2016/oct/29/angola-prison-rodeo-louisiana). Copyright Guardian News & Media Ltd 2017.

CHAPTER SUMMARY

This chapter was designed to introduce you to sport criminology—and is so doing, we explored the notion that sport can play a powerful role in contributing to crime. Instances of institutional corruption, harm-making, match-fixing, doping, and violence can go a long way to challenge the assumed beauty and goodness of sport. Further, as Armstrong and Hodges-Ramon (2015: paragraph 66) write, "Given that sport has become a nexus for criminal activity, it could be argued that introducing it into the lives of young people inadvertently offers them avenues to entertain criminal or at least anti-social and ethically questionable behaviors."

But this said, research has also shown that sport may be used to control crime and enforce social order. Indeed, there is certainly evidence to suggest that sport can be an effective vehicle to alter the lives of individuals, especially if it comes with good mentorship, education, and support. In the end, remember that sport is reflective of society—it will show both the good the bad and the ugly. And has the power to destroy lives or transform them for the better.

Extra-Inning: What in a Name?

The naming of college sports stadiums is big business (typically, a half million dollars or more, a year for several years). But what if your school accepted a deal from a corporation that you considered ethically dubious in its business practices?

Consider the case of Florida Atlantic University (FAU). In 2013, the university accepted a deal (later withdrawn after student protest) with the GEO Group for 12 years at $500,000 per year. GEO group is a Florida-based company specializing in privatized corrections, detention, and mental health treatment. Stated differently, they are a for profit prison that makes money off of incarcerating people—a moral quandary for many. The corporation had also drawn criticism for several alleged incidents of inmate mistreatment—including the deaths of persons allegedly denied medical treatment. After people began looking into the company's history, a GEO Group spokesman tried to whitewash the company's Wikipedia by removing references to those controversies (Vint 2013).

All of this led to FAU student petitions against the company asking that their university disassociate itself from GEO Group.

Questions

What do you think of this? Should students have a say in the naming rights of their university? Should a school concern itself with the negative association or symbolism of "brand association" and naming rights (please refer back to the chapter on sports mascots to help contextualize this discussion).

Reference

Vint, Patrict. 2013. "Too late for FAU's prison sponsor GEO Group to Erase its Wikipedia record." *SB Nation*, Feb 21. Retrieved November 13, 2017 (https://www.sbnation.com/college-football/2013/2/21/4011532/geo-group-fau-football-stadium-name).

Extra-Inning: Futuristic Sport Crime Films

Cultural critics suggest that Americans are predominately in love to with two core activities: crime and sport (Sirota 2011, Sperber 2011). Indeed, American society tends to have a tough-on-crime sentencing and incarceration mentality, with the belief that prisoners should be treated harshly (even though research shows that treating prisoners with dignity can reduce crime Dagan and Teles 2016).

And these punitive notions are often reflected in our material and cultural creations, especially film. In particular, the genre of sci-fi has a history of theorizing creative ways to combat crime vis sport. Here is a small sampling of this sub-genre of sci-fi:

The Running Man (1987) = Set in a dystopian United States, a very popular television show called "The Running Man" pits convicted criminal "runners" against professional killers. If the can escape/survive the various trials s/he is set free.

The Condemned (2007) = death penalty inmates are "purchased" by a wealthy television producer and taken to a desolate island where they must fight to the death against other condemned killers from all corners of the world, with freedom going to the sole survivor.

Death Race (2008) = Inmates are forced to participate in a road-race (with modified and weaponized cars) where the goal is to kill each other in order to be set free.

Gamer (2009) = In the future, gamers, through technological mind control, force death row convicts to battle each other to the death. If the person on death row survives, they will be set free.

The Hunger Games (2012) = Set in an alternative universe similar to a highly stratified American society, youth from across the nation are randomly selected to participate in a compulsory annual televised set of death match contests. The purpose is to suppress rebellion and criminal activity against the state by psychologically defeating and exhausting the population.

The Purge (2013) = Similar to the above, the movie is set in an alternative U.S. society, where an annual activity known as the purge is a governmentally sanctioned 12-hour time period where all illegal acts (including murder) are decriminalized. The purpose is to rid the society of persons deemed unworthy and a drain on societal resources.

As you will note, particular similarities exist in each of these films.

Questions

Why do these types of films (with their similar plotlines) continue to be popular? Why do we present the criminal population as dispensable and brutalization as entertaining? What do these films "say" about our obsession with vengeance, crime, and sport? Finally, what other films, fit into this genre and why?

References

Dagan, David and Steven Teles. 2016. *Prison Break: Why Conservatives Turned Against Mass Incarceration.* New York, NY: Oxford University Press.

Sirota, David. 2011. *Back to Our FutureL How the 1980s Explain the World We Live in Now.* New York, NY: Ballantine Books.

Sperber, Murry. 2011. *Beer and Circus: How Big-Time College Sports Has Crippled Undergraduate Education.* Henry Holt and Co.

CHAPTER REFERENCES

Apel, Robert and Raymond Parternoster. 2009. "Understanding "Criminogenic" Corporate Culture." Pp. 15–33 in S.S. Simpson, D. Weisburd (eds.), *The Criminology of White-Collar Crime.* New York, NY: Springer.

Armstrong, Gary and Luke Hodges-Ramon. 2015. "Sport and Crime." *Oxford Handbooks Online,* Retrieved November 4, 2017(http://www.oxfordhandbooks.com/view/10.1093/oxfordhb/9780199935383.01.0001/oxfordhb-9780199935383-e-87#oxfordhb-9780199935383-e-87-bibItem126).

Asinof, Eliot. 1977. *Eight Men Out: The Black Sox and the 1919 World Series.* Holt, Reinhart, and Winston.

Associated Press. 1996. "Cutting Edge?: Father Turns Son Into a Weapon by Sharpening Buckle on Helmet." *LA Times*, October 23. Retrieved November 13, 2017 (http://articles.latimes.com/1996-10-23/sports/sp-56796_1_buckle-on-helmet).

Associated Press. 1997. "Point-Shaving Scandal Hits Arizona State." *LA Times*, December 6. Retrieved November 13, 2017 (http://articles.latimes.com/1997/dec/06/sports/sp-61336).

Associated Press. 2013. "NFL, ex-players agree to $765M settlement in concussions suit." *NFL.com*, August 29. Retrieved November 4, 2017 (http://www.nfl.com/news/story/0ap1000000235494/article/nfl-explayers-agree-to-765m-settlement-in-concussions-suit).

Barker, Thomas and Marjie T. Britz. 2000. *Jokers Wild: Legalized Gambling in the Twenty-first Century.* Santa Barbara, CA: Praeger.

Bennett, Brian. 2013. "Woody Hayes' last game coaching." *ESPN*, December 30. Retrieved November 13, 2017 (http://www.espn.com/college-football/bowls13/story/_/id/10215217/the-punch-ended-woody-hayes-career).

Branca, Ashley. 2015. "Ex-NBA ref Tim Donaghy: 'Organized crime will always have a hand in sports' *The Guardian*, May 2015. Retrieved November 13, 2017 (https://www.theguardian.com/sport/2015/may/22/ex-nba-ref-tim-donaghy-organized-will-always-have-a-hand-in-sports).

Brown, Theresa, Kenneth E. Summer and Romy Nocera. 2002. "Understanding Sexual Aggression Against Women." *Journal of Interpersonal Violence* 17(9): 937–952.

Borden, Sam. 2017. "A Most Dangerous Game." *New York Times*, June 30. Retrieved November 4, 2017 (http://www.nytimes.com/2015/07/01/sports/the-most-dangerous-game.html).

CBS 60 Minutes. 2011. "Sports bettor Billy Walter's winning streak." *CBS News*, July 17. Retrieved November 4, 2017 (http://www.cbsnews.com/news/sports-bettor-billy-walters-winning-streak17-07-2011/).

Cobbs, Chris. 1985. "The Punch: Tomjanovich and Washington Both Still Feel the Pain From That Terrible Moment." *LA Times*, January 28. Retrieved November 12, 2017 (http://articles.latimes.com/print/1985-01-28/sports/sp-10262_1_kermit-washington).

Connor James M., and Jason Mazanov. 2009. "Would you dope? A general population test of the Goldman dilemma." *British Journal of Sports Medicine*. 43:871–872.

Crime Insider Staff. 2014. "NFL player who killed girlfiend in murder-suicide had brain damage." *Crime Insider*, September 30. Retrieved (https://www.cbsnews.com/news/nfl-player-who-killed-wife-in-murder-suicide-had-brain-damage/).

Crosset, Todd W., Jeffery R. Benedict, and Mark A. McDonald. 1995. "Male Student-Athletes reported for Sexual Assault: A Survey of Campus Police Departments and Judicial Affairs Officers." *Journal of Sport and Social* Issues 19(2):126–140.

Delaney, Tim and Tim Madigan. 2015. *The Sociology of Sports: An Introduction.* Jefferson NC: McFarland Press.

Easterbrook, Greg. 2015. "DraftKings and FanDuel Are Not Your Friends." *The New York Times*, October 5. Retrieved November 13, 2017 (https://www.nytimes.com/2015/10/07/upshot/the-big-winners-in-fantasy-football-and-the-rest-of-us.html?_r=0).

Epstein, Adam. 2009. "Incorporating the Criminal Law in Sport Studies." *The Sport Journal* Volume 19: http://thesportjournal.org/article/incorporating-the-criminal-law-in-sport-studies/

Galliher, John F. 1988. *The Criminology of Edwin Sutherland.* Piscataway, NJ: Transaction Publishers.

Goombridge, Nic. 2016. *Sports Criminology.* Chicago, IL: Polity Press.

Heckel, Aimee. 2015. "Dance Program Offers Women in Prison a Taste of 'Freedom.'" *Daily Camera,* November 11. Retrieved November 4, 2017 (http://www.dailycamera.com/lifestyles/ci_29173204/alchemy-movement-brings-dance-2b-free-colorado-women-prisoners).

Hill, Jemele. 2014. "Janay Rice, in her own words" *ESPN*, November 28. Retrieved November 12 (http://www.espn.com/nfl/story/_/id/11913473/janay-rice-gives-own-account-night-atlantic-city).

Hirschi, Travis. 1969. *Causes of Delinquency.* Berkeley: University of California Press.

Kaye, Diane. 2017. "War Machine faces life sentence" *CNN*, March 21. Retrieved (November 12, 2017 (http://www.cnn.com/2017/03/20/us/war-machine-guilty-christy-mack-beating/index.html).

Kerrigan, Nancy. 1996. Nancy Kerrigan: In My Own Words. New York, NY: Hyperion Books.

Ladika, Susan. 2017. "Sports and Sexual Assault." *CQ Researcher,* April 26. Retrieved November 4, 2017 (http://library.cqpress.com/cqresearcher/document.php?id=cqresrre2017042800).

Meek, Rosie. 2014. *Sport in Prison: Exploring the Role of Physical Activity in Penal Practices and in Correctional Settings.* Abingdon: Routledge.

Mez, Jesse, Daniel H. Daneshvar, Patrick T. Kiernan, Bobak Abdolmohammadi, Victor E. Alvarez, Bertrand R. Huber, Michael L. Alosco, Todd M. Solomon, Christopher J. Nowinski, Lisa McHale, Kerry A. Cormier, Caroline A. Kubilus, Brett M. Martin, Lauren Murphy, Christine M. Baugh, Phillip H. Montenigro, Christine E. Chaisson, Yorghos Tripodis, Neil W. Kowall, Jennifer Weuve, Michael D. McClean, Robert C. Cantu, Lee E. Goldstein, Douglas I. Katz, Robert A. Stern, Thor D. Stein, and Ann C. McKee. 2017. "Clinicopathological Evaluation of Chronic Traumatic Encephalopathy in Players of American Football." *JAMA* 318(4):360–370.

Moisse, Katie. 2012. "Lance Armstrong's Livestrong Legacy Stained by Doping-Cancer Link." *ABC News,* January 17. Retrieved November 4, 2017 (http://abcnews.go.com/Health/lance-armstrongs-livestrong-legacy-stained-doping-cancer-link/story?id=18220378).

Morris, Benjamin. 2014. "More on The Rate of Domestic Violence Arrests Among NFL Players." *FiveThirtyEight,* October 2. Retrieved November 4, 2017 (http://fivethirtyeight.com/datalab/more-on-the-rate-of-domestic-violence-arrests-among-nfl-players/).

Nitz, Alistair. 2012. "Doping Must Be Criminal Offence to Finally Eradicate It." *ROAR,* October 29. Retrieved November 4, 2017 (http://www.theroar.com.au/2012/10/29/doping-must-be-criminal-offence-to-finally-eradicate-it/).

Price, Satchel. 2014. "How 'Malice at the Palace' changed the careers of 6 key Pacers." *SB Nation,* November 19. Retrieved November 12, 2017 (https://www.sbnation.com/2014/11/19/7246943/malice-at-the-palace-anniversary-pacers-pistons-ron-artest).

Prison Yoga Project. 2017. "What we do." *Prison Yoga Project.* Retrieved November 4, 2017 (https://prisonyoga.org/what-we-do/).

Raftner, Nicole. 2008. *Criminal Brain: Understanding Biological Theories of Crime.* New York, NY: NYU Press.

Reimer, Alex. 2016. "Giants kicker Josh Brown admitted to abusing his wife, according to police documents" *SB Nation*, October 20. Retrieved November 12, 2017 (https://www.sbnation.com/nfl/2016/10/19/13341358/josh-brown-giants-domestic-violence-arrest).

Rennison, Callie Marie., and Mary Dodge. 2018. *Introduction to Criminal Justice*, 2nd ed. Los Angeles, CA: Sage.

Renzetti, Claire M. 2013. *Feminist Criminology.* New York, NY: Routledge.

Repetto, Nicole K. 2016. "Domestic Violence, Sexual Assault, and Elite Athletes: Analyzing Arrest and Conviction Rates." *Senior Honors Theses.* 485. *Eastern Michigan University.* Retrieved November 4, 2017 (http://commons.emich.edu/honors/485).

Rodenberg, Ryan. 2014. "Pete Rose's Reckless Gamble." *The Atlantic*, August 22. Retrieved November 13, 2017 (https://www.theatlantic.com/entertainment/archive/2014/08/why-pete-rose-still-cant-be-absolved/378866/).

Schefter, Adam, ESPN Chicago, and Associated Press. 2012. "NFL: Saints defense had 'bounty' fund." ESPN, March 4. Retrieved November 13, 2017 (http://www.espn.com/nfl/story/_/id/7638603/new-orleans-saints-defense-had-bounty-program-nfl-says).

Schwartz, Nick. 2015. "Report: Floyd Mayweather's Camp bans Rachel Nichols, Michelle Beadle from ttending fight." *For the Win*, May 2. Retrieved November 12, 2017 (http://ftw.usatoday.com/2015/05/floyd-mayweather-bans-rachel-nichols-michelle-beadle).

Sholtis, Emily and Anna Nicotera. 2016. "Inmates and Checkmates: Using Chess in Prisons. *Chess Club*, April 2016. Retrieved November 4, 2017 (http://saintlouischessclub.org/blog/inmates-and-checkmates-using-chess-prisons).

Siers-Poisson, Judith. 2014. "Student-Athletes Commit Rape, Sexual Assaults More Often Than Peers." *Wisconsin Public Radio*, January 2. Retrieved November 4, 2017 (http://www.wpr.org/student-athletes-commit-rape-sexual-assaults-more-often-peers).

Vancouver Sun, Staff. 2014. "Former Canuck Todd Bertuzzi, Steve Moore settle career-ending hit lawsuit." *Vancouver Sun*, August 20. Retrieved November 12, 2017 (http://www.vancouversun.com/sports/former+canuck+todd+bertuzzi+steve+moore+settle+career+ending+lawsuit+with+video/10130629/story.html).

Vogel, Carl. 2016. "Ten Years of Hoops in the Hood: An Oral History." *LISC Chicago,* July 22. Retrieved November 4, 2017 (http://www.lisc-chicago.org/news/2686).

Ward, Joe, Josh Williams and Sam Manchester. 2017. "110 NFL Brains." *New York Times*, July 25. Retrieved November 4, 2017 (http://www.nytimes.com/interactive/2017/07/25/sports/football/nfl-cte.html).

Wolfgang, Marvin E. 1963. "Criminology and the Criminologist." *Journal of Criminal Law and Criminology* 54(2):155–162.

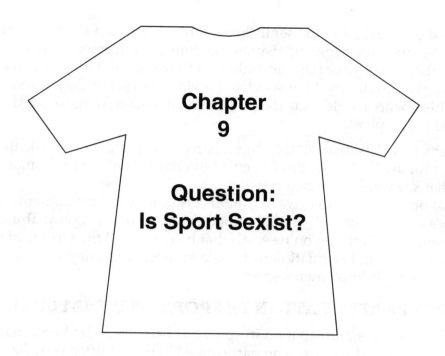

Chapter 9

Question: Is Sport Sexist?

Student Outcomes

After reading this chapter, you will be able to do the following:

- Discuss the historic and contemporary barriers to full sport participation for women.
- Identify female athletes and women's sports movements that have challenged sexism and advanced women's participation in sport.
- Detail the meanings of misogyny, abuse, sexism, and homophobia and illustrate with examples.
- Define and apply the concepts of gendered ideology and physical feminism.

In 2014, after winning her second-round match in the Australian Open, Eugenie Bouchard, was asked by a male interviewer to "give us a twirl" and show off her tennis dress. Noticeably embarrassed, Bouchard complied with a laugh and later said, "It was very unexpected." Social media erupted with chatter. Many called it sexist and questioned whether a male player would be asked to twirl after winning a match. Billie Jean King a 12-time Grand Slam winner and a longtime campaigner for equal rights in tennis responded by saying the act was "truly sexist . . . Let's focus on competition and accomplishments of both genders and not our looks" (ABC News 2015: paragraph 13).

Once she advanced to the semi-finals of the Australian she was asked in a post-game interview by Samantha Smith (a former British tennis champ), 'A lot of your fans are male, and they want to know: If you could date anyone in the world of sport, of movies – I'm sorry, they asked me to say this—who would you date?' (National Post and Associated Press 2014: Paragraph 6).

With criticism, Waldron (2014) commented, "[Y]ou'd never ask this sort of question of Rafael Nadal. . . . But Eugenie Bouchard? She's just a woman. No need to care what she thinks" (paragraph 5).

With this opening example, we highlight continuing and fundamental problems in women's athletics; namely the continued existence of **misogyny, abuse, sexism, and homophobia**. Building on research that has explored the worlds of sport and the attempted cultural regulation of female athletes, this chapter issues a critical analysis of these ills in women's sport.

WOMEN'S PARTICIPATION IN SPORT AS UNNATURAL

Historically, women's participation in sport has been trivialized and marginalized by a sexist culture and women who participated in it were often ostracized. Indeed, prior to the mid-1970s sporting activities for women were broadly absent (Gutmann 1991). It took legislation, the advocacy of women's groups, and the subversive actions of female athletes to chart a path of accepted and institutionalized play for women.

Consider the story of the first women to challenge their exclusion from the Boston Marathon. Before 1972, women were not allowed to run marathons, a sport then deemed "unsafe" for women. Cultural beliefs embedded ideas that such demanding physical activity was too damaging to the body and would cause irreparable damage to her reproductive health. Specifically, an argument held that sport could cause a woman's uterus to fall out. Please allow us a small digression on this issue: In 1898, an article in the German Journal of Physical Education argued that "violent movements of the body can cause a shift in the position and a loosening of the uterus as well as prolapse and bleeding, with resulting sterility, thus defeating a woman's true purpose in life, i.e., the bringing forth of strong children" (cited in Pfister, Gertrud 1990: 188).

In her book "Playing the Game: Sport and the Physical Emancipation of English Women, 1870–1914," McCrone (1988) writes that a woman's ovaries and uterus were thought to control her entire nature, from her disposition to her intellectual abilities.

On the basis of no scientific evidence whatsoever doctors of physiology related biology to behavior, figuring that women who displayed symptoms of aggression, ambition and competitiveness were incompletely developed and prone to disease. A woman who engaged in sport, therefore, could be sterile or transmit her unfavorable characteristics to her children who, in turn, would likely be degenerate (7).

Katherine Switzer, the first woman to officially run the Boston Marathon in 1967, recalled how, when she conducted an interview for the school newspaper, the high school girls' basketball coach told her that women would never play the men's version of basketball because "the excessive number of jump balls could displace the uterus" (Switzer 2007: 17). In a more recent example, this notion also came up in 2010 when Gian-Franco Kasper, president of the International Ski Federation, said that "the female uterus might burst during landing from a ski jump" (Beresini 2013: paragraph 6). This replicates a statement he made in a 2005 interview that ski jumping "seems not to be appropriate for ladies from a medical point of view" (Chadwick 2005: paragraph 29).

Returning now to our subversive athletes challenging the status quo: In 1966, Bobbi Gibb:

> . . . snuck into the Boston Marathon and became the first woman ever to (unofficially) run the world famous race . . . Following Gibb's lead, the next year Kathrine Switzer became the first woman to officially enter the Boston Marathon, registering under her initials K.V. Switzer and making it impossible for race officials to determine her gender. Unlike Gibb's race experience whereby the majority of her fellow runners cheered her on, Switzer's presence in the Boston Marathon was clearly unwelcome by race officials. (Epstein 2014: paragraphs 6, 8)

Jock Semple, one of the race directors, caught wind of Switzer's attempt. He tracked her down near the fourth mile marker and attempted to physically remove her race bid.

Bettmann/Contributor/Getty Images

Race official Jock Semple trying to remove Kathrine Switzer from the Boston Marathon.

In a series of famous photos that captured their encounter, Semple is shown trying to physically remove Switzer from the race, screaming, "Get the hell out of my race and give me those numbers!" (Kislevitz 2003:219). Tom Miller, her running partner, then boyfriend, and a member of the Syracuse University football team, gave Jock a body block and sent him flying through the air. Of the incident, she said, "At first, I thought we had killed him. I was stunned and didn't know what to do, but then my running coach just looked at me and said, 'Run like hell,' and I did" (Kislevitz 2002:220). Five years later, in 1973, opposition subsided and women were allowed to run in the race legitimately. Switzer eventually won the 1974 New York City Marathon in 3 hours, 7 minutes.

Women's participation and acceptance in sport was such a challenge because it was typically men who controlled power and access to such sporting worlds and whom extolled the belief that if girls and women play sports it would violate important morals grounded in culture and in "nature."

As Coakley (2000:241) points out:

> Strong women challenge the prevailing gender ideology that influences the norms, legal definitions, and opportunity structures that frame people's lives, relationships, and identities. Those who are privileged by this gender ideology describe strong women has abnormal and they put down certain women sports.

Movie Recommendation

A League of Their Own (1992)

A League of Their Own is a fictionalized comedy-drama about the Rockford Peaches, a team of the All-American Girls Professional Baseball League (AAGPBL). In real life, this league was founded by Phillip K. Wrigley and from 1943 to 1954 over 600 women played in the league (Official n.d.). While the Rockford Peaches were a real team, none of the characters are. Nonetheless, the movie presents a story that mirrors some of the historical issues faced by female athletes that persist, at least to some extent, to the present day.

Bettmann/Contributor/Getty Images

Sophie Kurys, star of the Racine Belles of the All-American Girl's Professional Baseball League, slides into the bag as a player from the South Bend Blue Sox looks on.

In the movie, two sisters, Dottie and Kit, are selected to be part of the Rockford Peaches team in the first year of the AAGPBL. Along with the other members of the team they prove to be outstanding athletes. However, they are pushed at all times to conform to gendered expectations lest they be considered too un-feminine. As stated by Ira Lowenstein who oversees the league in the film, "Every girl in this league is going to be a lady." As a result, the "girls" (all adults and some married) go through etiquette classes, learn to walk properly, receive beauty advice and are given uniforms that are skirted. In fact, one of the players, Marla, was almost not recruited in spite of her talent on the field because of her looks and mannerisms. Her father begged the scout to take her saying:

> I know my girl ain't so pretty as these girls, but that's my fault. I raised her like I would a boy. I didn't know any better. She loves to play. Don't make my little girl suffer because I messed up raising her. Please.

Additionally, on the field, the players find themselves heckled and the recipients of catcalls and discover that they need to do tricks plays to even keep the fans engaged.

By the end of the movie, it is made clear that a woman's place is in the home, not on the field. Ira puts words to this reality:

> This is what it's going to be like in the factories, too, I suppose, isn't it? "The men are back, Rosie, turn in your rivets." We told them it was their patriotic duty to get out of the kitchen and go to work; and now, when the men come back, we'll send them back to the kitchen.

From a sociological perspective, A League of Their Own brings up a variety of issues around gender. When we think about women in sports today, is there still pressure for athletes to look and act a certain way in order to be successful? For example, would Ronda Rousey have been as popular if she had looked like Marla from A League of Their Own? Are female athletes still considered un-feminine? There tends to be both a gender pay gap in sports and a difference in the size of the fan base . . . what does this say about how female athletes are viewed in society?

Official Website of the AAGPBL. n.d. League History. Online: https://www.aagpbl.org/index.cfm/pages/league/12/league-history

LANGUAGE AND GENDER INEQUALITY

This type of **gendered ideology** does not just affect female athletes—it also confronts women in sporting institutions in general. For example, in 2002, Martha Burk (then the director of the National Council of Women's Organizations) sent a letter to William "Hootie" Johnson (Chairman of the Augusta National Golf Club, Inc.) making a case for opening the all male club to women members. In response to Burk's request, Johnson responded in a press release that the club would not change its membership rules. During the ongoing controversy, Burk related that she was referred to as "a man hater, anti-family, lesbian") (Nelson 2003: paragraph 6). Despite Burk's efforts, it would be several more years for change to take place, but women were eventually invited to join Augusta in 2012. More recently, in a video produced by Just Not Sports (2016), female sports reporters are read cruel and misogynistic messages they've received from men on Twitter. The video specifically focuses on Julie DiCaro (a radio host and Sports Illustrated reporter) and Sarah Spain (an espnW reporter and ESPN Radio host) and examples of the tweets include: "You need to be hit in the head with a hockey puck and killed;" "Hopefully, this skank Julie DiCaro is Bill Cosby's next victim;" and "please kill yourself I will provide the bleach." Of the tweets, Spain states:

> [These men] hate you because you are in a space that [they] don't want you in. . . . How does this abuse end? We need more diversity in sports media. [For now] sports is still a man's world, and will be for the near future, leaving the few women in it as targets for some men who don't want them in their boys' club (Macur 2016).

Connections between women's subordination and language have long been recognized by gender scholars (Lakoff 2000; Layoff and Bucholtz 2004; Talbot 2010; Eckert and Mcconnell-Genet 2013). Language reflects and maintains the secondary status of women by defining them "and their place." Language places women and men within a system of differentiation and inequality—and it reflects the social value placed on different groups as well as the power dynamics that are found in society.

To this end, sport scholars have long noted and recorded audience members calling out and mocking female athletes during play. For example, Tom (2010:53) writes that female athletes are often bombarded by vitriolic—and often sexualized—discourse framing women athletes as "any combination of frivolous, talentless, inane, vain, trashy, promiscuous, exhibitionist.'" To this end, Dave Zirin (2008:244) noted that syndicated national radio host Tom Leykis once suggested that the Women's National Basketball Association change team names to things like: "the Denver Dykes, the Boston Bitches, the and the San Francisco Snatch." More recently, Raymond Moore, former CEO of Indian Wells Tennis Club, said that women players "ride the coattails of the men" and should "go down every night on [their] knees and thank God" that men paved the way for women to be finically successful in their sport (ESPN 2016: paragraph 2). Finally, in research conducted on female Mixed Martial Artists, it was noted that there was a tendency of male audience members to objectify athletes with derogatory statements. For example, the husband of a female fighter said the following:

> I was at my wife's first fight with her dad and we were standing next to these two guys and they were looking at my wife and her opponent [in the

cage] and one turned to the other and said, "I don't care who wins-I'm gonna fuck one of them." Not me, said the other one, "I'm gonna fuck the winner." It's hard hearing this shit, you know. It's unnecessary stuff like this that female fighters have to put up with. (Paul and Steinlage 2014:27)

Further, on the issue of words, labels, and their role in empowering or disempowering the athlete, I draw attention to school mascots and the gendered naming of sporting teams. Specifically, I call for a heightened awareness of the naming of women's teams by asking: are the names given to high-school, college/university, and professional teams equal to the names given to men's teams—or do they belittle them, diminish them, de-athleticize them, and reinforce negative gender stereotypes? In research conducted by Eitzen and Baca Zinn (1993), (see also, Eitzen 2016) the names and logos of over 1,500 co-educational 4-year colleges and universities were examined. They identified multiple gendered practices that diminish and trivialize women. I summarize some of their core findings:

- One, linguistic and symbolic markers become sexist when they privilege one sex over the other. For example, there is a dichotomy of power when men's teams and logos emphasize physical skill and traits such as courage, boldness, self-confidence, aggression and the logos and names for women's teams suggest that women are playful and cuddly (e.g., University of Central Arkansas men's team are named 'the Bears' and the women's team are the 'Sugar Bears').

- Second, sports imagery can be sexist with regard to terms 'girl' or 'gal'. The use of girl or gal stresses the presumed immaturity and irresponsibility of women. In the same light, the label 'lady' has several meanings that demean female athletes. Lady is used to evoke a standard of elegance, a characteristic that is decidedly un-athletic. Further, the term 'lady' may seem quite polite on the surface, but it does nonetheless suggest that a lady is hopeless and cannot do things for herself.

- Third, a problem also exists when women's teams are identified with a male symbol as a false generic (e.g., Rams, Stags, Friars, Midshipmen). This practice assumes that the masculine in language, work, or name choice is the norm whereas the feminine is ignored altogether. Further, it is also common to take this to the next oxymoronic level, with the use of a male name with a female modifier (e.g., the Lady Rams or the Lady Gamecocks).

Again, this is ironic given that in the current era, women are the majority among undergraduates and graduates on most college campuses. Yet, even in this time, gender marking remains a source of persistent inequality. Gendered names should be replaced with names and images that reflect changes in women's collegiate sports. As long as collegiate names are categorized by gender, a degree of negative linguistic and symbolic inequality will persist.

STRUCTURED AND INSTITUTIONALIZED HARASSMENT OF FEMALE ATHLETES

Beyond beliefs against women playing sport, the verbal harassment of them, and the perpetration of gendered linguistic inequality, physical abuse (or threats of) is also a significant problem in sports settings. And, it is one that often goes unreported because athletes are afraid that either their complaints will not be taken seriously, or that they will hinder their careers by making a report. Consider that in 2010, investigative reporters for ABC exposed a pedophile problem and widespread sex abuse of underage female swimmers by coaches in local and regional competitive swimming (an activity overseen by USA Swimming, the Congressionally sanctioned national governing body for the sport's 300,000 kids and 12,000 coaches) (Baker 2010). As of this writing, there have been "at least 68 coaches and swimming officials 'banned for life' from USA Swimming for sexual abuse or misconduct" (Kort 2014: paragraph 5).

But the problem is not just what coaches have done to underage athletes, it is the fact that national sports governing bodies, such as USA Swimming, did not take swift actions to protect vulnerable young competitors from such predators. Even when coaches would leave a swim club because of abuse allegations, there was no warning from USA Swimming to other clubs or to swimmers' parents about the coaches' behavior when they moved on to a new locale and new victims. In response to the sex abuse scandal, USA Swimming said it had strengthened its safe sport program "which includes mandatory training on code of conduct, enhanced background checks and lifetime bans for offenders" (Crouse 2013: paragraph 8).

In another example of structured harassment and abuse, numerous players in the Legends Football League (LFL) (formerly the Lingerie Football League)—in which bikini-clad women play tackle football—have accused the league of promoting a culture of harassment and protecting male coaches accused of such harassment. For example, in an infamous video posted on-line, Keith Hac then head coach of Chicago Bliss, is shown getting into an argument with a player who criticized him for confusing two plays. In frustration, and in an attempt to end (win) the argument he yells, "I'm gonna fuck you in the face!" (Escobar 2013: paragraph 2).

Surprisingly, the LFL posted the video on its own YouTube channel to promote the "intensity of the league." Indeed, the league, which also has a policy of fining players for wearing undergarments and too many clothes during play, has been accused of defending its all-male coaching staffs against sexual harassment. In one email exchange between the league owner, Mitchell Mortaza, and a player who had written to him about the harassment, Mortaza replied: "Let me give you a little advice and this goes for any other player creating unnecessary drama. Simply SHUT UP and play football" (Craggs 2009: paragraph 3).

Sport Case Study

The Legends Football League (LFL)

The Legends Football League (LFL) (formerly the Lingerie Football League) made its first televised pay-per-view appearance during halftime of the National Football League's (NFL) 2004 Super Bowl. The show incorporated a lingerie fashion show followed by a seven-on-seven "football game" between female models and actresses in uniforms consisting of lacy boy-cut underwear, bras, garter belts, and chokers (Knapp 2013). From this initial one time venture, the sport of LFL was born and has since morphed into a professional league with greater popularity than other women's football leagues. These other women's leagues (see IWFL, WFA, NWFA, and WPFL) have been largely ignored by the media and sponsoring agencies. As Knapp (2013:3) writes, "While these women playing football in football uniforms under standardized football rules struggle to receive mainstream attention, the women of the LFL, in their lingerie uniforms and playing a non-standard version of the game, thrive in comparison."

Ethan Miller/Staff/Getty Images

A major reason for the league's popularity is the marketing of players in revealing uniforms which have been described as, "tiny, curve-hugging, bun-exposing panties and provocative bras, accented by what amounts to downsized shoulder pads and hockey helmet" (Whitt, 2009: paragraph 11). While the uniforms of the LFL suggest a hyper-sexualization of female athletes for the purpose of sensual arousal, LFL ownership sees it differently. Mitchell Mortaza, the founder and chairman of the league stated:

> A lot of fans are coming to our stadiums and arenas expecting a big bachelor party . . . You know, just a bunch of T and A. And they're finding it couldn't be further from the truth. Yes, it's a sexy game, but these women are intense, their

football IQs are high (cited in Worner 2010: Paragraph 3) . . . the goal is to empower the women and show off their athletic prowess (cited in Duraku 2013: paragraph 5. Emphasis added).

Because sport is a human activity in which the body is the object of intense scrutiny, the sporting body "is the focus of not only the person who inhabits it but also spectators, trainers, and owners" (Besnier and Brownell 2012:444). In this way, the athletic body is always on display with increased opportunities for being "surveilled and gazed upon" (i.e., to be critiqued and judged by others, often using sexist cultural evaluations of beauty). And research indicates that female athletes are most often looked at as sex objects whether they want to be seen that way or not. Additionally, female athletes are typically judged and positively evaluated more by their appearance than by their athletic performance (Weber and Carini 2012).

Thus, while the members of the LFL do have the ability to "show off" significant moments of athletic prowess and display their powerful sporting bodies, they are nonetheless also objectified by the audience's gaze—and most observers do seem to read the uniforms as sexually suggestive "costumes" (Galloway 2012). Further, despite what league management reported above, they seem more heavily invested in promoting sexuality than athleticism.

Consider the fact that members of the LFL must submit to the possibility of accidental nudity on the field. Such moments of nudity are covered in the players' contracts:

Player has been advised and hereby acknowledges that Player's participation in the event and the related practice sessions and Player's services and performances hereunder may involve accidental nudity. In light of the foregoing, Player knowingly and voluntarily agrees to provide Player's services hereunder and has no objection to providing services involving Player's accidental nudity (Craggs 2009: paragraphs 5-6).

Athletes are also informed that they could not wear additional clothing that may inhibit opportunities for accidental nudity—and may be fined for doing so (The Smoking Gun, 2009). As Knapp (2012:10) notes, "in the season opener of the league's first year, at least one player was stripped of her bottoms during a tackle leaving her laying on the field pantiless." Further, Corr (2009) noted that the crowds' reaction to such "wardrobe malfunctions" was noticeably louder than any touchdown celebration at the games.

So why then do women play?

Despite these travails, many athletes say they play because they simply love football and feel that the LFL affords them the best opportunity to play. For instance, several have issued statements similar to the following:

I just appreciate playing football, I don't care what they put me in (cited in Smith 2011: paragraph 4).

It is a necessary evil . . . Maybe one day, girls won't have to wear lingerie to get people interested [in women's football] (Cited in Mosley 2011: paragraph 9).

And finally, a player with the Tampa Breeze, stated she'd rather wear a conventional uniform:

I mean, I don't like it. You'd rather wear full clothing. I have a bunch of scrapes on me. . . . But I believe the league will change to conventional uniforms in the future . . . You look back at basketball, you used to have to wear skirts. Obviously, it's changed, they have the WNBA now. So if you look back, women's sports has constantly evolved and I think that this sports league is going to end up changing the uniform (Cited in CBC News 2012: paragraphs 4-7).

While we doubt seriously that this will ever occur, this does signify that many women look at the Legends Football League as one of the few legitimate means to participate in a football—and it reveals the structural and cultural barriers that female athletes have to hurdle in order to play (and be valued) in the sport. Ultimately, the goal for women's sport would be to build legitimacy around athletic ability separate from sexuality.

References

Besnier, Niko and Susan Brownell. 2012. "Sport, Modernity, and the Body." Annual Review of Anthropology 41:443–459.

CBC news. 2012. "Skimpy Outfits Will End Someday, Lingerie Football Player Says." *CBCNews*, March 7. Retrieved November 4, 2017 (http://www.cbc.ca/news/canada/saskatchewan/skimpy-outfits-will-end-someday-lingerie-football-player-says-1.1230094).

Corr, Charlie. 2009. "Not Taking Chicago Bliss Seriously? That is the Point." Available: http://www.examiner.com.

Craggs Tommy. 2009. "You Will Be Shocked to Learn the Lingerie Football League is Not a Class Operation" *Deadspin.com*. Retrieved November 4, 2017 (www.deadspin.com/5429883/you-will-be-shocked-to-learn-the-lingerie-football-league-is-not-a-classy-operation-update).

Duraku, Liridona. 2013. "Female Athletes Tackle Inequality." *Pandora's Box-York College*, February 9. Retrieved November 4, 2017 (http://pbwire.cunycampuswire.com/2013/02/09/female-athletes-tackle-inequality/).

Galloway, Kate. 2012. "Lawyers' Lingerie League: Clothing as Control?" AmicaeCuriae, June 13. Retrieved November 4, 2017 (http://amicaecuriae.com/2012/06/13/lawyers-lingerie-league-clothing-as-control/).

Knapp, Bobbi A. 2013. "Garters on the Gridiron: A Critical Reading of the Lingerie Football League." International Review for the Sociology of Sport 0(0) 1–20.

Mosley, Tonya. 2011. "Lingerie Football Wants to Start a Youth League." *King5*. Retrieved November 4, 2017 (http://www.king5.com/news/Lingerie-Football-Wants-To-Start-A-Youth-League-132293863.html).

Smith, Emily Esfahani. 2011. "If the NFL Strikes, Lingerie Football will be the only Game in Town." *The Blaze*. Retrieved November 4, 2017 (http://www.theblaze.com/stories/2011/03/28/if-nfl-strikes-lingerie-football-will-be-the-only-game-in-town/).

The Smoking Gun. 2009. "Lingerie League Gets Litigious." *The Smoking Gun*, December 17. Retrieved November 4, 2017 (http://www.thesmokinggun.com/archivalyears/2009/121709/lfl1.html).

Weber, Jonetta D. and Robert M. Carini. 2012. "Where are the Female Athletes in Sports Illustrated? A Content Analysis of Covers (2000–2011)." International Review for the Sociology of Sport 48:196–203.

Whitt, Richie. 2009. "What's So Appealing About Gorgeous Women in their Underwear Tackling Each Other? Retrieved November 4, 2017 (http://www.dallasobserver.com/2009-10-29/news/what-s-so-appealing-about-gorgeous-women-in-their-underwear-playing-tackle-football-well-if-you-have-to-ask-you-won-t-want-to-see-the-dallas-desire/).

Worner, Elka. 2010. "First and Short . . . on Clothes." *Fox Business*, February 5. Retrieved November 4, 2017 (http://smallbusiness.foxbusiness.com/entrepreneurs/2010/02/05/sexy-la-pro-football-team-named-lingerie-league/. Last Accessed: 12/17/13).

Research clearly reveals that sexual harassment continues to be a problem in women's sport and deters girls and women from participating and developing as athletes (Women's Sport Foundation 2009). Indeed, what is needed is the development and implementation of policies regarding sexual harassment to help create organizational climates in which women and girls feel free to report such incidents.

SEXUALIZING FEMALE ATHLETES

As women participate in sports, they attract multiple types of attention. Schultz (as cited in Woods 2015) notes:

> A female athlete's strong and agile body, with its defined musculature, can be a magnet for millions of viewers. In addition, as clothing trends have changed, women have shifted from dowdy dresses, boxy pinnies, and kilted skirts to form-fitting swimsuits, gymnastics leotards and skimpy outfits . . . though the sport bra was a technical improvement for women and serves a utilitarian purpose—allowing them to move freely—it also symbolizes the duplicity in society's view of women both as strong athletes and as sex objects for men (p. 325).

Indeed, female athletes may be looked at as sex objects whether they want to be seen that way or not. Female athletes are often judged more by their appearance than their athletic success—and tremendous pressure is put on athletes to look hyper-feminine and sexy. For example:

- In 2004, the president of FIFA, the world governing body for soccer told women players that more spectators would watch them if they would wear tighter shorts (Christenson and Kelso 2004).

- In 2005, female golfers were told by commentators, "while women on the tour could hit the ball farther than 80 percent of male amateurs, to truly make front page news, they needed to do so in alluring ensembles" (Oppilger 2008:186).
- In 2010 at the AIBA (Amateur International Boxing Association) world championships, AIBA officials implemented a policy forcing female competitors to wear skirts instead of the usual shorts, noting that, "We can't tell the difference between the men and the women" (Bourgon 2010: paragraph 2).
- In other Olympic venues, The International Volleyball Federation recently required that female athletes wear bikini uniforms (i.e., the uniforms could be not exceed 6 centimeters in width at the hip) . . . and only changed the rule in response to pressures from countries whose religious and cultural customs prohibit such uniforms. The Badminton World Federation (BWF) instituted a rule that women must wear skirts, and an American Deputy President of the BWF defended the rule by claiming, "We just want them to look feminine and have a nice presentation so women will be more popular" (Fink 2010:52).
- Finally the WNBA recently showed players possible new "sleek and sexy" uniforms—part of a plan to attract more men to the games. To which WNBA superstar Brittney Grines, stated: "The shorts came in short or extra short," she says. "As soon as I heard that — 'sleek and sexy' — I was like, 'Um, excuse me, I play basketball'" (Ulaby 2014: paragraph 13).

When enough people trivialize women's sports by dismissing competent female athletes or defining them primarily as sex objects, it is difficult to consistently generate appreciation and celebration of women's sport and athletes as athletes.

Roller Derby

In its current form, women's roller derby is a full-contact team sport played on roller skates and organized as a women-only venue that is celebrated for combating the notion of women's supposed social and physical inferiority.

Today the sport exists as an amateur, women-only game, played on surfaces where a track could be laid out with a simple roll of rope and tape (venues have ranged from roller rinks to hockey arenas, sports halls, auditoriums, convention centers, and parking lots). This new incarnation has since attracted the attention of women across the United States and, increasingly, the world. In contemporary derby, amateur skaters play a full-contact sport, necessitating (in addition to quad roller skates) the use of helmets, mouth guards, and elbow-, wrist-, and kneepads. Further, skaters wear jerseys that are often printed with their "derby names" and numbers. In this context, derby names are often humorous, involving pseudonyms made up of puns, wordplay, cultural references, or inside jokes among players—though a growing number of skaters are choosing to skate under their real name.

Susan Montgomery/Shutterstock.com

Game Play and Structure

A roller derby "bout" (game) is composed of two 30-minute halves, during which each team skates five women at a time in shifts (called jams) that last up to 2 minutes. Athletes skate counterclockwise around an oval track, slightly smaller in circumference than a basketball court. There's one jammer (scorer) per team, per shift, who earns a point each time she laps an opposing skater. After her first, non-scoring pass through the opposing team, the leading jammer also has the strategic option of ending the jam prematurely by tapping her hands to her hips. The other eight players skate in a pack and make judicious use of their bodies (especially hips and shoulders) to clear space for their jammer and stymie her opposite number. Players are allowed to hit each other, hard, in shoulder-to-shoulder and hip-to-hip blocks. Further, with a continuous jostling for position, players' hips, thighs, upper arms, and front torsos are often in constant contact. Although fighting and elbowing incur penalties, skaters may move in front of other skaters ("body-" or "booty-blocking"), as well as thrust their bodies against other skaters in hopes of knocking them to the floor ("body-checking"). Finally, all participants in a derby event are volunteers, including the players themselves, the announcers, scorekeepers, and skating referees.

Physical Feminism

Scholarly studies of derby athletes suggest that the majority of those who play derby feel empowered by the opportunities for strong physical contact and derive pleasure from such physical expressions. Indeed, derby is a sport that allows women to gain bodily empowerment through "a positive redefinition of the body and the feeling wherein one is less alienated and insecure in her body and in her bodily world relation" (Liimakka 2011: 442).

Derby athletes will often post photos of their massive bruises from playing (called "kisses"—or badges of honor). Many players describe this as a type of physical feminism and they show that the player's bodies can take the hits yet overcome the pain and still continue to play. For women, derby is a powerful venue for discovering the joys of physical strength. In this way, it helps to challenge the idea that physicality is exclusively a male value. Further, derby can be a venue that combats the negative and disempowering effects of culture that promote physical inferiority of the female body.

References

Liimakka, Satu. 2011. "I Am My Body: Objectification, Empowering Embodiment, and Physical Activity in Women's Studies Students' Accounts." *Sociology of Sport Journal* 28 (4): 441–460.

Paul, John and Sharla Blank. 2015. "The Power and Joy of Derby: Women's Participation, Empowerment, and Transformation in a Flat-Track Roller Derby Team." *Journal of Feminist Scholarship* (9) Fall:51–72.

Documentary Recommendation

Strong! (2012)

All the men are always trying to get big and strong. But all the women, they're always trying to get smaller. There's no such thing in this culture as being big and strong and completely and totally accepted as a woman. No matter how much you can kick everybody's ass—Cheryl Haworth in the documentary Strong!

Cheryl Haworth is a weightlifting champion who became famous at age 17 when she won a bronze medal during the Sydney Olympics in 2000. Haworth also represented a different type of athlete—one who decidedly did not fit American culture's normal standards of athleticism and fitness. In the documentary, we learn about women's weightlifting and follow Haworth on her competitive journey. The film culminates with Haworth's final appearance, in the 2008 Olympics in Beijing. A powerful theme of the film includes Haworth's struggles to find confidence in her body, given the stigmas against larger women. In one particularly poignant moment, Haworth admits to having trouble balancing her athletic success with society's norms as she comes to grips with her life beyond weightlifting.

Despite the moments of self-doubt, Haworth provides viewers with a new image of physical fitness, strength, and beauty, and also with the confidence to challenge themselves.

Simon Bruty/Contributor/Getty Images

***

Documentary Recommendation

T-Rex (2016) takes viewers into the life of the then-17-year-old Claressa Shields—a young boxer from Flint, Michigan to the London 2012 Olympics and the first women's Olympic boxing competition. Ultimately, Shields takes the gold becoming the youngest boxing champion in nearly 100 years and the first female gold medalist in the history of the sport. But the film is also so much more than this amazing athletic feat—it's also about living in and attempting to escape Flint (known most recently for the lead poisoning water crisis, closed factories, unemployment, and crime), and dealing with disappointment as Claressa watches fellow athletes receive recognition and endorsements while none come forward to support her. At one point, a potential sponsor tells her she should soften her image, implying that she should be more stereotypically feminine and meek, and not talk about hitting people. She responds, "how am I to do that. I'm a boxer, it's what I do." This of course raising questions about race, class, and gender bias and what the media and culture expects from female athletes.

Of the experience, Claressa Shields says:

> You know what? I think the world has a definition of what a 'woman' is, and I'm changing that definition. It's not about being skinny and pretty and all of that. . . . I am a very strong woman. Inside my heart, and when you look at me, women like Serena Williams, and me we are built with very nice muscles. . . . I guess sometimes that can be intimidating towards men, or even towards some women who aren't built the same. So because of that . . . I felt like I got left out of a couple of things. There were times when I felt that maybe my gold-medal weighed less because I didn't get any attention. . . . I didn't even get on the Kellogg's Frosted Flakes box. [Yet], they had people there who didn't even medal in the Olympics. So that was hurtful (Tinubu 2017: paragraph 29).

Gregory Shamus/Staff/Getty Images

Reference

Tinubu, Aramide. 2017. "Interview: Olympic Gold Medalist Claressa Shields Talks 'T-Rex' Documentary, Fighting for Her Dreams & Her Hometown of Flint, MI." *Shadow and Act*. Retrieved November 4, 2017 (http://shadowandact.com/interview-olympic-gold-medalist-claressa-shields-talks-t-rex-documentary-fighting-for-her-dreams-her-hometown-of-flint-mi).

NO LESBIANS: HOW HOMOPHOBIA STILL RULES IN SPORTS

Another type of gendered harassment is the homophobia that generally comes with women's sport. It is a common practice in women's athletics to raise the specter of lesbian players and coaches, and to think them unworthy. We know that there are lesbians who play high-performance sport, yet because of the heteronormativity, many of them do not "come out" or reveal their sexual orientation. You would think this has changed with the success of LBGT social movements in American society, but athletes and coaches still face discrimination and the prospect of losing their scholarships and being cut from their teams (or losing jobs in the case of coaches). Thus, very few athletes and coaches feel safe enough to come out. Indeed, as Abdel-Shehid and Kalman-Lamb (2011: 84) write, "the world of sport is more than simply about winning and losing, it also has the effect of helping to reproduce the hetro-normative ideas that exist in other spheres of society."

Consider the following examples:

- In 2005, WNBA star Sheryl Swoopes became the first professional basketball player to come out of the closet (Granderson 2005). Later that year, an outstanding Division I basketball player, Jennifer Harris, was thrown off her college team because her coach believed that Harris was a lesbian. When Harris decided to sue the coach, athletic department, and university, she became the focus of the documentary Training Rules (Mosbacher and Yacker 2009). The documentary focuses on the women's basketball program at Pennsylvania State University under Rene Portland and her policy of gender discrimination based on her three team rules: No Drinking, No Drugs, No Lesbians.

Recommended Documentary

Training Rules (2009)

As noted above, during her 26 years of coaching basketball at Pennsylvania State University, Rene Portland had three training rules—no drinking, no drugs, and no lesbians. This documentary examines how the athletic department, enabled by the silence of a complacent university, allowed athletes to be dismissed from their team if they were thought to be gay. In 2006, student athlete Jennifer Harris, in conjunction with the National Center for Lesbian Rights, filed charges against the university and Coach Portland for discrimination based on sexual orientation. In turn, this lawsuit inspired others who faced the same fate during Coach Portland's time there to come forward. The film not only focuses on the stories of these individuals, but also investigates why organizations that were established to protect these athletes have done so little to end this type of discrimination.

Ultimately, the film explores how women's collegiate sport is broadly structured within a set of homophobic practices that collude to destroy of sporting careers of many of its most talented athletes, simply because they do not mirror hetero-normality. Penn State settled the Harris case, but that did not bring an end to homophobia in women's sports.

- In 2007, three female coaches and a female athletic administrator at Fresno State sued and won settlements charging the university with sex discrimination, discrimination based on perceived sexual orientation and creating a hostile climate for women. In this case, "male athletic staff actually held 'Ugly Woman Athlete' competitions and warned straight female coaches not to associate with female coaches on 'the other team' meaning lesbians." (Griffin 2015: paragraph 13)

- In 2010, Lisa Howe, Belmont University's women's soccer coach, was forced to resign. Although the official press release said that Howe made the decision to resign, soccer team members say that Howe told them privately that she was pressured into leaving after telling school administrators that she and her same-sex partner were going to have a baby (Robertson 2010). Belmont is a private Christian school and did not provide protection against discrimination for LGBT employees.

- In 2013, Brittney Griner, a former star player on the Baylor women's basketball team, told ESPN that:

Kim Mulkey, her college head coach, told players not to be open publicly about their sexuality because it would hurt recruiting and look bad for the program. 'It was a recruiting thing . . . The coaches thought that if it seemed like they condoned it, people wouldn't let their kids come play for Baylor.' (ESPN 2013: paragraphs 1–2)

As Griffin (2015) writes, the patterns we see:

> . . . paint an ugly picture for young women who might be interested in college athletics as a career. The message is . . . you are a second class citizen subject to a double standard in which your success and experience will not protect you from discrimination . . . If you are a lesbian, the message is, you better watch your back, keep it on the down low and even if you do stay in the closet, when athletic administrators want to come for your job [or your spot on the team], they will find a reason to justify their action. (paragraph 15)

LAWSUITS AND PROTESTS AS WEAPONS OF CHANGE

So, what may be done to combat this? The first step in combating this war on women coaches and athletes is to acknowledge the sexism, misogyny and homophobia that is so ingrained in college athletics that it makes these types of discriminatory acts against women in athletics possible.

Griffin (2015) argues:

> The only way to change athletics is to continue to file discrimination lawsuits. If money is the most important factor in college athletics today, let's continue to make schools pay for condoning and supporting discrimination. Defending a school against these lawsuits is a costly and losing proposition . . . Colleges and universities are paying out millions of dollars as a result of sexism, homophobia and misogyny in athletics and reaping lots of negative media attention in the process. If that is the only way to get the attention of college, university [and national] leaders, so be it. (paragraph 17)

As a final example for this section, please consider the Olympic and World Cup winning U.S. Women's Soccer team. In 2016, five players on the women's team filed a federal complaint, accusing U.S. Soccer of wage discrimination based on the fact that they earned as little as 40 percent of what players on the men's national team earned even though they have won three World Cup championships compared to zero championships for the men.

The five players said they were being shortchanged on everything from bonuses to appearance fees. U.S. Soccer pays women a smaller daily allowance (also known as per diem) than men when they are in camp at domestic and international venues. Per diem are 50 dollars a day to fees for women to 62.50 a day for men (in domestic travel). During international travel, men are given 75 dollars a day to the women's per diem of 60 dollars. U.S. soccer also pays women $3,000 per sponsor appearance, compared with $3,750 for men (Yourish, Ward, and Almukhtarn 2016).

The case, submitted to the Equal Employment Opportunity Commission (the federal agency that enforces civil rights laws against workplace discrimination), is the latest legal front in the attempt to equalize treatment for female athletes. A men's player, for example, receives $5,000 for a loss in a friendly match but as much as $17,625 for a win against a top opponent. A women's player receives $1,350 for a similar match, but only if the United States wins; women's players receive no bonuses for losses or ties. Further, a "close look at the figures published by U.S. Soccer from 2015 indicates that the federation spent $30 million to run the men's program compared to $11 million on the women's side" (Crooks 2016: paragraph 20). As Hampton Dellinger, the lead counsel for a coalition of international women's soccer players in a gender discrimination lawsuit against FIFA argues, "It's not just the pay gap; it's an overall support level between the two teams which seems so heavily one sided, particularly given the women's performance and what the women's team has been able to reap financially" (Cited in Crooks 2016: paragraph 21).

Finally, during the most recent four-year period, the revenue numbers "are more or less analogous with the men having generated $60 million compared to $51 million by the women's side" (Crooks 2016: paragraph 22). However, if one compares 2015 alone, the women's team has generated 20 million more dollars in revenue compared to the men's team (Santhanam 2016). Ken Reed (2016), sports policy director of League of Sports, concludes that only when "women athletes start bringing in revenue equal to the men . . . can we start talking about equal treatment" (paragraph 6).

Protest case study: The Women Rowers of Yale-Title IX Protest

With controversy (and some distain from gendered and generational traditionalists), Yale University finally began admitting women in 1969. And just as women held a secondary status on campus, so too did women's athletics—which was often viewed by administrators as equivalent to an intramural program. Wulf (2012) writes, "At Yale, the men took precedence. In the normal hierarchy of rowing, the heavyweights picked on the lightweights, and now both groups of male rowers looked down upon the women—quite literally. . . . women would be lifting in the weight room while the men stood over hooting and calling them names" (paragraph 6–7).

While the men had state-of-the-art facilities: boats, training facilities, and showers; the women had none of these things (despite the fact that the women were far more successful in competition). In fact, after every practice while the male rowers would shower, the women had to board a bus and sit in the cold, waiting to get back to campus to shower—and many of the women would get sick as a result. "Too often, cloaked in sweat-drenched clothes after workouts, the women waited outside in the wintry cold. . . . 'Sweathogs,' some of Yale's inconsiderate male rowers called them" (Dupont 2012, paragraph 6).

Now keep in mind these women these "had been admitted to one of the most prestigious universities in the world because of their intelligence, talents and strength of character. [There women included] future Olympians, . . . doctors, attorneys, professors, [an] owner of a WNBA team, a taekwondo world champion, and the head of an all-female plumbing company (paragraph 10). Yale picked the wrong sport to ignore.

The women had enough. Action was going to take place to force recognition and change to this second-class status: Nineteen members of the rowing team went to the office of Yale's Director of Physical Education, stripped naked (with the words Title IX painted on their bodies), and read the following the statement:

> These are the bodies Yale is exploiting. We have come here today to make clear how unprotected we are, to show graphically what we are being exposed to . . . On a day like today, the rain freezes on our skin. Then we sit on a bus for half an hour as the ice melts into our sweats to meet the sweat that has soaked our clothes underneath . . . No effective action has been taken and no matter what we hear, it doesn't make these bodies warmer, or dryer, or less prone to sickness . . . We are not just healthy young things in blue and white uniforms who perform feats of strength for Yale in the nice spring weather; we are not just statistics on your win column. We're human and being treated as less than such.

The scene was photographed, embarrassing Yale into action. The following year, a women's locker room was added to the boathouse, and women's sports began to be taken more seriously?

Questions

*Do you agree with this tactic of protest. How do your views on this form of protest differ from the actions of Colin Kaepernick?

*Are women's sports still secondary on campus? If so, how might this be reality be addressed?

References

Dupont, Kevin Paul. 2012. "'76 Yale crew stood up for women's rights." The Boston Globe, June 17. Retrieved November 4, 2017 (https://www.bostonglobe.com/sports/2012/06/16/former-yale-rower-chris-ernst-honored-for-forcing-changes-women-athletics/67fjt0fIH8lJ6Oy3bE7KmL/story.html)

Wuff, Steve. 2012. "Title Waves." ESPN, June 14. Retrieved November 4, 2017 (http://www.espn.com/espnw/title-ix/article/7985418/espn-magazine-1976-protest-helped-define-title-ix-movement).

Video Recommendation

The film *Suffragette* (2015) portrays the struggle by British women to win the right to vote.

Why is this film being recommended in a sociology of sport class? Well, beyond the study of gender, power and inequality, the historical suffragettes also engaged in a unique exploration of kinesics (the study of the mechanics of the body as well as the use of body movements to convey meaning and communication). The film portrays the numerous ways in which women were exposed to violence as their campaign for voting rights became more prominent. In fact, the women were often assaulted by male vigilantes and passerby's –in response, they taught themselves the martial art of jiu-jitsu.

Over time, this use of jiu-jitsu, combined with other communicative modes of protest, became known as 'Suffrajitsu.'

Questions

Do you agree with this mode of protest? How about it as an act of self-defense? How might the study/training of a physically demanding activity inspire forms of self-empowerment? (see earlier section on roller derby).

CHAPTER SUMMARY

When women play sports, they become strong physically, emotionally, and politically (McCaughey1997; Hargreaves 2000; Markula 2005; Liimakka 2011; Pavlidis and Fullagar 2014). Yet, concurrent with this fact, other realities continue to exist in women's sport. Woman's bodies are still sexualized and their athletic capital and sporting performances continue to be undervalued. Women are still marginalized in play, coaching, and reporting, and women continue to face routine harassment encased in sexism, homophobia, and fear of women invading men's spaces. What is to be done? As suggested in this chapter, we need more stories and modes of protest that critique the sexualization and marginalization of athletes; we need more gendered diversity in sports media, and women must continue to use the law and the courts as venues to protect women's access to sport in all of its forms.

Discussion Questions

*What are some of the historic (and lasting) myths associated with female participation in sport?

*What are some good sport films that center on female athletes and athletic achievement?

*Give an example of each of the following: misogyny, abuse, sexism, and homophobia in women's sport.

*Identify female athletes and women's sports movements that have challenged sexism and advanced women's participation in sport.

*Is women's sport taken as seriously as men's sport? Why/why not? Will equality in this regard ever be met?

*What has been your experience in sport? Have you had to deal with issues of gender stereotypes, sexism, etc.? How have you dealt with these issues (what are strategies of resistance?)

Extra-Inning

The Book *Feminist Figure Girl* (2015) chronicles the transformation of art history professor Lianne McTavish, at age 43, from a university professor into a muscled fitness/figure competitor—fitness competitions are a class of physique-exhibition events that bear a close resemblance to female bodybuilding, though its emphasis is on muscle definition, not size.

The author, who specializes in visual culture and the history of the body, explores her transformation into a fitness competitor through various lenses such as body image, fat studies, performance art, and feminism. In her work, she details the hard work it took to become a competitor—the years of lifting weights, and months of strict dieting (she said she ate a ton of chicken, bison, egg whites, sweet potatoes and oatmeal).

But the core notion of her book is the blending of bikinis and feminism—two seemingly oppositional things—together. McTavish argues that these things are compatible because she gained a sense of strength and ownership of her body through her fitness. She notes:

> I first I thought this is anti-feminist. But soon [I] began talking to "figure girls"— the ones who compete in the pageant-style face-offs—and realized they were motivated by far more than the judges' approval. They were all strong women who were not really interested in appearance. It was about personal challenge and strength. And so, I thought maybe I'm thinking too stereotypically about this. . . . though it may seem counterintuitive, feminist academics have lauded women who take up bodybuilding because it's considered a subversive act, one that blurs the line of gender roles and body types (referenced in Boesveld 2011: paragraphs 5–7, 9).

Questions

What do you think about this? Are bikinis and feminism compatible? How does Lianne's work mirror the physical and social experiences of Wacquant (Chapter 3), Ernestine Shepherd (Chapter 6), or Gottschall (Chapter 7)?

Icon Sportswire/Contributor/Getty Images

Malgorzata Flis, Amateur Bikini Competitor at the Fitness, Figure, Bikini and Physique Championships as part of the Arnold Sports Festival 2017

Reference

Boesveld, Sarah. 2011. "Alberta professor flexes her muscles for feminism." *National Post*, June 28. Retrieved November 4, 2017 (http://nationalpost.com/news/canada/alberta-professor-embarks-on-feminist-quest-to-be-musculed-figure-girl/wcm/df3be0f0-9137-49df-9246-c54c31205f02).

Extra-Inning: Is cheerleading a sport?

Research finds that although overall injury rates for cheerleading are lower than most other high-school sports, these injuries tend to be more severe when they do occur. Specifically, the American Academy of Pediatrics (the AAP) (2012) found that cheerleading ranked 18 out of 22 high-school sports in terms of injury rate but ranked second—behind gymnastics—in the proportion of injuries that resulted in an athlete needing to sit out for at least three weeks or for the entire season.

Further, concussions were the most common injury diagnosis, accounting for 31 percent of all cheerleading injuries. Other common cheerleading injuries in the report included ligament sprains, muscle strains, and fractures. As a result of these facts, the AAP want cheerleading called a sport over injury risk. They request that school sports associations designate cheerleading as a sport in order to make it subject to safety rules and better supervision. That would include on-site athletic trainers, limits on practice time and better qualified coaches, the academy says.

Additionally, just like other athletes, cheerleaders should be required to do conditioning exercises and undergo physical exams before joining the squad, the new policy says—these new policies should help erase misconceptions that cheerleading is not very athletic.

Question

Besides the physicality involved, what else defines cheerleading as a sport (don't forget the definition of sport in Chapter 1).

American Academy of Pediatrics. 2012. "Cheerleading Injuries: Epidemiology and Recommendations for Prevention." *Pediatrics*, October 22. Retrieved November 4, 2017 (http://pediatrics.aappublications.org/content/pediatrics/early/2012/10/15/peds.2012-2480.full.pdf).

CHAPTER REFERENCES

ABCNews. 2015. "Outrage After Female Tennis Star Asked to 'Twirl' on Court." *ABC News*, January 23. Retrieved November 4, 2017 (http://abcnews.go.com/Sports/outrage-female-tennis-star-asked-twirl-court/story?id=28420851).

Abdel-Shehid, Gamal and Nathan Kalman-Lamb. 2011. *Out of Left Field: Sport Inequality and Sports.* Halifax, Canada: Fernwood Publishing.

Baker, Katie. 2010. "USA Swimming's Monstrous Coaches And The 'Culture of Sexual Misconduct'" *Deadspin*, April 4. Retrieved November 4, 2017 (http://deadspin.com/5514226/usa-swimmings-monstrous-coaches-and-the-culture-of-sexual-misconduct).

Beresini, Erin. 2013. "The Myth of the Falling Uterus: Where did the myth that a woman's uterus would fall out if she participated in sports come from?" *Outside*, March 25. Retrieved November 4, 2017 (http://www.outsideonline.com/1783996/myth-falling-uterus).

Brown, Clifton. 2002. "GOLF; Augusta Answers Critics On Policy." *New York Times*, July 10. Retrieved November 4, 2017 (http://www.nytimes.com/2002/07/10/sports/golf-augusta-answers-critics-on-policy.html).

Bourgon, Lyndsie. 2010. "Why Women Boxers Shouldn't Have To Wear Skirts." *Slate,* January 18. Retrieved November 5, 2017 (http://www.slate.com/blogs/xx_factor/2012/01/18/women_s_boxing_and_the_olympics_why_boxers_shouldn_t_have_to_wear_skirts_.html).

Chadwick, Alex. 2005. "Women Lobby for Olympic Ski Jumping Event." *NPR*. Retrieved November 4, 2017 http://www.npr.org/templates/story/story.php?storyId=5011904.

Christenson, Marcus and Paul Kelso. 2004. "Soccer chief's plan to boost women's game? Hotpants." *The Guardian*, January 15. Retrieved November 5, 2017 (https://www.theguardian.com/uk/2004/jan/16/football.gender).

Coakley, Jay J. 2009. Sports and Society. Boston, MA: McGraw-Hill.

Craggs, Tommy. 2009. "You Will Be Shocked To Learn The Lingerie Football League Is Not A Classy Operation." *Deadspin,* December 12. Retrieved November 4, 2017 (http://deadspin.com/5429883/you-will-be-shocked-to-learn-the-lingerie-football-league-is-not-a-classy-operation-update).

Crooks, Glen. 2016. "The Numbers Fueling U.S. Women's Soccer Lawsuits Are Telling." *CBS New York,* April 4. Retrieved November 4, 2017 (http://newyork.cbslocal.com/2016/04/04/us-soccer-uswnt-lawsuit-red-bulls-revolution/).

Crouse, Karen. 2013. "After Sexual Abuse Conviction, New Scrutiny on Youth Athletics." *New York Times,* June 18. RetrievedNovember 4, 2017 (http://www.nytimes.com/2013/06/19/sports/after-sexual-abuse-conviction-new-scrutiny-of-youth-athletics.html).

Dator, James. 2016. "Serena Williams sends powerful message to Indian Wells CEO over sexist comments." *SBNation,* March 20. Retrieved November 4, 2017 (http://www.sbnation.com/2016/3/20/11273222/serena-williams-press-conference-sexist-comments-indian-wells-ceo).

Eckert and Mcconnell-Genet. 2013. *Language and Gender*. Cambridge University Press.

Eitzen, D. Stanley. 2016. *Fair and Foul: Beyond the Myths and Paradoxes of Sport*, 6th ed. Boulder CO: Rowman & Littlefield.

Eitzen, D. Stanley and Maxine Baca Zinn. 1993. "The Sexist Naming of Collegiate Athletic Teams and Resistance to Change."*Journal of Sport and Social Issues* 17(1):34–41.

Epstein, Elisabeth. 2014. "The Boston Marathon has been Breaking Gender Barriers Since 1966." *Huffpost*. Retrieved November 4, 2017 (https://www.huffingtonpost.com/elisabeth-epstein/the-boston-marathon-has-b_b_5186693.html).

Escobar, Samantha. 2013. "Lingerie Football Coach Says Sexual Threat To Player." *The Gloss,* May 22. Retrieved November 4, 2017 (http://www.thegloss.com/2013/05/22/odds-and-ends/keith-hac-lingerie-football-coach-im-gonna-fuck-you-in-the-face/).

ESPN. 2013. "Griner: No talking sexuality at Baylor." *ESPN,* May 27. Retrieved November 4, 2017 (http:// espn.go.com/wnba/story/_/id/9289080/brittney-griner-says-baylor-coach-kim-mulkey-told-players-keep-quiet-sexuality).

ESPN. 2016. "Indian Wells CEO lauds 'attractive' players in WTA." *ESPN,* March 21. Retrieved November 4, 2017 (http://espn.go.com/tennis/story/_/id/15026527/indian-wells-ceo-says-wta-rides-men-coattails).

Fink, Janet S. 2012. "Homophobia and the Marketing of Female Athletes and Women's Sport." In George. B. Cunningham (Ed.), *Sexual Orientation and Gender Identity in Sport: Essays from Activists, Coaches, and Scholars* (pp. 49–60). College Station, TX: Center for Sport Management Research and Education.

Gina Daddario, Gina and Brian J. Wigley 2006. "Prejudice, Patriarchy, and the PGA: Defensive Discourse Surrounding the Shoal Creek and Augusta National Controversies." *Journal of Sport Management*. 20:466–482.

Granderson, LZ. 2005. "Three-time MVP 'tired of having to hide my feelings.'" *ESPN,* October 27. Retrieved November 4, 2017 (http://espn.go.com/wnba/news/story?id=2203853).

Griffin, Pat. 2015 "College Athletics' War on Women Coaches." *Huffpost Sports,* January 1. Retrieved November 4, 2017 (http://www.huffingtonpost.com/pat-griffin/college-athletics-war-on-_b_6412950.html).

Hargreaves, Jennifer. 2000. *Heroines of Sport.* New York, NY: Routledge.

Kislevitz, Gail Waesche (Ed). 2003. *The Spirit of the Marathon: What to Expect in Your First Marathon, and How to Run Them for the Rest of Your Life.* Halcottsville, NY: Breakaway Books.

Kort, Michele. 2014. "When Sports Coaches Are Abusers." *Ms.blog Magazine,* September 19. Retrieved November 4, 2017 (http://msmagazine.com/blog/2014/09/19/when-sports-coaches-are abusers/).

Lakoff, Robin Tomlach. 2000. *The Language War.* Berkley, CA: University of California Press.

Lakoff, Robin Tomlach and Mary Bucholtz (ed). 2004. *Language and Woman's Place: Text and Commentaries.* Oxford University Press.

Liimakka, Satu. 2011. "I Am My Body: Objectification, Empowering Embodiment, and Physical Activity in Women's Studies Students' Accounts." *Sociology of Sport Journal* 28 (4): 441–460.

Macur, Juliet. 2016. "Social Media, Where Sports Fans Congregate and Misogyny Runs Amok." *New York Times,* April 28. Retrieved November 4, 2017 (http://www.nytimes.com/2016/04/29/sports/more-than-mean-women-journalists-julie-dicaro-sarah-spain.html?_r=0).

Markula, Pirkko (Ed). 2005. *Feminist Sport Studies: Sharing Experiences of Joy and Pain.* Albany, NY: State University of New York Press.

McCaughet, Martha. 1997. *Real Knockouts: The Physical Feminism of Women's Self-Defense.* New York, NY: New York University Press.

McCrone, Kathleen E. 1988. *Playing the Game: sport and the Physical Emancipation of English Women, 1870–1914.* Lexington, KY: University Press of Kentucky.

Mosbacher, Dee and Fawn Yacker (Directors and Writers) 2009. *Training Rules.* A Woman Vision Film.

National Press and the Associated Press. 2014. "Australian Open 2014: Eugenie Bouchard wins biggest match of her career, gets asked about dating in court-side interview." *National Post,* January 21. Retrieved November 4, 2017 (http://news.nationalpost.com/sports/tennis/australian-open-2014-eugenie-bouchard-wins-biggest-match-of-her-career-gets-asked-about-dating-in-courtside-interview).

Nelson, Mariah Burton. 2003. "Women of the Year 2003: Martha Burk." *Ms. Magazine,* Winter. Retrieved November 4, 2017 (http://www.msmagazine.com/dec03/woty2003_burk.asp)

Oppliger, Patrice A. *Girls Gone Skank.* Jefferson, NC: McFarland & Company, Inc.

Paul, John and Carolyn Steinlage. 2014. "Sound and Music in A Mixed Martial Arts Gym: Exploring the Functions and Effects of Organized Noise as an Aid to Training and Fighting." *Journal of Arts and Humanities* 3(4): 16–31.

Pavlidis, Adele and Simone Fullagar. 2014. *Sport, Gender and Power: The Rise of Roller Derby.* Burlington, VT: Ashgate.

Pfister, Gertrud. 1990. "The Medical Discourse on Female Physical Culture in Germany in the 19th and Early 20th Centuries." *Journal of Sport History.* 17 (2):183–198.

Reed, Ken. 2016. "U.S. Women's Soccer Team Being Treated Unjustly." *League of Fans,* April 7. Retrieved November 4, 2017 (http://www.leagueoffans.org/2016/04/07/u-s-womens-soccer-team-being-treated-unjustly/

Robertson, Campbell. 2010. "Lesbian Coach's Exit From Belmont U. Has Nashville Talking." *New York Times,* December 17. Retrieved November 4, 2017 (http://www.nytimes.com/2010/12/18/education/18belmont.html).

Switzer, Kathrine. 2007. *Marathon Woman: Running the Race to Revolutionize Women's Sports.* Boston. MA: Da Capo Press.

Santhanam, Laura. 2016. "Data: How does the U.S. women's soccer team pay compare to the men?" *PBS Newshour,* March 31. Retrieved November 4, 2017 (http://www.pbs.org/newshour/rundown/data-how-does-the-u-s-womens-soccer-team-pay-compare-to-the-men/).

Talbot, Mary. 2010. *Language and Gender.* Cambridge: Polity.

Tom, Emma. 2010. "Flip Skirt Fatales: How Media Fetish Sidelines Cheerleaders." *PLATFORM: Journal of Media and Communication ANZCA Special Edition* (April): 52–70.

Ulaby, Neda. 2014. "Coming Out in Basketball: How Brittney Griner Found 'A Place of Peace'" *NPR,* April 8. Retrieved November 5, 2017 (http://www.npr.org/sections/codeswitch/2014/04/08/300516000/coming-out-in-basketball-how-brittney-griner-found-a-place-of-peace).

Waldron, Travis. 2014. "Female Tennis Player Reaches Australian Open Semis, Is Asked What Man She Wants To Date." *Think Progress,* January 21. Retrieved November 4, 2017 (http://thinkprogress.org/sports/2014/01/21/3187181/female-tennis-player-reaches-australian-open-semis-asked-man-date/).

Womack, Mari. 2003. *Sport as Symbol: Images of the Athlete in Art, Literature, and Song.* Jefferson, NC: McFarland Press.

Women's Sports Foundation. 2009. *Play Fair: A Title IX Playbook for Victory.* Available: http://www.womenssportsfoundation.org/home/athletes/for-athletes/know-your-rights/parent-resources/~/media/PDFs/Educational%20Guides/ Play_Fair_Final.ashx.

Woods, Ronand B. 2015. *Social Issues in Sport.* 3rd ed. Champaign, IL: Human Kinetics.

Yourish, Karen, Joe Ward, and Sarah Almukhtar. 2016. "How Much Less Are Female Soccer Players Paid?" *New York Times,* March 31. Retrieved November 4, 2017 (http://www.nytimes.com/interactive/2016/03/31/sports/soccer/us-women-soccer-wage.html).

Zirin, Dave. 2009. *People's History of Sports in the United States: 250 Years of Politics, Protest, People, and Play.* New York, NY: The New Press.

**Chapter
10**

**Question:
Does Sport
Build Community?**

Student Outcomes

After reading this chapter, you will be able to do the following:

- Identify what is meant by the term community and the implications community can have on the individual.
- Identify and describe differing levels of communities within sport.
- Describe how sport interacts with various communities.
- See how your own life is associated with various communities, both sport-related and not sport-related.
- Identify examples of sport organizations' corporate social responsibility initiatives.

INTRODUCTION

Why do fans do all the things that they do during sporting events? Famously, fans around the globe support a variety of sports and have many traditions, which may include intricate or elaborate chants or dances and the wearing of symbolic logos or colors. Increasingly, fans or team supporters engage in a variety of pre-game or post-game rituals and gatherings. What purpose could these gatherings have for

241

r example, college football—in some places—is known for tailgat-
is a pre-game ritual where fans come together, sometimes hours
ne, to eat, drink, and be close to other fans. This "ritual" it would
distinct purpose outside of simply having fun.

The Ritual of Tailgating

Some (Albright 2014, Osgood 2014) link the first tailgating party to the Battle of Bull Run in 1861. It was the U.S. Civil War's first major battle, and civilians apparently arrived at the battlefield with drink and food to cheer on their "team," either the Union or Confederacy.

In an anthropological sense, scholars Bradford and Sherry, Jr. (2015) liken the modern tailgate festivities to the celebrations of ancient Greece and Rome and they note that the custom overlaps with the traditional harvest season. In summary: people eat and drink and build up community in the process. "It's one last blowout before we hunker down for winter" (Cited in Keen 2014: paragraph 3).

Sean Locke Photography/Shutterstock.com

Indeed, for many Americans, the football tailgate has become the contemporary equivalent of the harvest ritual. Further, for a considerable minority, the ritual often takes precedence over the game. In his study of tailgaters, sociologist Tim Delany (1998) found that as many as 35 percent of tailgaters never entered the stadium.

Questions

Have you ever tailgated? If so, what was the experience like for you? What do people "get out" of this modern "harvest" ritual?

References

Albright, Mary Beth. 2014. "History of Tailgating." *National Geographic,* November 5. Retrieved November 17, 2017 (http://theplate.nationalgeographic.com/2014/11/05/history-of-tailgating/).

Bradford, Toya Williams and John F. Sherry, Jr. 2015. "Domesticating Public Space through Ritual: Tailgating as Vestaval." *Journal of Consumer Research.* Available: https://www3.nd.edu/~jsherry/pdf/2015/Bradford%20and%20Sherry%202015%20Domesticating%20Public%20Space%20through%20Ritual.pdf.

Delaney, Tim. 2008. "The Social Aspects of Sports Tailgating." *The New York Sociologist* 3:1-10. Available: http://newyorksociologist.org/08/Delaney-08.pdf.

Keen, Judy. 2014. "Tailgating isn't just a party." *USA Today,* October 4. Retrieved November 17, 2017 (http://www.usatoday.com/story/news/nation/2012/10/04/tailgating-study-culture-history/1608741/).

Osgood, Matt. 2014. "War, Beheadings, and Booze, a Brief History of Tailgating," *VICE,* November 14. Retrieved November 17, 2017 (http://sports.vice.com/en_us/article/gv7n9q/war-beheadings-and-booze-a-brief-history-of-tailgating).

Building community, then, becomes a focus for sport sociologists, sport managers, and athletic and education administrators alike because *people* are at the center of sports. Individuals, as the famous sociologist Emile Durkheim identified, crave opportunities to come together and reaffirm communal bonds (Ritzer and Stepnisky 2014). In the previous example, tailgating is a chance for people to come together and find a common reason to be together with others, even if the people are very different or come from very different walks of life. In that moment, these individuals share something—a love (or disdain) for a specific team. People come together as a community and rally around an event, game, or team to represent their connection to a group. The social bonds tying a group together are so strong that the group's safety and continued existence becomes important.

Continuing with the example of tailgating at a college football game, we see there are some inherent positives about the communal ritual. But, as with all things, there are threats to the positives and, as Keen (2012) pointed out, some celebrations or rituals go too far. Alcohol abuse is a negative associated with the tailgating ritual and community and can even threaten aspects of public safety. The National Center for Campus Public Safety even hosts training events to address the alcohol abuse, violence, and vandalism associated with some tailgating environments as a way of introducing new social norms within tailgating culture (The National Center for Campus Public Safety 2016). Safety and security is important for not only individuals, but also for keeping communities safe.

It is obvious that tailgating is important to many fans. However, tailgating is simply one way of building a community associated with sports. Communities are built through many exercises or processes, which further (re)develop communal bonds. Since there are many different types of communities within sport, there are many different ways to build or strengthen a variety of communities. Consider, for instance, some of these other examples associated with sport and community:

- Athletes on a high-school team practicing long hours together
- A players' union in professional sport representing players' best interests
- Websites or blogs where fans discuss recent team activity
- Coaching clinics where coaches learn about relevant policies, strategies, and the latest information for keeping athletes safe
- Professional sport franchises working with local homeless shelters
- College athletes volunteering with Big Brothers Big Sisters
- A large sporting event, such as the NBA All-star game, working with a city's local environmental groups to lessen the event's carbon footprint on the city.

Throughout this chapter, we will attempt to answer the question of whether sport builds community. In order to answer this question, though, we need to understand what a community actually is and the various levels of social organization within sport. Then, we examine some of the interactions sport or a sport organization (e.g., franchise, athletic program, etc.) can have with a variety of groups. Before we begin, we must lay a few ground rules in order to clear up some of the ambiguity of discussing community. Our ground rules are as follows:

- We will discuss "community" from a larger, macro-oriented perspective.
- We will use examples of community processes, but we will not focus on specific rituals. (While speaking of rituals can be sociological and is always important, our point is to examine the concept of community, not its interactions.)
- Sport, as an activity, can only "build" community in context within other institutions and/or organizations. That is, we will draw on ideas or concepts that illustrate how the process of building a community can take place within the institution of sport, recreation, and physical activity.
- In this way, we will also talk about sport as a "religion."
- No one "community" is better or more important than another "community." (For example, the nationalistic pride associated with a community of fans rooting for Olympic athletes representing their country is no better or worse than the community of parents or fans associated with a little league softball team).
- Individuals can, and do, belong to multiple communities simultaneously.

Now that we are on the same page, let's look at another example. Major League Soccer team, the Chicago Fire, recently completed a rebranding strategy where they completely revamped not only the look of the team, but also the attitude of how to connect the team to its home city of Chicago. The new tagline for promotional materials reads: "Our city. Our club." According to the marketers at Gameplan Creative, Inc. the real issue was to have the soccer team truly embody and represent the spirit of Chicago. As a result, they landed on a strategy that represent the values and generalized image of the "community" of Chicago, which included emphasizing the blue collar work ethic of the city and region (Gameplan Creative 2014). The new and successful initiative has helped to rebrand this franchise into one that is not only supported by the community, but also embodies and represents the spirit and toughness of Chicago.

The Chicago Fire example illustrates an important point about the term community in modern society. We are talking about avid soccer fans in general, avid soccer fans in Chicago, casual soccer fans in Chicago, and avid or casual fans of soccer that may be from Chicago or have some other tie to that city or region, even if they do not currently live there. Technology has allowed us to build communities that transcend time, space, and place as compared to decades past when sport was more of a regional or local community.

WHAT IS COMMUNITY?

Community is a useful way for examining different groups or ideas and it is flexible enough to provide explanations for certain perceptions, actions or events. Coalter (2007), for example, discussed the role sport can play in developing the individual. But, his real focus was on how sport programming, in general, can have wide-ranging impacts on various levels of society, such as reducing crime in neighborhoods. Since the concept of community is so flexible, it behooves us to operationalize what the concept means so there is a consensus regarding what constitutes a community. Drawing on significant sociological ideas helps provide a starting point.

Berger and Luckmann (1966) argued that people define actions, thoughts, environments, and ways of understanding things around them during social interactions. Definitions are based on reservoirs of shared knowledge and the result of socialization processes. These interactions become habitual and, therefore, powerfully influence how people communicate or understand the social world around them. Many of the activities, institutions, and roles in society can be thought of as a social construction. The phrase **social construction** means the understanding we attach to things is the result of a culture's norms and values and how people define and redefine ideas or symbols. Sport, for example, is a social construction because people, ideas, actions, and organizations help to define the activity as a sport

(Coakley 2014). In many ways, then, a community is a social construction, too. This means a community can be thought of as a "cultural organism" involving knowledge, a possible physical location, traditions, or a shared sense of oneness (Bartle 2011).

Ferdinand Tönnies, ([1887] 1988) theorized about social institutions and community arrangements. Specifically, he compared modern and earlier social arrangements noting a **gemeinschaft** community is characterized by close-knit relationships with people sharing similar collective memories, backgrounds, life-experiences, and intimate social interactions. On the other hand, a **gesellschaft** community is where relationships are "governed by social roles that grow out of immediate tasks, such as purchasing a product or arranging a business meeting" (Schaefer 2004: 73). A gesellschaft community, often associated with modern urban life, tends to involve less social or emotional intimacy and the individual's self-interest is the dominant outlook. Sport is usually associated with the intimacy indicative of a gemeinschaft community. Indeed, Washington and Karen (2010: 278) note "[s]ports competitions create feelings of community that counteract the social fragmentation, distrust, and anomie of modern urban life." However, as we dissect the institution of sport more we see how gesellschaft helps us understand larger social dynamics within sport such as mega-event bidding processes, global sport sponsorship deals, and even player trades.

Documentary Recommendation

Watch the ESPN Films: 30 for 30 documentary entitled *Believeland* (2010). *Believeland* tells the story of professional sports, failure, and the community of Cleveland, OH. As you watch the film think about how the city grew from the beginning and what changes the city and its people endure; how Clevelanders see themselves; and how a variety of professional sport teams represent generations of people from northeast Ohio.

From the film's website (please note the film was created prior to the Cavilers winning the NBA Championship in 2016):

> There's a special place on the southern shore of Lake Erie, at the mouth of the Cuyahoga River known as Cleveland. It is the site of the Rock and Roll Hall of Fame and the home of the Indians, the Browns and the Cavaliers. But it's also the home of an agonizing losing streak. Of all American cities that have at least three major sports franchises, Cleveland is the only one that has failed to win a championship in the last half-century. Those sports teams, and the hearts they've broken over and over again, have inspired a different name for the city, and the title for this 30 for 30 film: "Believeland". Directed

by Ohio native Andy Billman, this evocative documentary will take you on a trip that goes back 50 years and captures the seminal ups and downs of the once-thriving metropolis — Superman, after all, was created there. Despite the economic and athletic misfortunes, and the T-shirt that reads "God Hates Cleveland," the people still believe and worship Jim Thome and Jim Brown and LeBron James. But they also can't forget Edgar Renteria and John Elway and Michael Jordan, the men who extinguished their dreams of a long-awaited championship. Painful as it is, "Believeland" is a celebration of faith, a testament to how much sports mean to Cleveland, and how much Cleveland means to sports (http://www.espn.com/30for30/film?page=Believeland).

Class Discussion

Think of your own sporting-identities as they are tied to geography and place. Why are you "connected" to this team? How do you describe your emotions as connected to this team and place? Solidarity is the social glue holding groups together and involves common interests. It is a way to describe the tie binding groups together. How does the concept of fan solidarity hold true in good times (when the team is winning) versus the bad times (when the team is on a losing streak)—and might losing actually bond "true believers" together more tightly?

Miller and Hess (2002), when discussing community policing efforts and strategies, note that a community can be defined in multiple ways resulting in many different types of communities. We are less concerned with the types of communities here and focus primarily on developing a working definition of what a community is and what it means to people. There are, however, two major components from their working definition of community which influences how we approach sport and community. Miller and Hess (2002: 55) note the following:

- A community involves a specific geographic area—served by one political entity—and includes all of the people, organizations, and entities that are part of that area.

OR

- A community refers to "a feeling of belonging—a sense of integration, a sense of shared values and a sense of 'we-ness.'"

You now have a sense for not only the usefulness or flexibility of the term community, but also the vagueness or ambiguity of the concept. Indeed, the concept of "community" is one of the vaguest terms in sociology which creates confusion for many students. For our purposes, then, a **community** involves either a **geographic element** (group of people, organizations, or dynamics within a specific area) or a **psychographic element** (the norms, values, feelings of solidarity, and social togetherness that transcends traditional geography). As sport continues to be exported across the globe and franchise or team affiliations go beyond regional, state, or even nation-state boundaries a psychographic understanding of community is useful for examining both sport's impact on various communities and growing sport participation/consumption from a business point of view.

Both the geographic and psychographic elements are important to understanding sport and community. Dave Revsine (2014) details the birth and rapid growth of college football in the late 1800s and early 1900s here in the United States. In his book *The Opening Kickoff: The Tumultuous Birth of a Football Nation*, Revsine illustrates how the game of football became not only associated with young men's development and but also how these football teams represented colleges, universities, towns, and then—eventually—entire parts of the nation. The geography was important to the origins of college football and over time the psychography helped to further expand the sport and religious-like fervor surrounding these games, especially as people started moving around the country more.

Psychographic research has become important in different aspects of sports business research, such as sports marketing or consumer behavior research (Hibma 2013). Within sport sociology or sport management, psychographic research includes a wide range of examples, such as the following:

- Studying the social impact a sporting event or tournament has on a suburban town
- Understanding "who" are the fans of a collegiate athletic department in order to better develop services and promotional activities
- Researching how 5th-grade girls' involvement in afterschool running programs impact their social development from 5th-grade through graduation from high school

All of these examples—and the many, many more not listed—illustrate how sport and community fit together. Ritzer and Stepnisky (2014) note how sociologist Emile Durkheim also spoke of people coming together and reaffirming communal bonds. The resulting **collective effervescence** is a feeling of exultation and (collective) emotional release indicating oneness, togetherness, and where the social fabric of the group is strong and tight. Think of a large sporting event and the excitement present during the hours leading up to, during, and after the game. That is the collective effervescent we are talking about. Sport—in general, and sports competitions, specifically—has the power to impact people and make them feel closer to a group.

Activity: Is Sport a Religion?

The English word *religion* has a Latin root ... *religare,* meaning "to bind together." Suggesting possibly the concept of a group or fellowship ... or a community (Johnstone 2007:8).

For many sociologists who study religion, sport mirrors and acts as a religion in that sport provides the foundation of fellowship and provides a degree of intimacy and collective energy indicative of a religious experience. In fact, to paraphrase the famed sociologist Andrew Greely (who was also a Catholic priest), religion is: a set of experiences that renew hope (give joy and teach people how to live with disappointment), a group identity bound by shared symbols of identity and allegiance, and community rituals that establish prolonged moods of feeling part of something larger than one's self (Greely 1996).

In small groups discuss how sport mirrors religion. Please compare and contrast the following:

Do religion and sport have:

Totems (Symbols that communities gather around for identity and unity)?
Symbols?
Rituals?
Holy days (What are some your favorite sports' holy days)?
Holy sites and shrines?
Persons who participate in pilgrimages?
Deities? Priests?
Grand rules, commandments?
Conversions?
Holy Books (Naismith's rules of basketball, anyone)?
An afterlife? (or hall of fames, maybe)?
Worshipers?
Fanatics? (Fan is short for fanatic).
Enemy "tribes"?
Religious metaphors, and regular invocations (prayer)?
Stories of who is good and who is evil (Red Sox vs. Yankees)?
Any instances of witchcraft and magic (hexes and the like)?
And so on. ...

Speaking of magic, did you know that:

*Frank and Jamie McCourt (former owners of the LA Dodgers) hired Vladimir Shpunt (a self-identified spiritual healer) to transmit positive energy to the Dodgers from his home in the Boston suburbs. Vladimir, who reportedly has only been to one Dodgers game, worked for the team for five years. He was given a stipend, plus a bonus of "certainly six figures and even higher" depending on whether the Dodgers won the National League West title and how far the team advanced in the playoffs (Shaikin 2010: paragraph 17).

*Gino Castignoli, a construction worker, attempted to hex the new Yankee stadium by burying a Boston Red Sox jersey in the bowels of the construction. He said:

> I became a Red Sox fan during my childhood, idolized slugger Jim Rice. . . As construction began for the new Yankee Stadium I got a call from the union to work on the project. . . I told them I would not go near Yankee Stadium, not for all the hot dogs in the world. But he relented, and hatched the plan to plant the jersey (He worked just a single day at the stadium project, but said it was worth it) (Associated Press. 2008. paragraph 15–19).

The Yankees reportedly spent $30,000 dollars to locate (they used jackhammers to break through about two and a half feet of concrete) and remove the jersey in an effort to "cancel out" the curse (Kimball 2008).

New York Daily News Archive/Getty Images

Question

What do you think of all of this? As sociologists, we cannot prove or disprove the existence of a higher reality; but as observers of human beings, we can say that sport and religion both share many facets necessary for the construction of group unity. In your opinion, can sport legitimately be called a religion?

References

Associated Press. 2008. "Yankess will donate once-buried Red Sox Jersey to Boston-area charity." *ESPN,* April 14. Retrieved, November 23, 2017 (http://www.espn.com/mlb/news/story?id=3344825).

Greeley, Andrew. 1996. *Religion as Poetry.* New Brunswick, NJ: Transaction Publishers.

Johnstone, Ronald L. 2007. *Religion in Society: A Sociological Analysis.* Upper Saddle River, NJ: Pearson.

Kimball, George. 2008. "Yankee's See Red" *The Irish Times,* April 17. Retrieved November 17, 2017 (http://www.irishtimes.com/sport/yankees-see-red-after-castignoli-s-full-toss-1.914137).

Shaikin, Bill. 2010. "Dodger's Tap into V energy." *Los Angeles Times,* June 10. Retrieved November 17, 2017 (http://articles.latimes.com/2010/jun/10/sports/la-sp-dodgers-psychic-20100610).

Sport Case Study

Religion and the International Pancake Race

While sport may mirror religion, please note that established churches and denominations will, at times, use sport to inspire religious observance. Take for example The International Pancake Race. The International Pancake Race is held annually (since 1950), between people in Liberal, Kansas, and Olney, Buckinghamshire, England. Each year the communities hold a 415-yard race to determine who can run the fastest while also flipping a pancake. The rules call for the participants to "flip" their pancake at least three times (at the start of the race, the middle, and just prior to crossing the finishing the line).

How is this religious?

The English tradition is centered around a community legend where a woman in Olney was making pancakes when the church bells began ringing to announce

Padmayogini/Shutterstock.com

church service. Carrying her frying pan and wearing an apron, she raced to arrive at church on time. Seen as a sign of the strength of religious devotion (mixed with whimsical fun), people started to adapt the legend into an actual sport.

Commemorated on Shrove Tuesday (the day before Ash Wednesday, the first day of Lent—a 40-day fasting period in preparation for Easter), participants mix up "rich, fatty" (tasty) foods, such as pancakes in order to indulge before the period of fasting begins.

The Liberal/Olney competition began when members of the Liberal Junior Chamber of Commerce learned about the Olney race and proposed a friendly competition with the English community. The event concludes with the presentation of awards and a church service (Kansapedia 2017). Both communities race at 11:55 am (their time) and immediately after the Kansas race, the results are compared by phone, email, or social media to determine the winning town and thus, the International Pancake running champion.

Questions

Note how many of our sporting subcultures are intertwined with religion—what do you make of this? How does sport (like religion) create community and ethnic identity?

Reference

Kansapedia. 2017. "Liberal Pancake Race." *The Kansas Historical Society*. Retrieved November 7, 2017 (http://www.kshs.org/kansapedia/liberal-pancake-race/18238).

Television Recommendation

Religion of Sports (2016)

In 2016, a series of six one-hour episodes titled Religion of Sports debuted. The purpose of the series, according to co-producer Gotham Chopra, is to "show why sports matter, how they provide meaning, purpose and significance in the lives of fans, athletes, or people involved in sports" (Roston 2016: paragraph 4). The series focuses on one sport each episode and the diverse subject matter includes minor league baseball, football/soccer, MMA, eSport, rodeo, and NASCAR. When asked about the connection between religion and sport, Chopra stated:

> I don't think this is just a comparative exercise or that sports are a metaphor for religion. I believe sports are a religion. Everything that we associate with religion and spiritual traditions exist in sports. We make pilgrimages to sports cathedrals and temples. We believe in curses and superstitions. We witness moments of redemption and revelation. To me, there's a genuine spiritual experience in sports . . . (Roston 2016: paragraph 6)

In reviewing the series for The Atlantic, Green (2016) provides some deeper insight into the underlying theme that connects the idea of sport as religion:

... [the] co-producers are trying to understand a resilient form of meaning making and community formation in the United States ... its central insight [is] that sports can be understood as a way that people find belonging ... For fans ... they provide a space for meeting and socializing with people who have common interests; and they offer shared experiences of excitement and disappointment and hopefulness (paragraphs 3, 8).

In short, the series is built around the theory of social bonding and creates an understanding of why people engage in and what they get out of sport. Given this, please consider the following questions. Part of social bonding theory is that when one is highly bonded, it reduces deviant behavior. However, there are instances when fans and players engage in violent behavior toward the other team ... how would you explain this from a sociological perspective? As a sports fan or player yourself (or thinking about a fan or player you know) do you see your participation mirroring that of being a religion you practice or is it something different ... explain? One of the themes of these episodes is the role of ritual and tradition ... what rituals and traditions can you think of that relate to sport and how does it serve to strengthen a community?

References

Green, Emma. 2016. "Tom Brady, Sociologist of Religion." *The Atlantic,* November 30. Retrieved November 17 2017 (http://www.theatlantic.com/entertainment/archive/2016/11/religion-of-sports-gotham-chopra-tom-brady-michael-strahan/508913/).

Roston, Tom. 2016. "'Religion of Sports' Gets Into the Depth of Sports Fandom." *PBS,* November 15. Retrieved November 17, 2017 (http://www.pbs.org/pov/blog/docsoup/2016/11/religion-of-sports-gets-into-the-depths-of-sports-fandom/).

COMMUNITY AND ORGANIZATION

Sport, as an institution, is exceedingly complex and functions on many levels ranging from global participation (e.g., FIFA's World Cup) to more localized or regional events (e.g., a middle school girls' basketball conference championship). The communities that develop in and around sports or sporting events indicate sport seems to bring people together. However, we do not have enough information to fully make the assertion that sport actually *builds* community. As a result, we need to further dissect the concept of community and examine the various organizational levels within not only sport, but also within the corresponding communities developing alongside sport.

In order to better understand the types of communities associated with sport, we need to examine levels of social organization. Social organization is simply how we organize groups of people and how daily social life is conducted or arranged. Leonard (1998) reviewed the various levels of social organization noting the three most common levels were interpersonal, group, and societal. Examining levels of social organization helps us to not only better understand sport's structure, but to appreciate the different types of community.

The interpersonal level of social organization is the most basic human interaction involving, at the least, two people. This level of organization is the least abstract and the most directly tied to personal experiences. Within sport, an example of the interpersonal level of social organization could include coaches and athletes, interactions among fans, or even between sport organizational personnel, such as between a baseball scout and the team's director of scouting. The group level of organization "refers to interactions that occur between groups, such as the negotiations between the National Football League (NFL) Player's Association and the team owners (i.e., labor vs. management)" (Leonard 1998: 78). The final and most abstract level of social organization is the societal level. The societal level involves the organization of the sport institution, which is made up of a variety of sport organizations, groups, and associations that organize, direct, and execute the important (or necessary) dynamics within sport. This includes many different aspects of the sport institution or industry such as sport media groups (e.g., ESPN), sport retail or manufacturers (e.g., Nike or Under Armour), and sport governance or governing bodies (e.g., United States Olympic Committee). The figure below graphically depicts the levels of social organization.

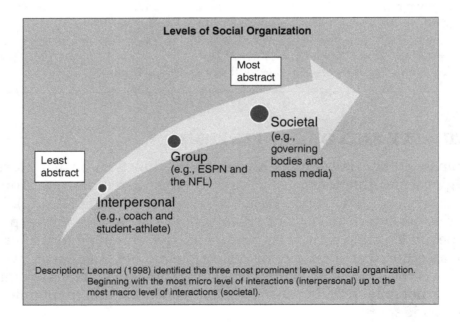

Description: Leonard (1998) identified the three most prominent levels of social organization. Beginning with the most micro level of interactions (interpersonal) up to the most macro level of interactions (societal).

LaVoi and Kane (2014:428), similarly, noted sport sociologists study sport by looking at "institutions and organizations (e.g., the International Olympic Committee [IOC]), microsystems (e.g., women's professional basketball teams), or subcultures (e.g., sport gamblers)." While these analytical categories are different from the levels of social organization Leonard (1998) identified, we can see similarities.

Both Leonard (1998) and LaVoi and Kane (2014) highlight that sport-based communities are the result of people—on some level—coming together and sharing a sense of purpose or direction. They come together for a reason. This is not to say, though, that a community cannot suffer from dysfunction or that everyone participating in the community views all issues the same way. Within many communities, disagreement, strife, and safety issues dominate conversations. For example, the NFL Player's Association (NFLPA) represents thousands of former and active players and has been a formal organization since the 1950s. There is likely, however, a lack of agreement on current NFL substance abuse polices with some players favoring drug testing for marijuana and others vehemently opposed to marijuana testing, since marijuana is more socially and legally accepted (depending on state legislation and decriminalization efforts).

INTERPERSONAL LEVEL

If we understand how society and sport are organized, then we have a better understanding of how to examine different communities associated with sport. Using the aforementioned levels of social organization, we can see how specific communities, which range greatly in size, scope, and impact, might not only organize, but also how they develop. A community having an interpersonal component to it echoes Miller and Hess' (2002) requirement that a community be comprised of at least two people sharing a sense of shared togetherness or having things in common. An interpersonal community within sport is similar to what Morgan (2011) calls an "internal community." An internal community is a group that is embedded within a larger group, community, or context. Within sport, an internal community example would be a group of pitchers on a professional baseball team here in the United States. The group of individuals, which could be less than 10 or 12 pitchers, spend a lot of time together not only practicing, but also viewing the baseball games separated from the rest of the team. The bullpen is usually located away from the dugout allowing these individuals to engage in interactions and lay the foundation for an internal community to develop.

Fan as Fanatic: When an Individual's Commitment to their Sporting Community Goes too Far.

If you break down the word *fan*, the origins are revealing. In English, the word comes from the Latin term *fanaticus*. In Latin, fanaticus indicated a religious devotee, one who would partake in orgiastic rites. . . . [this shows] that fandom stems from an emotional state that is not as simple as supporting your local sports team. There's something deeper and more endemic, a tie to madness, religious frenzy, or even magical spells (Gubar 2015: Introduction).

Please take a moment and discuss (with your fellow classmates): What makes a sport fanatic? What is it about sports that "sets the stage" for such behavior? Please identify some recent examples of sport fanaticism—and, using your sociological imaginations, ask, why did they occur?

***

As noted in Chapter 8, sport fanaticism is a topic worthy of sport criminology. Here are two striking examples of crimes committed by fans:

*An Alabama football fan used herbicide used to kill two beloved and "sacred" trees on the University of Auburn's campus after the Tigers won the national championship in 2011. That individual, Harvey Updyke, a former law enforcement officer, actually called into a regional sport talk show and bragged about doing the poisoning. According to Finebaum (2011: paragraph 8), "Updyke is such an Alabama zealot, he named his daughter Crimson Tyde and his son Bear. He wanted to name another child Ally 'Bama, but that was vetoed by his third wife. Even his dog is named Nick after Alabama coach Nick Saban." But Finebaum goes on to write, "Updyke is not an evil or violent man. His outstanding career in law enforcement is evidence of his contribution to society. In the end, it can be argued Updyke's biggest crime is really being a rabid college football fan" (paragraphs 21–22).

*In 2014, two men were sentenced to prison for the severe beating of a San Francisco Giants fan, Bryan Stow, after a game against the Los Angeles Dodgers in 2011. The beating left Stow with traumatic brain injury (his skull was severely fractured and he was repeatedly kicked in the head and ribs as he lay on the ground—please visit the Brian Stow foundation: http://bryanstowfoundation.org). The men, who were Dodgers fans, shouted profanities against the Giants as they led an unprovoked attack on Stow in the Dodgers' stadium parking lot after the game. Why? The offenders have not provided an explanation.

Scholars have attempted to determine causes for such actions. Commonly, such behavior is the result of too much drinking, mixed with masculine bravado, geographic and psychographic loyalty, and the perception of sport logo wear (totems) as representing racial and class antagonisms (Gubar 2015). In other explanations, one's sport identity and fanaticism is the result of "magical thinking:"

> It is a fan's attempt to gain control in a one-way relationship with the team. In other words, a fan has virtually zero impact on the on-field performance of a team, yet the actions exhibited by sport fans, such as sitting in a lucky seat or altering in-game behavior in belief that it will change the outcome, represent attempts to manage an uncontrollable relationship partner (Dwyer, LeCrom, and Greenhalgh 2016: 19).

Additionally, sometimes a sporting identity is "all one has" and any threat or perceived attack or affront upon the sporting franchise is an assault on one's own identity. Dwyer, LeCrom, and Greenhalgh (2016: 19) state: "Fanatics consume the object of their fanaticism as an end to itself, rather than a means to an end. In other words, fanatical consumption is a self-fulfilling prophecy where there is no conceivable end game [but to become a militant "member" of the team by aggressively defending any perceived attacks against it]."

Questions

Do you agree or disagree with these interpretations and explanations? What else may explain such fanatical behavior? How do we lessen such behaviors?

References

Dwyer, Brendan, Carrie LeCrom, and Gregory P. Greenhalgh. 2016. "Exploring and Measuring Spectator Sport Fanaticiam." *Communication and Sport*, December 2. Retrieved November 17, 2017 (http://doi.org/10.1177/2167479516679411).

Finebaum, Paul. 2011. "The Sad Saga of Harvey Updike." *Sports Illustrated*, October 13. Retrieved November 17, 2017 (http://www.si.com/more-sports/2011/10/13/harvey-updyke).

Gubar, Justine. 2015. *Fanaticus: Mischeif and Madness in the Modern Sports Fan*. New York, NY: Rowman & Littlefield.

GROUP LEVEL

The group level of social organization is an interesting concept when applied to sport communities. It focuses our attention on how various communities are at odds or work together regarding specific issues important to the individuals within their respective communities. For example, during the 2016 WNBA (Women's National Basketball Association) basketball season, various players decided to speak up about social conflict and support the Black Lives Matter (BLM) social movement by wearing non-team-sanctioned tee shirts that highlighted the deaths of minority men and women in acts of extrajudicial police violence.

In doing so, the players received warnings and then were fined by the WNBA for violating uniform policies. In the midst of this controversy several off-duty police officers—who worked security for the Minnesota Linx—left their jobs after they believed the WNBA players' social stance was aimed at police officers (Cauterrucci 2016). In this example, we see three communities (i.e., WNBA players, the WNBA, and police officers) interacting (with varying degrees of conflict) over important issues to each respective community's members.

Documentary Recommendation

ESPN Films 30 for 30: *Catching Hell* (2011)

Catching Hell tells the story of Steve Bartman, the man who was vilified and made a scapegoat for the Chicago Cubs' Game 6 loss in the 2003 National League Championship Series. What did he do that was so bad? He tried to catch a fly ball.

As director, Alex Gibney states at the beginning of the film: "This is really a story about the fans almost more than the players. . ." He goes on to say that the level of anger deposited on Steve Bartman for just trying to catch a ball from the stands was ironic given that Wrigley Field is known for its positive, friendly fans and is nick-named the "friendly confines" because of it . . ."it's the one time that the fans went to a really dark place."

Ironic as well was the fact that Bartman was not the only fan reaching for the ball, he was just the one that happened to touch it and potentially kept Moises Alou from making the catch. And, not only was it not the potential deciding out of the game, but the series went to a Game 7 which the Cubs failed to win. An article about the film, that included quotes from an interview with Gibney, noted that Bartman was immediately singled out after the incident, "the entire stadium focused their ire on him and almost tried to kill him . . . he was a perfect scapegoat" (Conan 2011: para-graphs 5-6, 9-12).

This incident puts an interesting sociological twist on the idea of community within sport. We primarily assume that all individuals rooting for the same team are part of a unified community. However, in the case of Steve Bartman, we see how quickly a community can turn on one of its own when they need something or some-one to blame for their frustrations with their team. In fact, things were so bad for Bartman that he stayed basically hidden and refused interviews until he released a brief statement through a spokesperson after the Cubs won the World Series in 2016: "He was just overjoyed that the Cubs won, as all the Cubs fans are" (Chiari 2016: paragraph 2).

Questions

Given this incident, what do you think it says about the strength of a sport commu-nity? Did the fans turning against one of their own serve a social purpose for them? Despite being shunned by the "Cubs community," Bartman apparently still consid-ered himself a "member" . . . how does this fit with what we know about the role of community in this context and what purpose might it have served for him? Do you think a unified sense of joy in sport or a unified sense of hate in sport makes a stron-ger sense of community . . . why?

References

Chiari, Mike. 2016. "Steve Bartman Comments on Cubs Winning World Series." November 4. Retrieved November 17, 2017 (http://bleacherreport.com/articles/2673998-steve-bartman-comments-on-cubs-winning-world-series).

Conan, Neal. 2011. "'Catching Hell' Director Defends a Baseball Scapegoat." June 2011. Retrieved November 17, 2017 (http://www.npr.org/2011/06/22/137347080/catching-hell-and-blaming-steve-bartman).

The group level of social organization does not; however, need to be a place of conflict. The group level can also consist of communities working together to achieve mutually beneficial community ends, such as Sporting Kansas City's (team in Major League Soccer) literacy and STEM (science, technology, engineering, and math) initiatives within the greater Kansas City metropolitan area (Rosen 2015).

SOCIETAL LEVEL

The societal level is the final level of social organization Leonard (1998) identified. This level is more closely associated with a gesellschaft community because of the larger, macro-oriented relationships. For example, during the 2016 College Football Playoff there were 15 main business sponsors that included soft drink companies, insurance companies, and fast food chains (College Football Playoff ND). These business or media interactions take on a utilitarian feel where each group, business, or community is working towards a financially beneficial outcome that serves the best interests of each group. Sport has the power, at times, to slowly erode some of these large societal level distances. A community could be an entire nation-state, for example, with most of the country's inhabitants rooting for hundreds of Olympic athletes representing their country or region. Because globalized interactions are so large and often devoid of human emotion, it is easy to see how sports competitions can bring people together.

Indeed, recent trends in sport management, show sport organizations are increasingly expected to take a lead role in social and community development. Addressing areas of social concern, then, is a great example of the group and societal levels of social organization coming together in one interaction. For example, though we critique the historic role Major League Baseball (MLB) has played in the Dominican Republic in chapter 3, MLB is nonetheless attempting to use its substantial organizational resources to not only develop the nation's baseball infrastructure, but also positively impact underserved communities throughout the country. According to the *MLB en la comunidad* initiative, their new focus is meant to "promote positive play, education, civic pride, environmental awareness and humanitarian values" (MLB/DR 2016: paragraph 2). Additionally, MLB is partnering with the U.S. Agency for International Development to focus on the education, health, youth development and economic development of identified communities. Already, over $2 million has been set aside or fundraised to go towards specified initiatives (MLB/DR 2016).

SPORT AND COMMUNITY INTERACTION

Corporate Social Responsibility (CSR) is a business-based initiative where corporations give back to specific communities in social, environmental, cultural, or philanthropic ways (DeSensi and Rosenberg 2003). Indeed, Bradish and Cronin (2009) stated that CSR includes the ethical responsibilities of organizations and the need for accountability to not only organizational stakeholders, but also to society in general. There are a host of sport-related examples of CSR as evidenced by the special 2009 publication of the *Journal of Sport Management*, which devoted an entire issue to the topic of CSR. Within the issue, a host of topics were covered, including: an examination of community development through various sporting events (Misener and Mason 2009); a study on the impact of CSR initiatives on fan loyalty and product consumption patterns (Walker and Kent 2009), and a review of the internal and external motivating factors for how and why sport organizations participate in any given CSR initiatives (Babiak and Wolfe 2009).

There has been work done, as well, on specific mega events or professional sport franchises. Babiak and Wolfe (2006) examined the CSR initiatives associated with Super Bowl XL, which was hosted for the first time in Detroit, MI. The economic environment of Detroit was greatly impacted by economic recessions in the 1990s and 2000s resulting from, in part, certain automobile manufacturing layoffs. Babiak and Wolfe's (2006) research examined how the NFL's Super Bowl impacted the host community in a positive way. During this time, the NFL made contributions to small businesses and minority owned businesses, helped work with environmental groups and specialists to ensure the Super Bowl would not have an invasive impact on the ecological environment, and supported many developmental programs, such as working with local schools, libraries, and building computer labs. Focusing on Detroit, as well, Heinze, Soderstrom, and Zdroik (2014) noted how the Detroit Lions have continued CSR efforts in the city and have taken a strategic approach by focusing on specific, high impact areas. These broadly defined initiatives were identified by working with local community, neighborhood, and education groups. Some of the CSR initiatives focus on community health, wellness, and economic development. Attempts are being made so that these efforts and the resulting changes are not only impactful, but also sustainable over time.

Class Activity: CSR and Sport

FIFA (Federation Internationale de Football Association) is the global governing body for soccer. While soccer's popularity is at an all-time high, there have been recent high-profile scandals involving bribery, skimming money, receiving kickbacks, and other forms of corruption or fraudulent behavior (Davis 2013). Understanding the negative context FIFA is embroiled in, consider some of their CSR initiatives.

View the following CSR-related website for FIFA. (Here: http://www.fifa.com/ sustainability/); full PDF reports are located at the bottom of the page. After researching some of these reports and initiatives, please answer the following questions:

(1) What types of initiatives are associated with this organization's CSR?
(2) What specific things are they doing to impact their community?
(3) Is their CSR approach meaningful, impactful, and strategic?
(4) What other things could/should they be doing?
(5) Do the charges of corruption impact how you view their CRS programs? Why or why not?

Also:

In previous chapters, we have spoken about the Functionalist view of society. Functionalism is a social theory that sees society as working together and different institutions have their own specific "functions." We have listed the "functions" of sport before, such as providing integration/socialization and a consensus of norms and values in society. How do the social, integrative, and normative functions of sport (from the functionalist point of view) relate to the concept of CSR as well as to the larger notion of community building as presented in the chapter? Should sport be used to build a sense of community amongst people or should it simply be viewed as another entertainment or for-profit entity?

Reference

Davis, Noah. 2013. "The series of scandals have not only tainted FIFA, but undermined trust in the game as well." *Americas Quarterly*. Retrieved November 6, 2017 (http://www.americasquarterly.org/content/series-scandals-have-not-only-tainted-fifa-undermined-trust-game-well).

SPORT, DISASTERS, AND COMMUNITY

Over the past two decades, sport organizations and sporting competitions have become extremely visible during community, regional, national, and international disasters. As we have already discussed, sport organizations and franchises are increasingly expected to be actively engaged in their communities. When the "community" involves, for example, all 50 states and many other countries around the world, you can see the extent to which sport's involvement is noticeable. Consider the following examples from recent history:

- September 11, 2001—Terrorist attacks in the U.S. prompt increased security concerns. In the wake of the attacks MLB and NFL franchises become public "figures" in leading the U.S. people back to what President Bush called "normalcy." The patriotic displays during these sporting events highlighted the American community and the values important to its peoples.

- August 23–31, 2005—Hurricane Katrina hits and destroys many communities in the United States Gulf Coast (especially impacting the city of New Orleans). While the region is still recovering from the impact of the hurricane, many people come to the see the eventual return and play of the New Orleans Saints (who were initially displaced by Katrina) as a symbol of New Orleans's perseverance and healing.
- April 16, 2007—A college student brings terror to a college campus by killing over 30 students on Virginia Polytechnic Institute and State University's campus. The football team under the leadership of Frank Beamer became a symbol of the larger VA Tech community and the healing that took place.
- April 15, 2013—The Boston Marathon is attacked by two terrorists who planted and exploded several bombs along the 26.2 mile course killing three people and injuring over 260 others. In the wake of the attack Boston Red Sox player, David Ortiz, took the microphone at a home game, declaring, "This is our (F-ing) city" rallying the community. His speech became one of the important moments in the community's collective healing (Doyle 2016: paragraph 4).

In the wake of all of these disasters and tragedies, sports competitions or sport organizations have—to some extent—been a part of the healing of the affected communities—and you can probably think of many other such examples where sport was part of the story.

Miller (2007) noted how **therapeutic communities** develop in the wake of (some) disasters and reviewed the seminal work of Allen Barton. Barton (1969) identified some of the factors associated with a therapeutic community responses to a disaster. Regarding important social factors in the wake of a disaster, Miller (2007:48) stated:

> Barton's model also identifies social factors influencing willingness to help within communities. Barton (1969:261-8) refers to the influence of group culture on people's helping behavior by recognizing that there is a "normative mechanism" at work. If many people in a community help, the local perception is likely to be that people are expected to help, establishing a helping norm in the group culture (Barton 1969:261-3).

The normative mechanism and community expectation, then, is that sport organizations are part of their community and have a variety of resources that can be directed toward or mobilized to address a community disaster. The informal code of helping becomes routinized within the community and provides an example of helping and a rallying point for other community members' involvement. In other words, sport organizations serve as a beacon for community involvement during times of crisis. Miller (2007: 58) discussed the importance of legitimacy during disaster responses and noted:

[T]he legitimacy of social institutions refers to people's acceptance that they are fair and just, deserving of support and cooperation. Citizens' view of social institutions are critical during a crisis in that it is these institutions that attempt to prepare for, warn about, help during and recover after, disasters. If they are seen as trustworthy, residents will be more receptive [to] disaster-related efforts.

Sports are social activities that—for many people—bring individuals together into communities. Sport organizations or sporting competitions are an integral part of geographic or psychographic communities and are embedded within the communities. Because of the social responsibility allocated to large community organizations, such as those related to sport, these organizations lead the community in responding to a variety of different disasters by providing resources, a place to mobilize efforts, a mechanism to mobilize relief efforts, or a chance to be a part of the healing process.

How Sports Helped the Country Return to Normalcy After 9/11: An Oral History

After September 11, sports gave the world an outlet from the pain, death, destruction, and debate of the attacks. There were home runs . . . and there were touchdowns. There were wins and losses on an inconsequential level. There was entertainment. Something that allowed people to feel again, even if it was just for a short time—Thomas

Excepted from: "Thomas" responds to 9/11. Collected on the Bleacher Report Website. Available: http://bleacherreport.com/articles/56317-how-sports-helped-the-country-return-to-normalcy-after-911.

***

What about you? Has sport ever been a "therapeutic community" for you following a misfortune or a dramatic transition of change? Do you have an oral history you would like to share regarding the healing power of sport in the face of tragedy?

CHAPTER SUMMARY

We started this chapter with a simple yet power question: Does sport build community? In order to answer that question we needed to develop a working concept, understanding, or definition of what a community actually is or does. Drawing upon ideas and scholars from the social or behavioral sciences, we noted that a community could involve a geographic or psychographic element associated with a sense of belonging or togetherness. The implication here is that "community" does not simply mean the people you are living around. The explosion of social media outlets or various online echo-chambers means people can find like-minded folks all over the world in regards to almost any topic more than ever before. Our social networks and communities, as a result, can be understood by looking at the various levels of social organization, which provides interpersonal, group, and societal ways of understanding various communities.

Next we discussed how sport organizations and communities interact. The concept of Corporate Social Responsibility (CSR) involves at its core the sport organization recognizing they are part of a community (or multiple communities) and they have an obligation to give back to their community (or communities). The process of "giving back" can take many forms and the organization's resources will help dictate the ever changing flow of resources between organization and community. Sport organizations and sporting competitions find a variety of ways to not only interact with communities but to help them with resources or tools to further develop their communities whether it involves education, economic development, health and wellness issues, or issues of environmental impact and sustainability.

Finally, we identified how sport can be associated with the concept of therapeutic communities in the wake of a variety of disasters or tragedies. It is important to note here that sport organizations are not the sole parties responsible for assisting tragedy-struck communities. There are many not-for-profit organizations, civic groups, religious groups, governmental agencies or even concerned and giving citizens that help not only respond to disasters, but also help in the long, long rebuilding process. Sport can be a polarizing force amongst fans, non-supporters, and educational or governmental administrators. Sport—generally speaking—though, does bring billions of people across the globe together. Sport can also serve as a social event whereby people belonging to a community can come together and reaffirm their communal bonds. In short, sport can build, rebuild, or identify different parts of a community. Whether you are participating in sport, are a fan of a sport or specific team, or simply know of a sporting team associated with your town, neighborhood, city, state, or country the power of sport lies in the social properties associated with it that help bring people together. Sport can build, rebuild, or identify different parts of a community.

Discussion Questions

*Identify some local or personal examples of sport building a sense of community.

*Can sport erode a sense of community or be a divisive force? Explain your rationale with examples.

*This chapter devotes a sizable amount of time and space to Corporate Social Responsibility. Within sport business, a commonly used phrase is "good sports makes for good business." What does that mean to you?

*In your opinion, are CSR initiatives done so sport organizations can get more fans to attend or buy their products? Or, do most of the CSR initiatives stem from an altruistic point of view on behalf of sport organizations?

*Can you think of global examples of sport(s) building community?

Extra-Inning. Sport Case Study: Lumberjack World Championships

Imfoto/Shutterstock.com

Sport and sporting competitions often develop out of cultural lifestyles of community events. Indeed, the close-knit communities Ferdinand Tönnies ([1887] 1988) spoke of often have "ways of life" where everyone comes together to socialize and strengthen their community. The logging community in the upper Midwest of the United States is no exception. It is a region where immigrants settled and began cultivating and industrializing the abundance of natural resources in the area, such as large waterways, strong agricultural potential, and large forested areas. As a result, strong cultural identities and communities began to develop there—as with many other parts of the world—based upon the work that dominated in the communities. The fur trapping/trading and logging communities near the Great Lakes provide one example of how history, immigration, culture and community can influence the development and evolution of sport.

The Lumberjack World Championships is an annual event hosted in Wisconsin for the last 60 years (http://www.lumberjackworldchampionships.com/index.php). It is an event that brings together many of the world's best outdoor, lumberjack athletes. The Lumberjack World Championships were associated with the logging industry so prevalent there and important in the history and development of that region. Essentially, daily work skill sets, such as ways of using various saws and climbing trees, were celebrated and translated into competitive activities.

For a brief history, see http://www.lumberjackworldchampionships.com/lumberjack-history.php. The Lumberjack World Championships offer over 20 men's and women's events. Many of the events include names uniquely associated with the logging culture and community, such as the boom run, axe throwing, or log rolling. Over a hundred athletes compete annually and last year almost 12,000 spectators attend championship games. The events bring together not only the outdoor athletes but also hundreds of community members who volunteer for the events. To view 2015 highlights of the event, see https://www.youtube.com/watch?v=yZEnAH3QjaI.

CHAPTER REFERENCES

Babiak, Kathy and Richard Wolfe. 2006. "More Than Just a Game? Corporate Social Responsibility and Super Bowl XL." *Sport Marketing Quarterly*. 15:214–222.

Babiak, Kathy and Richard Wolfe. 2009. "Determinants of Corporate Social Responsibility in Professional Sport: Internal and External Factors. *Journal of Sport Management*. 23 (6):717–742.

Bartle, Phil. 2011, October 24. What is Community? A Sociological Perspective. *Community Empowerment Collective*. Available: http://cec.vcn.bc.ca/cmp/whatcom.htm.

Barton, Allen H. 1969. *Communities in Disaster: A Sociological Analysis of Collective Stress Situations*. Garden City, NY: Doubleday & Company, Inc.

Berger, Peter L. and Thomas Luckmann. 1966. *The Social Construction of Reality: A Treatise in the Sociology of Knowledge*. Garden City, NY: Anchor Books.

Bradish Cheri L. and J. Joseph Cronin. 2009. "Corporate Social Responsibility in Sport." *Journal of Sport Management*. 23 (6):691–697.

Cauterucci, Christina. 2016, July 25. "The WNBA's Black Lives Matter Protest Has Set a New Standard for Sports Activism" *Slate.com*, July 25. Retrieved November 17, 2007 (http://www.slate.com/blogs/xx_factor/2016/07/25/the_wnba_s_black_lives_matter_protest_has_set_new_standard_for_sports_activism.html).

College Football Playoff. ND. "CFP National Sponsors." *collegefootballplayoff.com*. Available: http://www.collegefootballplayoff.com/sponsors.

Coakley, Jay. 2014. *Sports in Society: Issues and Controversies,* 11th ed. Boston, MA: McGaw.

Coalter, Fred. 2007. *A Wider Social Role for Sport: Who's Keeping the Score?* New York, NY: Routledge.

DeSensi, Joy and Danny Rosenberg. 2003. *Ethics and Morality in Sport Management.* Morgantown, WV: Fitness Information Technology.

Doyle, Ricky. 2016. "David Ortiz's 2013 Speeches Exemplify What He Means To Red Sox, Boston." *NESN,* September 23. Retrieved November 17, 2017 (https://nesn.com/2016/09/david-ortizs-2013-speeches-exemplify-what-he-means-to-red-sox-boston/).

Gameplan Creative, Inc. 2014. "Fueling the Fire—Igniting Professional Soccer in Chicago." *Gameplan Creative.* Retrieved November 17, 2017 (http://www.gameplancreative.com/case-study-chicago-fire-soccer/).

Heinze, Kathryn L., Sara Soderstrom, and Jennifer Zdroik. 2014. "Toward a Strategic and Authentic Corporate Social Responsibility in Professional Sport: A Case Study of the Detroit Lions. *Journal of Sport Management.* 28:672-686.

Hibma, Maggie. 2013 "What are Psychographics?" *Hubspot,* October 28. Retrieved November 17, 2017 (http://blog.hubspot.com/marketing/what-are-psychographics-faqs-ht#sm.00000fjp2ed quhegmpm751761zxbv).

Keen, Judy. 2012, October 4. "Tailgating isn't Just a Party, Research Shows." *USAToday.com,* October 4. Retrieved November 17, 2017 (http://www.usatoday.com/story/news/nation/2012/10/04/tailgating-study-culture-history/1608741/).

LaVoi, Nicole M. and Mary Jo Kane. 2014. "Sociological Aspects of Sport." Pp. 426–447 in *Contemporary Sport Management.* 5th ed. Edited by P. M. Pedersen and L. Thibault. Champaign, IL: Human Kinetics.

Leonard, Wilbert Marcellus II. 1998. *A Sociological Perspective of Sport,* 5th ed. Upper Saddle River, NJ: Pearson.

Major League Baseball in the Dominican Republic (MLB/DR). 2016. "Social Responsibility." *MLB* Retrieved November 17, 2017 (http://mlb.mlb.com/dr/social_responsibility.jsp).

Miller, Lee. 2007. "Collective Disaster Response to Katrina and Rita: Exploring Therapeutic Community, Social Capital, and Social Control." *Southern Rural Sociology* 22 (2):45–63.

Miller, Linda S. and Karen M. Hess. 2002. *The Police in the Community.* Belmont, CA: Wadsworth/ Thomson Learning.

Misener, Laura and Daniel S. Mason. 2009. "Fostering Community Development Through Sporting Events Strategies: An Examination of Urban Regime Perceptions. *Journal of Sport Management* 23 (6):770–794.

Morgan, Jacob. 2011. "Understanding the 3 Types of Communities in Social Business." *The Future Organization,* January 24. Retrieved November 7, 2017 (http://thefutureorganization.com/three-types-social-business-communities/).

National Center for Campus Public Safety. 2016. "Best Fans In America: Working to Change the Culture of College Football Tailgating." *The National Center for Campus Public Safety.* Retrieved November 17, 2017 (http://www.nccpsafety.org/training-technical-assistance/webina best-fans-in-america-working-to-change-the-culture-of-college-football-tail).

Revsine, Dave. 2014. *The Opening Kickoff: The Tumultuous Birth of a Football Nation*. Guilford, CT: Lyons Press.

Ritzer, George and Jeff Stepnisky. 2014. *Sociological Theory*, 9th ed. Boston, MA: McGraw Hill.

Rosen, Steve. 2015. "Sporting KC teams up with Black & Veatch for STEM education program." *The Kansas City Star*, April 1. Retrieved November 17, 2017 (http://www.kansascity.com/news/business/article17143256.html).

Schaefer, Richard T. 2004. *Sociology Matters*. Boston, MA: McGraw Hill.

Tönnies, Ferdinand. [1887] 1988. *Community and Society*. Rutgers, NJ: Transaction.

Walker, Matthew and Aubrey Kent. 2009. "Do Fans Care? Assessing the Influence of Corporate Social Responsibility on Consumer Attitudes in the Sport Industry. *Journal of Sport Management* 23 (6):743–769.

Washington, Robert E. and David Karen. 2010. *Sport, Power, and Society: Institutions and Practices*. Boulder, CO: Westview Press.

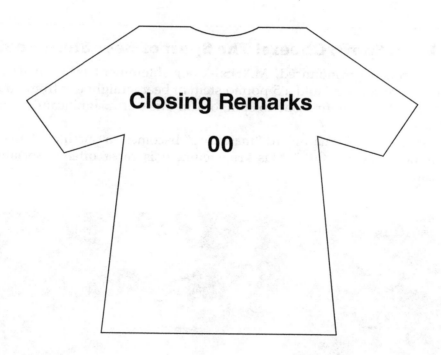

Closing Remarks

00

Throughout this book, we have tackled 10 questions in an attempt to dissect and examine the sociological underpinnings of sport and identify the good, the bad, and the ugly about sport in society. While the book was centered around 10 broad questions, we hope that you came away with an appreciation of the endless number of questions and issues the topic presents and the fact that there is not always an easy answer. After all, defining what is and what is not sport likely still has you scratching your head in some cases (e.g., is playing poker really a sport or how about that hotdog eating contest? The answer is, in our opinion, always yes!).

But apart from these debates, the important thing to remember is that for most of us, sport is a part of our lives; whether we watch them, play them or have family members and friends who do so with an enthusiasm we are unable to escape. Sport not only mirrors the world around us, but gives us greater insight into who we are.

Finally, keeping in mind that sociology is the study of society allows us to put sport in a much larger context than just recreation or entertainment. It both reflects and shapes the society we live in; it can give us meaning and purpose; it creates a sense of community with the ability to unite or divide us, etc. We learned that our sporting culture consists of sometimes competing values such as the notion of fair play versus a win at all costs philosophy. We also learned that sport brings out our commonalities while also laying bare the ugly forms classism, sexism, racism, and nationalism. When it comes down to it, sport helps define us as individuals, communities and societies and that is why sport is such an integral part of creating and understanding the sociological imagination.

One Final Sport: Cheers! The Sport of Beer Stein Holding

Masskrugstemmen (pronounced, MAHSS-kroog-shtemmen) is a Bavarian sport, and the rules are simple: Hold a 5-pound stein of beer straight out from your body, parallel to the floor. The first one to spill, or dip one's arm significantly (no longer parallel), loses.

In translation, the German word "masskrug" becomes "a one-liter stein of beer," and "stemmen" means "lift." Masskrugstemmen is most often associated with Oktoberfest.

Alexander Raths/Shutterstock.com

Now that you've come to the end of your academic term (and the final pages of this book), we wish you good cheer. Now go enjoy a beverage of your choosing and the company of goods friends.

Visit the homepage of the US-Stein-Holding-Association: http://www.ussteinholding.com/info/what-is-beer-steinholding-faqs

INDEX

CPSIA information can be obtained
at www.ICGtesting.com
Printed in the USA
LVHW061802080822
725426LV00005B/75